ONLY THE STRONG SURVIVE

THE ODYSSEY OF ALLEN IVERSON

L A R R Y   P L A T T

ReganBooks

An Imprint of HarperCollinsPublishers

Photographs on pages i, iii, ix, 1, 11, 23, 33, 49, 59, 73, 93, 123, 153, 173, 189, and 223 by Bill Cramer; pages 4, 88, 117, 136–37, 166, 180, 194–95, 206, 212, 219, 245, 248, and 258 by AP/Wide World Photo; and pages 16 and 70 courtesy of Sue Lambiotte.

HarperCollins books may be purchased for educational, business, or sales promotional use. For information please write: Special Markets Department, HarperCollins Publishers Inc., 10 East 53rd Street, New York, NY 10022.

FIRST EDITION

Designed by Brenden Hitt

Printed on acid-free paper

Library of Congress Cataloging-in-Publication Data has been applied for.

ISBN 0-06-009773-6

02 03 04 05 06 WBC/RRD 10 9 8 7 6 5 4 3 2 1

For Bet (as in Black Entertainment Television), my true heart . . .

Invisible Man/You got the whole word watching . . .
—Mos Def, "Hip-Hop"

I think in a combination of abstract visual patterns and muscular sensations; it is only later, when I wish to speak or write to another person, that I translate these thoughts into words.
—Albert Einstein

CONTENTS

ACKNOWLEDGMENTS

This project grew out of conversations some three years ago with Ann and Allen Iverson about penning the Iverson family autobiography. This is not that book; instead, this is an originally reported, part bio, part meditation on the phenomenon that is Allen Iverson. But I am still deeply indebted to both Allen and Ann, for their tolerance of my questions over the years and their constant good cheer. Allen, in particular, has always been a straight shooter. I have tried to write about him with affection, but secure in my conviction that he'd have little respect for hagiography.

I am indebted to Dana Albarella and her posse at Regan Books, who were committed to this book from the start. David Black is, as always, not only an all-star agent, but a great friend.

David Teel of the Newport News *Daily Press,* a superb columnist, researched and shaped the Virginia sections of this book with great care and expertise. He interviewed countless sources, and his perspective on Allen and the times that spawned him was always dead-on. As a result of our close working relationship, I'm happy to say David has become a good friend as well.

Mark Kram and his generous editors at the *Philadelphia Daily News* provided me with an exclusive jailhouse interview with Allen's biological father, Allen Broughton. In addition, Mark was, as always, eager to share his uniquely thought-provoking take on Iverson.

Andrew Corsello may be the strangest genius I've ever met. His input on the manuscript was invaluable. He reminds me of Bubbachuck: a defiant, spiritual creative artist who is always "keepin' it real."

Corsello is a charter member of *my* posse. We call ourselves Cru Thin, 'cause we're a little light in the muscle department but have really high SAT scores. There's Scott MacDonald, whose creative thinking about Iverson's place in the culture at large runs through these pages. There's Ben Gay Wallace, whose insight into human nature, combined with his ignorance of all things athletic, made him a valuable manuscript reader.

Bob Huber is not only a good friend and trusted confidant, but a onetime annoying officemate as well. Rounding out the Cru: Ken Shropshire, Bob Baber, Joey Joe, Eric Reilly, Tex Cobb, Janet Ake, John Lucas, Iain Levison, and Vernon Maxwell. An all-star lineup of folks to watch big games with.

Over the last few years, I interviewed and/or picked the brains of close to one hundred sources for this book, and am indebted to each and every one. Space prevents me from listing them by name. You all know who you are and how much I appreciate your candor. In addition, special thanks to the Philadelphia 76ers, particularly the ever-professional PR department, headed by Karen Frascona and Chris Wallace.

There were countless writers whose stories about Allen Iverson I relied on for background material and who I now humbly salute: John Smallwood, Phil Jasner, Stephen A. Smith, Ashley McGeachy-Fox, Rick Reilly, Gary Smith, Thomas Boswell, and J. A. Adande, among others.

Also, Kevin Maguire and Suzann Vogel provided expert editorial assistance, and Rich Rys conducted some great last-minute interviews while I was pounding out pages.

Thanks to many magazine editors over the years, including: Eliot Kaplan, Ilena Silverman, Stephen Fried, Loren Feldman, Bill Shapiro, and Tim Whitaker.

Finally, a big shout-out to my wonderful parents, siblings, nieces, and nephew. And a special nod to Alex. I couldn't have written this book without his support and unflinching affection. He had me at "Meow."

introduction

TUPAC WITH A J

Bubbachuck was looking like a damned Ethiopian bodybuilder. That's what he likes to call himself when he's shirtless, the bones of his wispy upper body jutting out at sharp angles. Allen Iverson without a shirt is a striking sight; he does not have the physical presence one would expect from a man who regularly challenges NBA behemoths under the boards and in the lane, men a foot taller and in some cases nearly twice as heavy. He's listed at six feet, 165 pounds, but on this May 2001 morning, in the bowels of his team's practice facility, he appeared willowy thin. A buck-fifty and maybe five-eleven, tops—somebody who could easily be mistaken for a rambunctious ballboy, rather than a man who was about to be named the National Basketball Association's Most Valuable Player.

On this day that would name him, in his words, "the best in the world at what I do," Iverson knew how the accolade would be spun in the media. He was having none of it. He knew it would be presented as his redemption, even though he saw it as just another moment of vindication, another in a series of "I told you so" moments.

That is why his thoughts were strictly on those whom he never felt the need to prove anything to: the crew from back home. Iverson was raised on the rough streets of Newport News, Virginia, a small Southern city with a strong migratory connection to New York City. On those streets throughout the 1980s and early '90s, he'd brashly tell whoever would listen that he'd one day star in the NBA or NFL. Older guys, guys with rap sheets and shady connections, would shake their heads and laugh, but they'd look out for him, too—because they saw a prodigy in the making, someone they could help make it out.

Still bare-chested, Iverson eyed two outfits laid out before him. His business adviser, Que Gaskins, awaited his verdict. Gaskins had received a phone call the night before from Gary Moore, Iverson's personal assistant. Moore was the grade-school football coach who took in a twelve-year-old Bubbachuck—an amalgam of two uncles' nicknames—when things got crazy at home; Ann, Allen's single mother, all of fifteen years his senior, couldn't care for him. Now Moore couldn't make it back to Philly from Virginia in time for the press conference; could Que find Allen something to wear in front of the cameras?

"I just want him looking fresh and clean," Moore said.

"Well, we know he ain't wearing no suit," Gaskins said, prompting both men to laugh. Iverson's disdain for business suits was well known. "If he's going to go urban, it should be sophisticated urban."

So Gaskins laid out in front of Iverson a baby-blue velour Pelle Pelle sweatsuit and a black sleeveless Sean John ensemble. "These are phat," Iverson said, looking them over. "And I will wear them, but I ain't wearing 'em today."

Bending over and rummaging through his locker, Iverson extracted a black T-shirt recently given to him by one of his friends from back home. BAD NEWS HOOD CHECK, the T-shirt boldly read in front; a list of street corners adorned the back—the toughest spots in Newport News, the very corners where Iverson came up. There was Sixteenth Street, where the troubled Ridley Circle housing projects were located, just blocks from the Stuart Gardens Apartments, where Allen lived for a time. There was Jefferson Avenue, where the hustlers hawked their illicit wares a chest pass down from the Boys and Girls Club.

"I want all my niggas back home to see this," Iverson said, pulling the shirt on. If hip-hop culture is all about carving self-identity while maintaining your roots, then Iverson is all hip-hop culture; its defiance fuels his demeanor, both on court and off, and its music was the sound track of his turbulent upbringing, from the very first time he heard Kool Moe Dee and Biggie Smalls flow about their lives as though they'd been living his. Of the twenty-one tattoos that adorn his body, two pay homage to Newport News and four salute Cru Thik—his crew from back there, many of whom stay with him in Philadelphia during the basketball season.

When Iverson, wearing the Hood Check T-shirt, Timberlands, a scarf encircling his braided hair, and some $300,000 worth of ice dangling from his earlobes and around his neck, took the podium that day on May 15, 2001, it was much more than just another press conference to name a league's MVP. It was, in a sense, the end of an era, nothing short of a generational handoff. Suddenly gone were the days when a black athlete had to be deferential and nonthreatening in order to be loved. Iverson's team was winning and his name had just surpassed Anna Kournikova's as the most searched on the Internet, in or outside of sports. Of course, the talking heads would go on to paint a portrait of Iverson as a man who had undergone an epiphany. They'd give us a New and Improved Iverson: onetime bad boy morphed into heroic moral exemplar. But the press

Iverson after being named the NBA Rookie of the Year in May 1997. The NBA would refrain from publicizing the award because of Iverson's white skull cap.

accounts said more about those who wrote them than about Iverson. The new conventional wisdom revealed a hunger to squeeze Iverson into a safe, familiar narrative. Which is a pastime made particularly hard by Iverson, because as well as he plays, he just refuses to play along.

For Iverson is neither hero nor villain, and he knew it that day. Instead, he is what the artwork burned into his skin shows him to be, a product of hip-hop culture never before seen in the "crossover"-oriented world of sports. The sound bites of his MVP press conference would focus on Iverson making nice with his old-school coach, Larry Brown, with whom he had feuded in the past—and would again in the not-so-distant future. But a widely ignored part of his remarks that day spoke to the singularity of the event. Iverson looked to the back of the room, squinting, until his eyes settled upon his beaming, high-fiving friends—his once much-derided "posse." They were dressed like him: baggy-jeaned, tattooed. These are the guys who took care of his mama and baby sister when he was in jail, the guys who kept a vigil for him on the other side of the prison's fence for five months, even though, not wanting to be seen in his county jumpsuit, he refused to make eye contact with them.

But on this day of his vindication, Iverson searched them out and his gaze never wavered. There was Ra, his eyes, as always, visibly red-rimmed. There was Eric Jackson or, as Iverson called him, "E." There was Marlon Moore and there was Andre "Arnie" Steele, who was busted in 1998 behind the wheel of Iverson's Benz CL 600 V-12 after allegedly taking part in a drug deal, and who was convicted in 1990 of cocaine possession with intent to distribute.

"What makes me proudest is that I did this my way," Iverson said, still looking straight at his boys, echoing the refrain long crooned by a previous generation's entertainer who was seen by some to have similarly remained loyal to gangsta roots. "I never changed who I was."

Months later, Iverson came face-to-face with the dark side of his "keeping it real" ethic. How real, after all, is too real? On the eve of the 2001–2002 season, five months after being named MVP, four months after winning over fans with his hustle and determination against the mighty Los Angeles Lakers in the 2001 NBA Finals, and just two months after marrying his high-school sweetheart, Tawanna Turner, the mother of his two children, Iverson learned that his best friend, Ra, had been murdered in Newport News. Shot eight times. Killed after arguing with a guy over who could rap better.

"I don't want to die in no projects, man, laying in the grass, people walking by, and be bleeding to death," a crushed Iverson whispered to his former bodyguard Terry Royster when he called to tell him the news. They talked about a supposed friend of Ra's—and theirs—who goes by the name of Fiend. He was there and could probably have prevented the altercation from escalating—but didn't. Now Fiend was nowhere to be found. "It just don't seem real, you know what I'm saying?" And then he paused. "But it's also *too* real. I don't want nobody telling Tawanna and the kids I died like that, over something so stupid."

He donned a black elbow pad with Ra's name on it. From then on, he'd tap it before every foul shot. "Some people see too much too soon," Gary Moore had once said of Iverson, who witnessed his first murder at eight years old. In one summer alone, eight of his friends were felled by gunshot wounds. With Ra's death, Allen Iverson would once again take his pain and use it as fuel to excel on the basketball court, the one constant sanctuary of emotional escape he had found in his twenty-seven years on this earth.

Whether he is proclaiming to the media throng that he's "maintained who he is," privately agonizing over the cost of keeping things too real, or, most recently, staring down felony weapon charges, Allen Iverson has left an indelible cultural mark. More than any other athlete on the public stage, he is, by virtue of his groundbreaking game and his unwillingness to sanitize his ghettocentric style, at once a product and a shaper of his times.

Since 1993, Iverson has heard himself described as a thug and a drug dealer and an ex-con. His response? To simply *represent.* After years of hearing himself judged, he made of his body his own personal billboard and advertised his ethic on his very own skin. (Not surprisingly, Iverson had all but two of his tattoos etched onto his body only *after* he became a multimillion-dollar basketball star.) White men in suits—like the white men in suits who sent him to jail at seventeen—lectured him about what he'd have to do to "cross over," to garner mainstream acceptance as a modern-day "role model" sports star. Instead, he defied the sports punditocracy and NBA old guard with the tattoos and by catalyzing a youth culture trend as the first basketball star to braid his hair in cornrows, a style prevalent among black prison inmates.

The sportswriters and league elders alike were used to athletes, from Julius Erving to Michael Jordan, who subscribed to their middle-class "role model" mores; they were mystified by Iverson's in-your-face persona. It was a classic culture clash; they saw Iverson as a basketball player, when, in fact, he had already transcended his sport and become a hip-hop icon.

"In a sense, Allen Iverson is Tupac with a jumpshot," says cultural critic Michael Eric Dyson. "Like Tupac, he carries his history with him. Usually, America says to somebody, If you want to be successful, you gotta be blanched, you gotta be whitewashed. This is the United States of Amnesia—we want to distance ourselves from everything. Get over your blackness. Now here comes this basketball player who understands that the ghetto is a portable metaphor for how he has faced odds and won. Like Tupac, he says to America, 'It's not that I've transformed—*you* have changed your understanding of what is capable of coming out of a black body from the ghetto with writing all over it and cornrows, the very things that once signified the worst elements of blackness to you.'"

Indeed, cared for by drug dealers, abandoned by his biological father, raised by another man who was constantly in and out of prison for dealing crack cocaine, Iverson often seems to be living a rap lyric. When he first heard Biggie Smalls, it was as if the Notorious B.I.G. were speaking directly to him: "Either you slinging crack rock/Or you got a wicked jumpshot..." The previous generation of ballplayers, from Erving to Jordan, embodied the integrationist vision found in the politics of their day and were made over for the comfort of white America, even while Madison Avenue marketed the likes of Joe Namath and John McEnroe as rebels in the tradition of James Dean and Elvis. They had to make concessions Iverson would never consider. Erving, for instance, cut his trademark Afro in 1979 when he decided he wanted to be a businessman. Jordan, early in his career, spelled out his marketing strategy: "I smile a lot and I get along with everybody. People understand me as much as I want them to."

Now comes Iverson's story, containing the four elements that characterize the generation of black youth that came of age during the Reagan eighties: basketball, rap, dope dealing, and the ethic of "getting paid." He is known for basketball's crossover move, having done for dribbling what

Erving did for the dunk: turn it into a weapon of intimidation. But he has also garnered *cultural* crossover acceptance—without compromising. Like rap mogul Master P, who has gone from (reputed) drug dealer to music impresario to tryouts with the NBA's Charlotte Hornets and Toronto Raptors, Iverson embodies the New Crossover, where (seeming) street-level authenticity trumps Madison Avenue glitz. It's no accident, after all, that some 70 percent of hard-core rap CDs are bought by white kids in the suburbs, or that Iverson's sneaker and jersey sales at malls across America dwarf the numbers racked up by Kobe Bryant, dubbed "Karaoke Jordan" by USC cultural studies professor Dr. Todd Boyd.

As the baby boomers age, a vibrant, even dominant youth culture is up for grabs. Kids raised on MTV and hip-hop are eager to embrace sports stars who have what marketers call "edge," who reflect antiestablishment mores. "Madison Avenue has seen how powerful the urban consumer is," says Gaskins, Iverson's cornrowed, baggy-jeaned business adviser, who holds an MBA from the Kellogg School of Management. "They've seen [urban fashion company] FUBU [For Us, By Us] explode on the scene, they've seen Lauryn Hill maintain her identity while getting the cover of *Time* magazine. There's a new audience out there that craves authenticity and embraces characters like Allen, who won't let himself get pimped out."

At a time when P. Diddy is partying with Donald Trump and Martha Stewart in the Hamptons and the oft-obscene rapper Lil' Kim is doing Calvin Klein ads, Allen Iverson has similarly come to embody the New Crossover by suggesting a new way to think of the American Dream. It's no longer solely about "rags to riches." It's still about attainment, yes, but it's also about achievement born of a ballsy, antiestablishment style; in rap song after rap song, after all, none other than the Donald is celebrated as much for his renegade mind-set as for the fortune he's amassed.

And so we get Allen Iverson, holding a defiant press conference at the end of the 2001–2002 season in which he blasted the press and, by extension, his old-school coach, for publicly questioning his practice habits. The media compared it to a Mike Tyson–like public meltdown, yet people ate it up. Here was a sports star unafraid to speak his mind, or to turn the dynamic around on his interlocuters.

And then we get a series of felony and misdemeanor charges against Iverson in the summer of 2002, for allegedly threatening two men with a gun when he was in search of his wife late one night. His mug shot adorned newspaper front pages, Jay Leno made him a running gag, and the sports columnists called for Iverson to be traded, without citing even *one* on-court reason for such a move.

At the same time, far from the hand-wringing pundits, there were different perspectives. On the streets, people—usually black people—wore FREE IVERSON T-shirts. On Philadelphia playgrounds, kids and young adults of all ages wore Iverson number three jerseys. Not only that, countless wore long, protective sleeves on their left arms, from their biceps to just below their wrists. Iverson, of course, had played the entire season like that to protect a still-tender surgically repaired elbow. Yet, because he had, the sleeve had been adopted as an inner-city style statement. Yes, at all of twenty-seven years old, Allen Iverson had achieved rarified status: that of a true American antihero.

NEWPORT B

I grew up in Newport N
but we call it Newp
'cause a lot of bad shit h

It sounded like the house was about to collapse. The boom was so loud, it would send Butch Harper to the window, time and again, just to make sure. Yep, he'd chuckle to himself. They're throwing that kid around again.

Harper, an environmental engineer and substitute teacher in the Hampton, Virginia, school district, lived at 35 Jordan Drive, a tree-lined street of shoe-box one-story, two-bedroom homes in the Aberdeen section of Hampton, the neighboring town of Newport News. Next door, in a faded yellow house with a cramped backyard, lived a large, boisterous, rotating cast of Iversons. There was the matriarch, Mrs. Mitchell, and her eldest granddaughter, Ann, known as "Juicy." There was Ann's sister, Jessie, called "Li'l Bit," who ran track at nearby Bethel High, and there were the boys, Stevie and Greg, not to mention an ever-present cast of cousins and aunts and uncles and friends. They slept, thirteen of them, in the two bedrooms. "I smelled my share of stinky feet," Ann Iverson remembers today.

And there was Juicy's son, Bubbachuck, the kid who, at all of four and five years old, would be there, every time Harper looked out his window, day and night, playing football with the older boys. They wouldn't coddle him; far from it. Harper would watch this tiny kid—the football was almost as big as he was!—pivot and stutter-step and run, eluding his frustrated elders. He was always in motion—that is, until they caught him. Then they'd hit him, and they'd hit him so hard he'd go slamming into the back of the house; sometimes Harper swore he could feel the reverberations under his feet next door. But the kid would get up, time and again, shaking his head, not letting them see him stagger, and then he'd be right back out there, running and cutting and running some more.

Harper got some peace and quiet when the Iversons got booted from the comfort of Jordan Drive three years later. They settled at the Stuart Gardens Apartments in Newport News's east end. Stuart Gardens wasn't the projects per se—but it was close enough to the dicey cluster of government-provided housing that, over the years, its residents had come to see themselves as indistinguishable from those, say, in the troubled Ridley Circle Homes just blocks away.

The east end of Newport News was only a ten-minute drive from Aberdeen, but the differences were vast. When it came time for Allen to play in a rec league, Ann—no stranger to the perils of the street—didn't want her son walking from Stuart Gardens to the Boys and Girls Club or the Dorrie Miller Rec Center in downtown Newport News. So she called Harper, who was also commissioner of the Aberdeen Athletic Association. He waived the rule that forbade those living in Newport News from playing in Hampton leagues, and vice versa.

That's when the legend began to form, well below the surface of media attention. The Bubbachuck phenomenon was grassroots all the way. In barbershops and on street corners, from the take-out line at Wilkes Bar-B-Q on Victoria Boulevard to the makeshift pews at the Gospel Spreading Church of God in the shadow of the projects, people started talking about this eight-year-old who just couldn't be caught, let alone brought down.

Football came first. Gary Moore, who had been a collegiate baseball standout at Hampton University, coached him in Aberdeen and couldn't believe what he saw: a lethal combination of speed, quickness, fearlessness, and toughness. Just as he did on Jordan Drive, the kid would spring back up no matter the ferocity of the hit that had—finally!—taken him down.

But Ann wasn't satisfied. "You're going to basketball practice today," she told an eight-year-old Allen one day after school.

"Hell if I am," he snorted. "Basketball's soft. I'm a football player."

Ann stood in the doorway. "Well, you ain't coming in until you go to basketball," she said, arms crossed. Grudgingly, alternately sobbing and cursing his mother, Allen Iverson headed for the basketball courts for the first time in his life.

Once there, he was surprised to see all his buddies from football. He sat back and watched for an hour, picking things up. So that's a layup, he observed, when a player scored close to the basket. That's a jumpshot, he noted. When he got in his first game, knowing only one speed, he was a blur. After two possessions in which he literally did whatever he wanted, it dawned on him: I'm the best player here.

Allen's de facto father, Michael Freeman, known as "House Mouse" on the streets, would take a ten-year-old Bubbachuck to the courts at Anderson Park and knock him around, one-on-one. "Get yer ass up," the five-foot six-inch Freeman would growl every time Allen would hit the asphalt. Freeman was an aficionado of playground ball; his favorite team was Dr. J's high-flying Philadelphia 76ers, who had been changing the once-staid NBA. Along with such colorfully ghettocentric characters as World B. Free and Darryl "Chocolate Thunder" Dawkins (who, after a magazine writer made an oblique reference to his "Devastating Dunker" in the locker room, penned an eloquent letter to the editor: "Been looking at my dick, motherfucker?") and, later, Andrew "The Boston Strangler" Toney, Erving was making the once-taboo one-on-one street game a fundamental staple of NBA play. That was the game that Allen was first introduced to, one born of creativity and freedom, where shots were celebrated for their degree of difficulty, regardless of whether the ball actually made it through the twine. From the earliest age, Allen Iverson was shown that basketball is art, not craft, that playing and self-expression go hand in hand.

Eventually, Allen started to run with the older guys in the early evening at Aberdeen Elementary School. Uncle Stevie and Greg were among them, as were a bunch of the older guys who would spend the next few years looking out for Bubbachuck, including Tony Clark, a mentor. Soon the legend extended to basketball. Mike Bailey, the basketball coach at Bethel High, had heard the stories about this Bubbachuck kid, this playground phenom, a skin-and-bones energy freak who would outrace all the older guys, despite the fact that he was *dribbling* while sprinting. Bailey had to see for himself. He walked into the gym at Jefferson Davis Middle School, where, it was rumored, Bubbachuck would be. He poked his head in and saw a kid in desperate need of Ritalin throw a behind-the-back pass out of bounds. He also saw that every eye in the gym was on this indefatigable child.

It would take some time—years, really—for the basketball establishment to take note of Iverson. For now, he was an underground phenomenon, a gift to a town in need of one. For a time in the 1980s, Newport News was flourishing. The Newport News Shipyard, at the height of the Reagan era's upsurge in defense spending, was the area's largest employer—some thirty-two thousand locals were on its books. When the 4-P.M.-to-midnight shift let out, the town would be ensnarled in a bumper-to-bumper traffic jam in the dead of night.

By the late eighties, though, the Cold War was over and the Shipyard was faltering. But even when the Shipyard boomed, other policies of the Reagan eighties started to have a deleterious effect. Throughout the country, an underclass began to develop; the gap between those doing well and those barely making it broadened. The top 10 percent prospered while the bottom 90 percent treaded water, at best, waiting for their promised windfall to "trickle down." Corporations, finding themselves competing in a newly global marketplace, began exporting low-skilled manufacturing jobs. Words like *downsizing* and *outsourcing* entered the national lexicon.

Iverson saw the adults around him bounce from odd job to odd job, or turn to hustling in the burgeoning underground economy. Those dealing crack cocaine seemed to be the only businessmen making it in the new economy. As the drug-dealing character of Nino Brown, played by Wesley Snipes, pointed out in 1991's *New Jack City,* "You got to rob to get rich in the Reagan era."

Ann, by turns, drove a forklift, was a typist at Langley Air Force Base, manned a cash register at a local grocery, and welded at the Shipyard, where she met Freeman, the man who raised Allen and fathered Allen's two sisters, Brandy in 1979 and Ieisha in 1990. Freeman had spent a good part of his adult life in and out of prison for dealing crack cocaine. As far as Allen was concerned, his stepfather had only been trying to put food on his family's table. Unlike the fictional Nino Brown, he wasn't chasing some new twist on the American Dream; he was just trying to stay afloat. Watching Ann, Freeman, and others in the neighborhood, Iverson began to get the message, even then: sports would be the only way out.

It's a message Ann had long accepted as the gospel truth. Many of our feel-good sports narratives portray the mother of the indigent athlete pushing education—sometimes even after the kid has made it, as when Isiah Thomas, later in life, completed his undergraduate degree at his mother's urging. But Ann Iverson didn't subscribe to the "you need something to fall back on" school of thought. No, her baby was born to make it. When folks started talking about her son as if his mere presence had been divinely granted, she didn't humbly object. No, Ann Iverson had long known that God had a plan for her and her baby.

Like her son, Ann Iverson doesn't just smile; she emits joy. First, her mouth, framed by liberal swipes of righteous ruby lipstick, begins to widen, revealing gleaming white teeth, and then the smile keeps expanding, wide and bigmouthed, until Ann Iverson is beaming the way her red Jaguar's headlights beam. But the smile predated the red Jag; it was there, in fact, on June 7, 1975, in the maternity ward of Hampton General Hospital, when her boy was handed to her; suddenly the pregnant lady who hadn't stopped talking and bitching and demanding more drugs to ease

Boo Williams's thirteen-and-under AAU team. Iverson, twelve (second row, second from the left), is the smallest but already best player.

the pain of childbirth, this mouth that ran a mile a minute and had nurses rolling their eyes, started to beam when she took in one specific sight: the length of her baby's arms, which dangled down to his kneecaps.

"He gonna be a ballplayer!" she cried.

She knew it then, just like she knew it when the whole clan landed on Jordan Drive in Hampton—you think that's coincidence, she'd say, that my baby lives on a street the same name as the guy who is The Man of the NBA?

Because she knew God had a plan for her, see. She'd inherited from her grandmother, Ethel Mitchell, a strong spiritual sense, and she just believed. In her view, Allen was her Baby Jesus; she even later claimed—in the hallowed pages of *Sports Illustrated*, no less—that he was immaculately conceived, which would make her the Virgin Mary.

Ann grew up in Hartford, Connecticut, a tomboy who climbed trees and kicked little boys' asses. Her mother was a waitress; her father was long gone. In the fifth grade, she met Allen Broughton. They started dating in seventh grade.

Like Ann, Broughton was a basketball player, a teammate of Rick Mahorn's. (Mahorn would later spend a year as her son's teammate in the NBA.) She and Broughton were in love, according to Broughton, who is currently serving time in Connecticut for assault after stabbing his girlfriend six times in 1998. It was Broughton she was talking to on the phone the night her mother, Ethel, was rushed to the hospital for an appendectomy. Doctors botched the operation and Ann's mother died on the table. The hospital paid the Iversons $3,818.18 to settle any future legal claims.

Ethel Mitchell committed to raising her grandchildren over her husband's objections. "I've already raised mine and I don't want to raise no more," he said.

"I guess you better be on your way, then," Mitchell told him. Without her husband, she moved her brood to the comparatively safer streets of Virginia, where she'd grown up. Before the move could take place, however, Ann decided to lose her virginity with Broughton on her fifteenth birthday, though she claims he never penetrated her. Not so, recalls Broughton. "We were in love and we wanted to make a baby and be together," he says. They were in the eighth grade and consumed by the tragedy of their impending separation. "I wanted her to have a part of me," says Broughton.

The possibility of divine intervention notwithstanding, Ann and Broughton certainly passed on basketball genes to their son. Ann played point guard in high school, rumbling the length of the court while five months pregnant. Broughton, five-six, was the playmaker on the men's team. He was lightning quick and tough—almost as tough as Ann.

Once the move took place, Ann and Broughton kept in touch for a time. He even visited once, buying baby clothes for Allen. "We were kids, man," Broughton recalls today. "Kids making a kid." Ann soon met Michael Freeman, and they had Allen's sister Brandy together. She had started a family with another man. Allen Broughton was out of the picture.

So this was the school skipper extraordinaire. She had heard a lot about him, but she hadn't been prepared for just how engaging he could be, or how talented. And she wasn't even thinking of his athletic skills.

Sue Lambiotte was a teacher and president of the Peninsula Literacy Council. Along with her husband, Butch, a lawyer, the Lambiottes were steeped in sports. All four kids had grown up playing. Clay Lambiotte, Sue's youngest, played in Boo Williams's Summer League with a thirteen-year-old Iverson, which is how Sue came to be on Williams's board of directors, which is how she first came across Bubbachuck.

Boo Williams is well known and widely respected in basketball circles. In 1982, Williams came back home to the Peninsula area after starring at St. Joseph's University in Philadelphia. He started a summer league with $400 in his pocket. Over the years, it has grown into one of the premier summer programs in the country, and Williams has earned accolades as one of the nation's great barnstorming Amateur Athletic Union coaches. AAU coaches often come under fire as the scourge of college sports; unregulated and operating in the shadows, they have been accused of steering their high-school ballplayers to sneaker companies and college coaches with whom they have forged under-the-table deals.

Williams, though, enjoys a stellar reputation compared to most. And he has coached some of the most talented basketball players in the country. Alonzo Mourning, J. R. Reid, Joe Smith, and Bryant Stith have all passed through his program. The thirteen-and-under team that went to a national tournament in Kansas with Sue Lambiotte as a chaperon was no exception. In addition to Iverson, Williams put on the floor Tony Rutland, who would star in high school with Iverson and go on to play with

Tim Duncan at Wake Forest; Aaron Brooks, now a quarterback with the New Orleans Saints; and Damon Bacote, who would go on to play hoops at the University of Alabama.

During that trip, Lambiotte was taken by the happy-go-lucky class clown that was Allen Iverson. In Kansas for a week, Lambiotte insisted on taking the team to local museums. There was no need for a tour guide, however, as Iverson—a talker, when he gets going, right out of the mold of his mother—kept his teammates in stitches with his own running commentary. When he wasn't cutting up on his teammates, he was breaking into dead-on impersonations of them or quickly drawing their caricatures on loose-leaf paper. Lambiotte was amazed at the frequency and depth of his artistic expression. He'd find the one distinguishing characteristic in his subject's makeup—later, in Shaquille O'Neal's case, it would be his slightly crossed eyes—and he'd exaggerate the detail to uproarious proportions.

During practice at the University of Kansas during that trip, the then–head coach of the Kansas Jayhawks walked into the gym. There he saw the shortest player on the court, chirping loudly and goofing off while his coach tried to capture his frantic, easily diverted attention. "Who's that little kid?" Larry Brown asked, not knowing that he'd just laid eyes on the player who would grow up to be the most important, and maddening, he'd ever coach.

This Bubbachuck was not what Lambiotte had expected. She had been warned about him. She knew how, already, he was well on his way to becoming one of the most truant students in the history of his school district. She had heard the stories of how, when he didn't show for a practice or tournament, Boo and his coaches would fan out across town, inevitably finding the kid on a dimly lit playground court, shooting around by himself—sometimes well past midnight.

Iverson's lack of reliability was one of the reasons Williams hadn't already brought him up to play on the main barnstorming team. In the spring of Iverson's eighth-grade year, Williams and his coaching staff debated whether to give the high-maintenance Iverson a chance. Coach Carroll Williams lobbied against Iverson. "We don't want to mess with this kid," he said. "He doesn't want to come to practice."

Coach Bill Tose was the lone dissenter. He'd heard that the kid was a problem and he'd listened to other coaches insist that Iverson was a great playground player who would never amount to anything. Basketball lore was full of such flameouts, guys who never realized their potential, either because of their inability to tame their improvisational styles to conform to team play or because they succumbed to bad grades, drugs, or crime. But when Tose had worked with Iverson one-on-one—when the kid showed, that is—Iverson had always been immensely coachable. In fact, he had always *helped* him coach, like that time when Tose got on Antwain Smith during a time-out for being passive; when Smith responded with a ferocious alley-oop dunk on the inbounds play, there was Iverson right up in his teammate's face—Tose didn't even know the kid had been listening in the huddle!—yelling encouragement: "That's what he's talking 'bout! That's what he's talking 'bout!" Besides, Tose argued, every thirteen- and fourteen-year-old deserves a tomorrow.

Williams, noting that Tose was often the softest touch among the group, opted to elevate Rutland instead, in part because his game—as an outside shooter—would mesh better with that of Michael Evans, an older kid out of Norfolk. Williams was convinced Evans would be the program's next superstar—following in the sneaker prints of Reid and Mourning. (Sure enough, as a senior at Norfolk's Granby High School, Evans would go on to be ranked as the nation's number two point guard behind Jason Kidd; because of injuries and academic neglect, his college career never panned out.)

But then Evans couldn't make a tournament in Memphis, so Iverson was picked to go in his place. During the fourteen-hour drive to Memphis, Williams started to regret it: he'd never heard someone talk for fourteen consecutive hours. Often, it was just Bubba bitching. One favorite complaint was the beat-up rental van: "Coach, why don't Alonzo buy you a damned real van, man?" he called out. "Tell you what, when I make it in the NBA, I'll get you a real van." Williams laughed at the kid's presumption. ("I'm still waiting on that van," he jokes today.)

He didn't regret having Iverson on the court, though. The team went on to capture second place, losing in the finals to the Arkansas Wings, led by future NBA star Corliss Williamson, a behemoth even then. Iverson wasn't cowed; he challenged Williamson at every turn. He earned all-tournament honors and the team took home the runner-up trophy. During the long van ride back home, he cracked everybody up by opening his window and flinging the trophy onto the side of the road. "We don't take no second place," Iverson said. "That's not what we came to do."

"But that still would've been a nice dust collector," Tose deadpanned.

Meantime, Iverson's life away from the court was still turbulent. The coaches had addresses for him, but were never quite sure where he was spending the night. They'd still conduct nighttime searches, trying to track him down. The family had been evicted from Stuart Gardens; for a time, he went to stay with Gary Moore while Ann and the two girls moved into a shelter.

Mike Bailey, the Bethel head coach, took Allen in for three weeks that summer between ninth and tenth grade to make sure Allen attended summer school. Bailey's wife, Janet, taught English at the high school, and had even taught Gary Moore during his Bethel days. Early on, Bailey made a deal with Iverson: you're going to come to study hall at my house, and we're going to stay on top of everything you need to do to stay eligible so you can go to college and make something of yourself for your family.

It wasn't easy. The first time he went to pick up Allen to come over, he showed up outside the locker room after football practice as they'd arranged. No sign of Allen. But then, pulling out of the Bethel parking lot, Bailey spied a 1981 black Toyota Tercel. That was Michael Jackson's car, a sweatbox with no air-conditioning. Jackson, whom Iverson called "Thrilla," was a tailback on the football team and one of Iverson's closest friends. They bonded when, as twelve-year-olds, Jackson was the only kid who could beat Iverson in a footrace. Jackson, a stellar student, drove Iverson to and from school every day—doing his best to get Bubbachuck there on time. Now Bailey pulled up alongside Jackson.

"You seen 'Chuck?" he asked. "We're supposed to meet for study hall."

"Haven't seen him, Coach," Jackson replied, his eyes darting nervously. Bailey glanced into the backseat; in his peripheral vision, he saw a form crouched low on the floor behind the driver's seat. Bubba.

"Well, if you see him, tell him I'm not giving up," Bailey said. "Tell him I'll see him tomorrow." The next day, Bailey successfully corralled Iverson on the football field.

Bailey's commitment might have appeared self-serving to an outsider. His job, after all, was to win basketball games, and Iverson, for all the headaches he caused, could do that for him. But others attest that Bailey truly loved Iverson like a son. This was because, like Lambiotte, he saw some potential that had gone untapped. He'd had experience in dealing with inner-city black kids. The hardest thing to combat was their fatalism, the sense that they were doomed, that no one was there for them. He knew so many kids who lived for today, even if it meant they'd die tomorrow. Hearing Iverson talk about how he just had to make it to the NBA, how he wanted to use sports to help his family, Bailey sensed that, unlike so many of his generation, he lived for the next day. Lived for his family. Hell, he'd already promised Ann that, when he signed with an NBA team, he'd buy her that candy-red Jaguar she'd always wanted. The kid was fixated on the possible while others around him were succumbing to hopelessness.

So that summer, Bailey took him in for three weeks while Iverson took a history class he had failed. Bailey would wake him up at 5 A.M. and watch as Iverson ironed his T-shirt, trying to smooth over its holes. He'd fret when Friday came, because along with it came the call of the streets. Bailey would cruise Newport News on Sunday night, trying to find him. One missed class, after all, in such a truncated semester, resulted in a failing grade. One Sunday night, Bubba was nowhere to be found. A distraught Bailey headed home.

The next morning, Bailey checked the history class. There was Iverson. He'd scratched together enough pennies to afford a taxi from the streets of Newport News to the school at dawn. Another time, he called Bailey at 6 A.M.: "Coach, my ride didn't show. Can you pick me up?" After three weeks, he'd gotten a B.

But that's not what sticks most in Bailey's mind of this, his first summer of Bubbachuck. No, what Bailey remembers is what made him realize that, to reach Iverson, he'd have to "coach him with my heart." In their first sit-down together, when Bailey spelled out all that he'd be expecting of Iverson—the study halls, the promptness, the attitude—he wasn't even sure if Iverson was listening. Iverson was looking down or looking away, rarely making and holding eye contact. Bailey finished by asking, "Now, what do you expect from me?"

And this thirteen-year-old who had no recollection of meeting his father, whose de facto father was hustling on the streets when he wasn't doing time, who, almost every day, found himself among a hushed crowd jockeying around yellow police tape while cops crouched over yet another chalk outline, this thirteen-year-old raised his head and looked Mike Bailey squarely in the eyes. "Will you always be there for me, Coach?" he asked.

chapter 2

ONLY THE STRONG SURVIVE

this is a cross of daggers knitted together,
reading ONLY THE STRONG SURVIVE. BECAUSE
that's the one true thing I've learned in this life.

That was one crazy-ass summer," Allen Iverson would say, some ten years later, of the summer of 1992. It was the summer that the basketball establishment was stunned into taking note of the five-foot ten-inch prodigy from the forgotten streets of Newport News. It was the summer death seemed all around, everywhere Iverson turned. And it was the summer Iverson met many of those who would play meaningful roles in his life.

The Iversons had moved to 3710 Victoria Boulevard, to a one-story rectangle of a house two doors down from Wilkes Bar-B-Q; Ann did her best to get bills paid, but each month began with one certain uncertainty—which would be the first to be shut off, the electricity, phone, or gas? In the living room, there was a tattered couch and easy chair. The only other piece of furniture was a bookcase displaying Allen's 209 trophies and 62 plaques.

A burst pipe under the house resulted in an ever-present sewage stench and constant backups, forcing Allen and his sister Brandy to wear boots inside so as to sidestep the raw debris that often floated across the floor. Allen could tolerate it, but he couldn't stomach watching two-year-old Ieisha live in such conditions. From the first day Ieisha came home from the hospital, Allen was smitten, often rushing home from school to see this little sister who looked just like him, who had his big hands and feet. She also had his toughness, according to Ann, whose pregnancy with Ieisha was troubled. Born nine days late, Ieisha was admitted to Norfolk's King's Daughters Hospital, where doctors told Ann not to expect her baby to make it. From there, it was on to Georgetown University Hospital for treatment of, among other maladies, recurring seizures.

Allen hated to see Ieisha living in the decrepit house on Victoria Boulevard, the location of which made for an ironic incongruity; just a quarter mile away sat Darling Stadium, where thousands had cheered for Iverson the previous fall during Bethel football games.

Iverson played wide receiver as a freshman, when he was timed running a 4.7 forty-yard dash, the same speed posted by NFL superstar Jerry Rice in his rookie year. As a sophomore, Iverson moved to quarterback and also played safety and returned kicks. Without taking any time off between football and basketball seasons, he went on to average 27.1 points a game, leading Mike Bailey's team to a 15–8 record, the school's best in ten years. The test, for Bailey, was getting Iverson to peacefully coexist with the team's other star, Tony Rutland, who was also a sophomore. Bailey referred to them as "The Terrible Twos." When he'd take one out of a game, he'd take the other out, too, and sit between them on the bench, trying to foster chemistry, talking them through their inevitable spats that usually began with one or the other moaning, "Man, I was open!"

But now it was summer, AAU time. Bust-out time. By summer's end, basketball cognoscenti across the nation would be touting Iverson in the same reverential tones Newport News locals had been using for years. Boo Williams, who coached Alonzo Mourning in his most dominant summers, still shakes his head when he thinks of Iverson's summer of 1992. "I can't explain it, but it was the greatest display of basketball I've ever seen," Williams says. "Not even Alonzo ever had a summer like Bubba's."

Iverson had always been fast, but now he'd become a blur. Stealing the ball from him was out of the question; his low-to-the-ground dribble combined with his quickness and jumping ability to make him unstoppable. But perhaps the best explanation for his suddenly dominant play could be found in the tumult swirling around Iverson away from the hard courts. Life at Victoria Boulevard was a struggle; he'd stay on the playground till all hours, not out of some workmanlike desire to perfect his game, but because heading back home, where it was likely dark, cold, and smelly, was so daunting. "It ain't supposed to be like this," he told Bailey one night when he sought to crash over at the coach's house.

Other times, he'd head over to Gary Moore's, or to Tony Clark's place, book bag in tow. Clark was twenty, a mentor who kept at bay the street tricksters looking to gain instant notoriety by fucking with Bubbachuck. A former athlete and high-school dropout, Clark preached the wisdom of education to Iverson: "Don't end up like me—stay in school," he'd say. If Bubba came over without his books, Clark would send him right back home for them—no matter the time of day or night. That summer, Clark was murdered by his girlfriend. Stabbed in the neck. When he heard the news, a disbelieving Iverson raced to his mentor's place, where he saw a river of dark purple blood staining the street and sidewalk.

"I still ain't over that one," Iverson says matter-of-factly today.

Eight other acquaintances died that summer, all from gunshot wounds. It felt like a daily occurrence: Iverson would be on the playground, fooling around, when some kid would come running with an account of trouble. The whole neighborhood would turn out, it seemed, and Iverson would hang near the back of the throng—"scared as shit," he remembers today—catching glimpses here and there of the lifeless body of someone he'd regularly played ball with.

That summer found Iverson hanging with some new friends. One was Rasaan Langford, or "Ra," a good-natured court jester who, along with Eric "E" Jackson, turned Iverson on to rap. They'd hang out till all hours, freestyling. Iverson had been raised on Ann's music, R&B. Finally, here was something that described *his* life. He got hooked on the poetic stylings of Kool Moe Dee, and, later, would flip when Biggie Smalls seemed to perfectly capture both his own upbringing and his ambitions to make it big, as in Smalls's song "Juicy," which was dedicated to "All the teachers that told me I'd never amount to nothing": "We used to fuss when the landlord dissed us/No heat, wonder why Christmas missed us/Birthdays was the worst days/Now we sip champagne when we thirst-ay . . ." Biggie took all his boyz—known as the Junior Mafia—with him wherever he went; when he made it big, they made it big. Iverson decided early on that that was how it was going to be with Ra and "E" and some of the other guys, like Marlon Moore and Arnie Steele. Together, they called themselves, first, Dynasty Raiders and, later, Cru Thik. They made a pact: If Allen made it out through hoops, the others were along for the ride. If one of the others blew up as a rapper, Allen would be there, too.

To this day, Iverson considers Ra and "E" the two best rappers he's ever heard. That summer, taking a cue from them, he started writing his own raps, having finally found a creative form to rival that of basketball. But no other talent of his could approach what he was suddenly able to do on the basketball court, not drawing, rapping, or even playing football. No, in the summer of 1992, Iverson became something special in basketball, and this fact was not unrelated to all the turmoil around him. If he was, as those who witnessed him that summer attest, an artist on the court, he was using suffering to fuel his creativity, as so many artists had done before him.

"The basketball court was my one escape," he recalls today. "I mean, I'd go out there and it was the one place I could just do my thing and have no worries, forget about everything."

The coming-out party began at the state tournament in Richmond. Back then, only the state champion advanced to play in the nationals, so the stakes were high. In the title game, Rutland hit a game winner off a penetration and no-look assist from Iverson. Afterward, the team stopped at a barbecue joint in Richmond. Iverson was, as usual, a nonstop chatterbox. But, even for him, the braggadocio was reaching new levels.

In the parking lot, he approached coaches Williams, Bill Tose, and David Six. "I'm as good as Mike, you know," he said. "I can take Mike."

The coaches all looked at one another and snickered. "Maybe you can," Tose said. "But Mike Evans is pretty good. It'd be a good matchup."

"No, no, no," Iverson corrected him. "I can take *Mike*. Mike Jordan." At the time, Iverson had just painted Jordan's likeness on his bedroom door. When it came time to move, in fact, he was found trying to unhinge the door to take it with him.

In late July, Iverson put on a Jordan-like display at the AAU seventeen-and-under nationals at Wake Forest's Joel Coliseum. Most of his teammates, and most of those they were going against, were all heading into their senior seasons. Iverson was not only younger and shorter than everyone else, he was less experienced, too. His teammates were Rutland, Bacote, Joe Smith, Faisal Abraham (who would play at Marquette), and Tarik Turner (St. John's). They were going against the most-hyped players in the country, but it didn't matter. It became the Allen Iverson show.

Iverson averaged 25.5 points over eight games, with a high of 37. He made threes from NBA distances and dunked off alley-oops, rising above seven-footers. He scored 33 in a triple-overtime win over the Cleveland team, including all 7 of his team's points in the final overtime. He led his team with 24 in the semifinal win over the Arkansas Lakers. In the final, Iverson had 25 points, 6 rebounds, and 5 assists in an 82–78 win over the much-heralded Charlotte Sonics starring Jerry Stackhouse, Jeff Capel, and Jeff McInnis. He was named MVP of the fifty-seven-team event.

"I knew I was this good!" Iverson announced to his teammates, clutching his MVP award and the championship trophy all the way back to Newport News.

"You gotta understand," says Boo Williams. "Almost nobody knew who this rascal was. People were just stunned."

The success made Iverson's off-court demeanor easier to good-naturedly tolerate. "Socks, shoes, uniforms, playing time: ain't nothing right according to Bubba," Williams says, laughing. "He's a constant complainer. But he never cheated you with effort."

Coach Koz, a bear of a man with a growl of a voice, had a shirt-and-tie rule on game day. Dennis Kozlowski was not only Bethel High's football coach, he was also its athletic director, and his rule was sacrosanct: if you didn't wear a shirt and tie to school, you didn't play. On the day Allen Iverson's junior season was to begin, a security guard told Koz that his star quarterback was wearing a T-shirt.

Kozlowski was perplexed. Last spring, after Iverson had led the Bruins to a 10–1 record, the sophomore was a finalist for the annual Peninsula Sports Club and *Daily Press* Athlete of the Year award, announced at an annual banquet. Kozlowski had personally taken Iverson shopping for a shirt and tie back then—and that had been only five months earlier. What happened to the clothes he had bought him?

"One of my mother's boyfriends took 'em, Coach," Iverson replied.

"C'mon," Kozlowski said, taking his player shopping again. It wasn't the first time he'd had to go beyond what many coaches might do for a star player. The previous year, Iverson's sophomore season, Kozlowski got wind that Iverson wasn't eating regularly. He called him into his office and told him that he could get him placed on the school's Underprivileged Meals Program so he wouldn't have to pay for lunch.

Iverson's eyes widened, and with wounded pride in his voice, he protested, "I ain't underprivileged."

"Well, forget what it's called," Kozlowski said. "Would you do it if nobody knew you were doing it?"

Iverson grudgingly agreed that yes, if no one were to find out he was getting meals for free, he'd eat them. So Kozlowski approached Mrs. Johnson, a white woman who ran the cafeteria staff, which consisted of all black women. He explained the situation to her and she explained it to her staff; to them, Mrs. Johnson was helping out one of their own. All involved saw to it that Allen not only ate, but that it never cost him anything.

Shortly thereafter, Kozlowski received a call from a friend on the Newport News police force. Turns out, a drug task force had recent video footage of Allen buying narcotics. Kozlowski was stunned; Iverson had always been vociferously antidrugs. Plus, unlike so many other kids, he had always, as Coach Bailey observed, been aware of just how much he had at stake. The police, Kozlowski was assured, were not going to do anything with the tape—provided he straightened the kid out. He called Allen into his office, and after telling him their conversation would be just between them, confronted him with what he'd been told. Angry denials—"Coach, I don't do drugs!"—were followed by, finally, an embarrassed admission.

"Coach, I was running an errand for my mom," he said.

It was, the coach would later recall, the hardest heart-to-heart he'd ever had with a player. "Do you really want to help your mom?" Kozlowski asked him.

"More than anything," Iverson said.

"How do you think you're going to do that?"

"C'mon, man, you know," Iverson replied. "By going to the NBA or NFL."

Kozlowski took a deep breath, trying to make the moment as dramatic as possible. "But if you get caught with drugs, the dream ends," he said. "I know you love your mom, but, in the future, if she asks you to get anything for her, just send some of your friends. Don't go yourself." He made Allen promise to heed his advice.

By the time his junior season rolled around, Iverson's football team was on a roll and his local celebrity was approaching mythic proportions. A kid himself, he couldn't go to the Coliseum Mall, for example, without being mobbed by kids seeking his autograph. "It was crazy, man," remembers Jamil Blackmon, a street-smart hustler at Hampton University at the time; he promoted rap concerts on the weekends and always seemed to have wads of cash at his disposal. Ann, according to Blackmon, had been trying to convince him to become her family's benefactor. "Every time he touched a ball, whether at Aberdeen Elementary, Anderson Park, or Bethel, there was a crowd. He had people crowding around him in restaurants like he was Michael Jordan. Guys who are celebrities in the game now, I know they never experienced anything like what he went through when he was that age."

Blackmon befriended Iverson and started looking out for him. Often, Iverson would stay at Blackmon's apartment on Marcella Drive in Hampton. Just as Tony Clark had done, Blackmon would send him home if he arrived without his schoolbooks. Ann would open the door and laugh as Allen moped his way inside. "He sent your ass home again, huh?" she'd say. When Ann needed a bill paid, she'd often turn to Blackmon. "And the way Juicy was, it'd be like, 'This four-hundred-dollar phone bill is due in ten minutes, or they're cutting off my shit,'" Blackmon recalls. Meantime, Ann kept pitching Blackmon on taking her and her family under his wing; he kept promising to consider it. "Once my baby gets rich, you'll never want for nothing," she'd say. "You and me, we'll have mansions right next to each other."

Before any mansions could be purchased, though, there was a high-school football state championship to contend for. Iverson was having a dream season in what many considered to be his best sport. "As unbelievable as he is in basketball, he was more amazing in football," recalls Gary Moore, his first football coach.

As a sophomore, Iverson intercepted 13 passes and accounted for over 1,500 yards of total offense. Now, as a junior, he easily surpassed those numbers. He amassed 2,204 yards, ran for 21 touchdowns, passed for 14 more, and picked off 8 passes. But a litany of statistics doesn't do his game justice. As in basketball, he would do things on the gridiron that defied belief. Like the time his touchdown punt return was called back on account of a holding penalty against one of his teammates. Fielding the ball upon the rekick, Iverson found an even higher gear and repeated the touchdown run, using almost the exact same route. "It was like everyone else was playing football and he was playing PlayStation," recalls basketball coach Mike Bailey, who would cringe every time his star player got hit during a football game. "Everybody looked at each other and wondered, 'Did we just see a replay, or was that really live?'"

Kozlowski was a staunch believer in psychocybernetics. He'd preach the value of visualization long before such mental gymnastics were in vogue. He had Allen read the book *Psycho-Cybernetics*, by Maxwell Maltz, a plastic surgeon who maintained that, even after reconstructive nose surgery, many patients would still see their old nose when they looked in the mirror; such was the power of the brain's imagery. Kozlowski would tell Iverson to tie his shoe while continuing to carry on a conversation with him. Iverson would be speaking to him, looking up at him, while kneeling and tying his shoe. "See that," Kozlowski said. "See how you didn't have to look at yourself tying your shoe? See how you didn't even have to think about it? I want you to play like you just tied your shoelaces—automatically. The way you do that is by having an image in your mind of what you do before you do it."

"Allen took psychocybernetics to a new level," Kozlowski recalls. Today, Iverson doesn't like to talk about how he does what he does on the basketball court. "I just do it," he says. Partially, like any artist, he is wary of overanalyzing his gift. But it could also be that he's known since high school that the real explanation defies easy answers, that the answer is, at heart, both beneath and above the level of language, and connected, on some level, to his psyche. In other words, missed in all the hand-wringing about his lackadaisical practice habits in the NBA is the possibility that so much of his work is *cerebral.* Unlike, say, Jordan, who was a craftsman, someone who would take hundreds of jumpshots a day, Iverson imagines possibility and then acts it out.

"Let me tell you about Allen's workouts," says Terry Royster, his bodyguard from 1997 until early 2002. "All the time I've been with him, I never seen him lift a weight or stand there and shoot jumper after jumper. Instead, we'll be on our way to the game and he'll be quiet as hell. Finally, he'll say, 'You know how I usually cross my man over and take it into the lane and pull up? Well, tonight, I'm gonna cross him over and then take a step back and fade away. I'm gonna kill 'em with it all night long.' And damned if he don't do just that. See, that's his workout, when he's just sitting there, thinking. That's him working on his game."

Imagining himself doing great things had its desired effect his junior year of high school. Iverson was named Virginia's Football Player of the Year, and he led the Bruins to the state title game against E. C. Glass in Lynchburg. The day before the big game, Kozlowski took the squad to practice at Lynchburg's Heritage High School. It was a rainy, cold day, but Kozlowski wanted to run through some game situations one last time. When it came time to practice punt returns, Iverson took his place deep in the backfield, awaiting the kick. He fielded it, took two steps, and then, as the play was going on, simply stopped and stood there, motionless. Kozlowski whistled the play dead and approached his star.

"What are you doing?"

"Coach, we shouldn't be out here," Iverson said. "It's cold, the ground's wet."

Kozlowski was taken aback. "Allen, you're on a team—everybody else is practicing," he said. "Now let's do it again, get it right, and we can all go back to the hotel."

The next punt came to Iverson, and again, he caught it and stood still. Kozlowski blew his whistle—and his top. "That's it! You're out!" he yelled. "You're not playing tomorrow! Go stand over there!"

For the next hour, the team practiced in a drizzle while Iverson huddled under the awning of a shed. One of the assistant coaches approached him.

"Are you crazy? Don't you want to play tomorrow?" he asked.

"I don't care," Iverson said. "We shouldn't be out here. I'm *right*. And you all know I'm right."

Iverson may have been surprised by Kozlowski's hard-line response. After all, Iverson was still setting all sorts of truancy records in the school district, and yet he hadn't been sat down for a single football or basketball game. Indeed, one Bethel administrator at the time recalls an argument with Iverson over whether he'd missed sixty-nine *or* seventy-five days to date in that school year. (Many of his absences came because he was home caring for Ieisha.) Perhaps he figured that, if he hadn't been held accountable for skipping school all that time, no one would dare bench him on the eve of the championship game.

The next morning, led by Michael Jackson and Xavier Gunn, the seniors appealed to Kozlowski to reverse his decision. "We've come this far together and we want to play together tomorrow," Gunn said.

The players were unanimous. Kozlowski said he'd leave it up to them, but not before warning them: "We might be doing a disservice to Allen in the long run."

That day, Iverson intercepted two passes, passed for two touchdowns, and scored two more—including a breathtaking punt return in which not one defender could so much as touch him—and the Bruins won, 27–0. Many of the Bethel faithful had come down for the game. They were, just as at all the Bethel home games, a truly mixed crowd: black, white, young, old, united by this team and this special player. And they were jubilant, especially when Allen, interviewed on the sideline, was asked what was next. "We gonna get us one in basketball," he said, referring to the state championship. He knew that in three days—and after just one basketball practice—he would begin trying to make that prediction come true. He'd score 37 points to beat Kecoughtan High, where his new girlfriend, Tawanna Turner, was a student.

But, as he danced and hugged and smiled his mother's beaming smile on the sideline the day he won the state football title, he didn't know that the unity sparked by him and his team would be short-lived. An event loomed in the future that would set his hometown against itself, white versus black, young versus old. He had no way of knowing he was about to be at the center of his town's biggest racial maelstrom since the assassination of Martin Luther King Jr.

chapter | 3

PRAYING HANDS

A set of hands between my grandma's initials—Ethel Selena
Mitchell, who died when I was real young—and my mama's
initials, Ethel Ann Iverson. They taught me to pray every
day, 'cause when you send prayers up, lessons come down.

Whorized her hen the trouble came, there were those who thought it all had its roots in the simplest of things, nothing more than high-school rivalry run amok. It's impossible to tell, of course; no one will ever know precisely why it went down the way it did, any more than they will know *what* exactly happened the night that Allen Iverson's life, as well as his hometown's history, changed.

It is true that Bethel High School was a relative upstart, particularly in athletics. After all, the school had only been around since 1968, and it was only in the era of Iverson that its teams had begun dominating. Its cross-town arch rival, Hampton High, was the more established school. By virtue of its longevity, Hampton had graduated much of the town's power elite: countless judges, lawyers, and business owners. Bethel's backers were wary; Iverson was in the process of following up the state football title by leading the Bruins on a state basketball championship run. Would the town's powers-that-be take steps to guard against Hampton losing out on two more championships next year, when Iverson would be a senior?

Most objective onlookers viewed such fear as melodramatic. But those in the trenches of area high-school sports, guys like Coaches Kozlowski and Bailey, insisted that anything was possible. They knew firsthand the passion of this particular high-school sports rivalry. Add such incendiary emotions to the always combustible context of race relations and there was no telling what could happen.

Before the trouble, though, there were basketball games to be played. Early on, against Hampton, Coach Bailey (already known as a demonstrative sideline coach) was at his most animated. In fact, Iverson had once penned a caricature of Bailey on the sidelines, shirt all rumpled and untucked, hair unruly and unkempt. Here was that caricature come to life as Bailey constantly yelled instructions to his point guard. "Allen! Pass the ball ahead!" he called.

Iverson wheeled around at midcourt. "Coach! Stop telling me how to play all the time!" he yelled.

"I'll do just that," Bailey said, and he pulled Iverson from the game; in the ensuing huddle, Iverson muttered "fuck you" to his coach. He had 29 points at the time and Hampton led, 65–51. Bailey kept him on the bench through the third and fourth quarters and the final score was 101–67, Hampton. It was an uncharacteristic move on Bailey's part; he was not known to be stern when it came to Iverson. Walking off, Bailey approached his star. "Do you like me not coaching you?" he asked. "It's real easy when you're sitting on the end of the bench for me to not say much to you."

Iverson looked away, said nothing.

In the locker room, Iverson's teammate and close friend Xavier Gunn called a twenty-minute team meeting. "Allen, you're selfish," he said.

Iverson leaped to his feet. "How can I be selfish when I average ten assists a game?"

"Not the basketball part," Gunn replied. "You gotta be right all the time. When Coach Bailey said what he said to you tonight, when we say things to you sometimes, you always gotta be right."

No one raised his voice. Iverson stewed in silence, taking in the criticism from significantly lesser talents. In the next game, against Menchville, he decided he would prove a point: he wouldn't take a shot. He'd show Bailey and Gunn and everyone else just how unselfish he could be. Bethel found itself down 41–25 at halftime. Iverson had made some beautiful passes, but his teammates—never expecting, or wanting, to be taking *this* many shots—were befuddled by this apparent new strategy. Bailey knew he had to do something, so in front of the team, he decided to appeal to his star's most prominent and laudable quality: his competitiveness.

"Allen, if you honestly feel that not taking a shot is the best way to win a game, then by all means, pass the ball—I have no problem with that," Bailey said. "As long as your decision making is driven by what's going to make us win, we'll all be all right. We all have confidence in your judgment and competitiveness."

Iverson said nothing. As would often be the case, Bailey wasn't even sure he was getting through, so sporadic was Iverson's eye contact. But Bailey knew from experience that Iverson was a much better listener than he appeared to be. In the second half, Iverson started draining threes and penetrating at will. With him leading the way, Bethel scored 37 points in the eight-minute fourth quarter and won, 86–74. Iverson had 21 of his game-high 40 in the final quarter.

"That game was our turning point," Bailey recalls. "I think Allen saw that his teammates, and me, would both stand up to him *and* stand by him. And that's the key with him. It's why he's so loyal to those guys from back home. They've stood by him."

The Bruins won nineteen straight games after the Menchville win, but as Iverson would say, all was not "peaches and cream" from then on. In early February 1993, Bailey benched him again, after Allen missed a practice. Cleverly, the coach got Ann and Gary Moore on board with the punishment before telling Iverson of his fate. "I know you do what you do because you love him," Ann told Bailey.

Still, Iverson would not speak to his coach. The next game was before another overflow crowd. Before the game, a security guard interrupted Bailey's team meeting. Fans were going to have to use the locker-room bathrooms, Bailey was told—too many were crowding into the rest rooms upstairs. Bailey objected. "You don't like it, too bad," said the security guard.

Now Bailey and the guard were face-to-face, exchanging unpleasantries. Suddenly, squeezing between them was Iverson, staring the security guard down, wagging an index finger. "You don't talk to this man that way," he said calmly. Immediate silence ensued; both men backed off. He's not speaking to me, Bailey thought, incredulous, and now he's telling other people how *they're* supposed to act toward me?

Shortly after that win, Iverson was at a party at the Sheraton on Hampton University's campus. A twenty-two-year-old bouncer tossed a guy, who came back with an Uzi. After the shots, the assailant calmly walked back out. Iverson and two of his teammates were upstairs. They heard the shots and huddled together until it was safe to come down. When they did, they heard the victim laughing that one of the bullets had hit him in the ass. He died later that night.

Mike Bailey heard that his star player had been at the scene of a homicide. He had always known, given the type of people looking out for him—people who were doing good by him, but who didn't always do good themselves—that the kid was perpetually one ill-timed moment away from calamity. This was too close, he felt.

The next night, Bailey's players celebrated another win in the locker room, but Bailey quieted the party. "This is not a moment we should be celebrating," he said. "We should be reflecting. Because three members of our team were someplace last night that wasn't the best place to be. I'm not saying they were doing anything wrong, but we don't need to be doing these things. We need to reflect on what's at stake. Think about, what if it was you, shot at a party? Think about your loved ones, how they'd react. Reflect tonight on what's truly important. That's all I'm saying."

The players were silent as the meeting broke. Bailey stood in front of Iverson and both men wrapped their arms around each other and hugged. "I wanted to do this a week ago," Bailey said.

"Me, too," Iverson said.

"What stopped us?"

"Pride," Iverson said.

Bailey and his star walked out of the locker room together, and Bailey offered a piece of advice he'd forever regret. "You know what you need to do, Bubba? You need to do high-school things, like any other teenager would do," he said. "You know, go to the movies. Or get a bunch of guys together and go bowling, blow off some steam."

Hampton and Newport News, Virginia, commonly referred to as the Virginia Peninsula, changed sometime after midnight on Valentine's Day, 1993, when a brawl broke out at the Circle Lanes bowling alley. The fallout wasn't apparent right away. But over the course of the next year, as groups chose sides and sharpened their rhetoric, as the media onslaught began, it became clear that the character of a town was being inexorably tested. The Hampton and Newport News area, as part of the New South, had prided itself on its racial comity. Any quick scan of the stands during Bethel or Hampton sporting events showed this—showed blacks and whites, side by side, united in a common purpose.

But then came the bowling-alley incident, where how you perceived what happened determined who you were, just as who you were determined *how* you saw things. The divergence of opinion, almost without exception, broke down along racial lines.

Allen Iverson, Michael Simmons, Melvin Stephens Jr., and Samuel Wynn were among a group of black students bowling in lanes nine and ten and were, according to witness testimony, being boisterous. Twice, bowling-alley employee Brandon Smith, a student at Bethel, approached them to ask Simmons not to stand on the chairs. A little after midnight, Iverson, with a friend in tow, made his way toward the snack bar. Nearby was a group of white bowlers from the wealthy neighborhood of Poquoson. According to testimony from one of them, six-foot two-inch, two-hundred-pound Steve Forrest, Iverson approached them and, unprovoked, said, "What's your problem? What are you looking at?"

Iverson and others maintain that Forrest, who had been convicted of felony cocaine possession in the past, called Iverson a "nigger" and "little boy." The two were soon squaring off, an arm's length away. According to Forrest, he told Iverson he didn't want any trouble, which is when, he testified, Iverson's friend Michael Simmons came up and blindsided him with a punch to the back of the head. Iverson claims that Forrest broke their stare-down by swinging a chair and hitting him on the head, at which point someone, seeking to protect him, grabbed Iverson and ushered him outside. He didn't throw a chair or punch anybody, he maintained.

That's how it started. What followed was a dizzying, violent mess of a brawl that sent bowlers scurrying down lanes, seeking to hide behind the pins. Simmons was a wannabe filmmaker, a senior, and he'd been documenting the last semester of his high-school career. He had a video camera with him that night, which was on and which stayed on, capturing the jumpy, scrambled, confused mess of a rumble. There were people screaming and falling, chairs being hurled, and sounds of sobs and curses echoing through the air. Things quickly calmed down, but escalated again soon after. One witness said that Iverson reentered the bowling alley, or had never left, though others refute that claim. Brandon Smith would go on to identify Iverson as the assailant who hit a twenty-three-year-old white college student named Barbara Steele over the head with a chair; Steele, who was knocked unconscious, required six stitches around her left eye and later suffered amnesia. Smith would later testify that he tried to help Steele, but that Iverson knocked him over the head with a chair, shattering his glasses.

All in all, the melee might have taken two minutes. But when it was over, more than one witness told the *Daily Press,* the local newspaper, that the bowling alley looked like a "war zone." According to the *Press,* in the stunned silence after the violence, the only thing that could be heard was Michael Jackson's hopeful voice over the piped-in sound system: "It doesn't matter if you're black or white . . ."

Just hours after the brawl, Dennis Kozlowski's phone rang. A former student of his, a white alumnus of the Bethel track team, was on the other end of the line. He'd been knocked around in a bowling-alley brawl earlier, he said, and he wanted to give Kozlowski a heads-up. Iverson was the only recognizable face there, and the cops were going to blame the whole thing on him.

The next day, Ann Iverson got Simmons's amateur tape into the hands of Boo Williams and Mike Bailey. Before turning it over to the authorities, they watched the grainy footage some fifty times and were convinced Allen was nowhere to be found on the tape. Bailey instinctively knew why this was: Allen was being protected. The whole reason his friends came running in the first place was that they had Allen's back; it only made sense that one of them would, as Allen maintained, get him out of there. "If you understand that culture, the one who can make it, they're going to protect him," Bailey says. "I can't tell you how many times I'd be driving around some pretty iffy sections of Newport News looking for Allen in the middle of the night and I just couldn't believe where I was. I once said to Allen, 'What's going to happen to me when I go to these neighborhoods looking for you?' And he said, 'Nothing, Coach. They know you're with me.' "

Most observers of the video couldn't tell if Iverson was in it or not. It didn't incriminate, but neither did it exonerate him. Shortly after the brawl, the *Daily Press* reported that Iverson was under investigation, violating its own policy against publishing the names of juveniles accused of crimes. But what had happened at the bowling alley was hardly a well-guarded secret; the whole town was talking about it, so the paper was obliged to write about it. Kozlowski asked Iverson if he wanted to speak to his lawyer.

"Gary Moore's got someone for me," Iverson replied. "Gary's gonna handle it." Moore arranged for Iverson to be represented by seventy-three-year-old Herb Kelly, a lawyer of counsel to Hampton University, where Moore was employed, but someone who hadn't tried a case in court for over a decade. More ominous was the fact that Kelly wasn't considered politically connected to the Hampton establishment.

Many in the Iverson camp were concerned. Once the *Daily Press* got on the story—soon the national media would swarm in—it ceased to be about the facts. There were also politics to consider; the white victims were from Poquoson, a traditional bastion of wealth and power.

On February 16, just two days after the incident, the much-hyped basketball rematch between Bethel and Hampton took place in front of eight thousand fans at the Hampton Coliseum, the largest crowd to see a Peninsula District game in fifteen years. Bethel authorities and Iverson's loved ones were a wreck; Iverson seemed like the only person unaffected by the controversy surrounding him. He led his team to a 69–67 win over Hampton, ending the Crabbers' seventeen-game winning streak. He scored 23 points, and five days later was named to the *Parade* magazine high-school all-America team, with averages of 31.1 points, 11 rebounds, and 10 assists per game.

Just two days later, the newly minted all-American was placed under arrest. As would be the case throughout his life and career, Iverson would feed off the drama he found himself starring in. He would locate the calm eye at the storm's center and nestle in. Later, in the pros, he developed an almost comical knack for orchestrating blowups with his old school coach Larry Brown, creating a psychodrama with himself at its center—only to rise up out of the squabbling in epic fashion. It was a pattern reminiscent of another tortured artist who also happened to express himself in the field of sports, tennis great John McEnroe. Like Iverson, McEnroe was an artistically inclined "natural" with poor work habits who, in order to summon his genius, needed to raise the stakes to the point where his outbursts would create a "me versus the world" tension.

So it was that, just hours after he was arrested, booked, and released, all eyes were on seventeen-year-old Allen Iverson as he took to the floor for the Peninsula District Tournament semifinals against Ferguson High. In attendance that night was the singer/songwriter Bruce Hornsby, who lived in Williamsburg and fancied himself something of a basketball player.

He'd heard about this kid who'd been arrested earlier that day. And then he sat there, slack-jawed, watching this slight, speedy junior put aside all the distractions—his very future, at all of seventeen, was in peril!—en route to scoring more than half of his team's points. Iverson lit up Ferguson for 42 points in an 81–78 Bethel win.

Iverson could control his world on the basketball court, which is why it was always such a comfortable escape for him. Off the court was another matter. While Iverson took his team on a thrilling run toward the state championship, worries among Iverson loyalists escalated when Judge Louis Lerner disregarded the recommendation of the juvenile probation officer, Ernest Madison, and opted to charge Iverson and the others as adults. Iverson was seventeen at the time of the incident and had a clean record, save for a conviction the previous fall for reckless driving and driving without a license; he'd subsequently failed to meet with a juvenile probation officer five times. Moreover, the charge was particularly ominous sounding: maiming by mob. Ironically, maiming by mob was a seldom-used Virginia statute put on the books to prosecute Ku Klux Klan members, a way to hold individuals accountable for the havoc wreaked by the group.

A July trial date meant that for the rest of the basketball season, charges would hang over Iverson's head. Even though the state championship loomed, for Iverson and the entire community, the worst was just beginning.

The road to the state championship promised more roadblocks beyond the distraction of Iverson's legal travails. It also contained a six-foot nine-inch pothole named Joe Smith. Smith, a close friend of Iverson's, starred at Maury High, the team to beat statewide. He'd go on to star at the University of Maryland before becoming the first overall pick in the 1995 NBA draft. Briefly, in 1997, he and Iverson played together on the Philadelphia 76ers.

But for now, Smith was an obstacle. Bethel was a small team; no one topped six-two. But Bailey had a secret strategy that, when unveiled, led those who were watching to wonder if they were really seeing what they were seeing. At the right moment, he was going to have Iverson, at all of five feet eleven inches, guard Smith.

As expected, Smith was having his way with the Bethel defense. But he was a one-man team. Of the 50 points Maury ended the game with, 37 were Smith's, a career high. He had scored 35 of those with two and one-half minutes to go, when Bailey put Iverson on Smith. Some in the crowd started laughing as Iverson "bodied up" against Smith down low. Though he towered over Iverson, Smith was rail thin—more of a finesse than a power player. Amazingly, there was Iverson, pushing Smith out of the lane, keeping him from getting position down low. Smith's teammates looked for him a couple of times, but Iverson wasn't allowing Smith an angle to receive an entry pass. Smith's teammates would pump-fake the ball to him and then pass it elsewhere; someone else would end up taking the shot. So it was until the buzzer sounded; Iverson held Smith scoreless down the stretch, save a meaningless bucket at the buzzer, and Bethel eked out a 52–50 win, earning the school's first-ever trip to the Group AAA Tournament quarterfinals.

As Bethel's run continued, the line for tickets on game days would form four or five hours before tip-off. By the time of the state semifinal game against Woodbridge, all of the Peninsula had caught Bethel fever. But, in the first half, it looked like the dream was over. Woodbridge's Damion Keyes, at six-four and 250 pounds, was dominating inside. He was just too big and too strong for the undermanned Bethel defense. At halftime, Bethel was down 11 points, Keyes had scored 18, and Iverson had three fouls. Bailey and his players were at a loss as to how to counter the Woodbridge attack.

"Let's go to a matchup zone," one of the players called out.

"Uh, we've never played zone, let alone a matchup zone," Bailey pointed out.

There was silence. It was not, Mike Bailey would later concede, one of those great Knute Rockne–like moments. Finally, bewildered, he simply looked at his team and said, "Forget it. Let's just go play."

Once on the court, Iverson sidled up alongside his coach and put his arm around him. "I can guard him," he said, nodding toward Keyes.

"Are you crazy?" Bailey said. "You got three fouls, he weighs two-fifty and you're one-sixty. You're crazy!"

"Coach, I can guard him."

"I'm not wasting my best player," Bailey said. "Why don't these other guys have the heart you have? Why don't your teammates want to guard him?"

Grudgingly, Bailey let Iverson open up the second half checking Keyes. Again, it made for a comical sight as Iverson put his bony hip alongside Keyes's beefy one and tried to hold his ground. Even today, in the NBA, Iverson is a surprisingly proficient low-post defender, thanks to his singularly stubborn will—combined with his high-school experiences against the likes of Smith and Keyes. When he came into the NBA, Iverson's size was thought to be a major liability; bigger guards, the thinking went, would exploit him under the basket. It has never happened because Iverson has never let it. Against Keyes, as against NBA players later, he decided to use his strengths to minimize his disadvantages. And his strength, as usual, was his quickness.

As expected, Woodbridge began the second half by dumping the ball into Keyes on two consecutive trips down the floor. Both times, Iverson waited until the last possible instant and then darted out from behind his man to steal the ball and score two straight layups. It sparked a comeback that, in the fourth quarter, was imperiled when Iverson, having dunked after stealing another pass, turned an ankle. He was barely able to make it to the sideline, where the trainer worked on him while Bethel's hopes faded. But Bailey knew. He remembered that time, two years earlier, when Iverson saw every doctor in Hampton after spraining his ankle, in search of the one who would give him the go-ahead to return to the court. Sure enough, two plays later, he got up. "I'm ready, Coach."

With Bethel down three with twenty-six seconds left, Woodbridge double-teamed Iverson in the forecourt. He ran right at the double team, freezing one defender before blowing past the other and rising for a contested three-pointer. Overtime.

In the extra session, Iverson overpenetrated and was called for an offensive foul—his fifth and final foul. Having blown such a big lead, Woodbridge seemed demoralized, but who would pick up Iverson's slack? Bailey called on seldom-used sophomore Lovett Gaither, who scored 9 points in the overtime to seal the win.

On the sideline down the stretch, it was as though there were two coaches, Bailey and Iverson, who was part cheerleader, part assistant coach. In the NBA, Iverson has not been known as a vocal team leader, but in high school evidence of his leadership abounded. Prior to the start of his junior year, for instance, Bailey had decided to cut Kelly Rodgers. Rodgers was the team's strongest rebounder, but he frequently violated one of Bailey's few ironclad rules: he didn't play hard every single play. Bailey had had enough, until Iverson came to him.

"Coach, we need him," Iverson said.

"Allen," Bailey explained, "it's not fair to you or your teammates to play a guy who takes plays off."

"Let's do this, Coach," Iverson said. "Let him be my responsibility. I'll get him to play."

Bailey mulled it over, finally hammering out a deal with his star. "Okay," he said, "but your name is going to be Rodgers from now on. He screws up, and it's you who pays the price."

From that moment on, Bailey would watch while Iverson would take

Rodgers aside, during practice and games, always cajoling effort out of him. Bailey never again had a problem with Rodgers, who became an integral part of the Bethel team.

There was also Iverson's locker-room banter, nonstop teasing that drew the squad together. He nicknamed everyone on the team, including Tony Rutland—the Pippen to his Jordan—whose mother was Korean. Rutland was dubbed "Kong Fu." Melvin Stephens, who often suffered bloody injuries in practice, became "Lip Therapy."

Then there was Bobby, the special-education student who served as a manager for the team. Early in the season, Bobby approached Iverson. "Allen, I got a new play for you," Bobby said. Bailey, watching, knew that Iverson was already growing tired of how everybody was always telling him how to play. Just don't hurt this kid's feelings, Bailey thought, watching nervously.

"Turn around, I'll show you," Bobby said. Once Iverson turned, Bobby started scratching out a crazy array of directions on his back with both index fingers—for about thirty seconds. "That's it!" Bobby said.

Iverson spun around, eyes wide. He snapped his fingers. "That'll work, Coach!" he said, and Bobby beamed for the rest of the season, especially when Iverson and the others continued to call him Coach.

Fourteen weeks after winning the state football title and boldly predicting that a basketball one was to follow, Iverson delivered. The night before the big game, he rounded up his teammates and organized them into a late-night Monopoly tourney, during which he displayed his competitiveness.

The next day, he ran rampant on the court. Iverson and Rutland combined for 58 points (Iverson 28, Rutland 30), as the 27–3 Bruins beat John Marshall High at the University of Virginia's University Hall, 77–71. The go-ahead basket, fittingly, came when Iverson penetrated and dished to Rutland; ever since their turbulent "Terrible Twos," as Bailey used to call them, they'd not only come to mesh on the court, but to respect and admire each other off it. In fact, Rutland was playing overseas when Iverson, having just completed his fourth NBA season, heard that Rutland's father was in the hospital back home. One day, a Bethel administrator went to see Larry Rutland in the hospital. Poking her head into his room, she saw the NBA star sitting by his bedside, deep in conversation.

When the state championship was won, Iverson and Rutland embraced and the crowd started chanting "Iverson! Iverson! Iverson!" He shook his head no and pointed to his chest, leading them, letter by letter, on a new chant: "B-E-T-H-E-L!"

Next came the celebration, but not before Iverson had to borrow fourteen dollars from an assistant coach to help pay for twenty-eight dollars' worth of in-room movies he watched at the hotel during the team's stay at the University of Virginia. Then it was time for the championship ceremony back at Bethel, where the players wore tuxedos. The local TV stations all turned out.

"Iverson," an announcer asked, "is this your first experience in a tux?"

"First experience," Iverson replied, shy as ever when the TV lights were on him.

"How do you like it?"

"I don't like it," he said, breaking into a devilish half smile. "I don't like wearing my pants this far up."

With basketball over, there was little to do but wait for the summer trial date. In the spring, Bailey received a call from Bruce Hornsby, who hadn't been able to shake the image from his head of this basketball prodigy whose future was in jeopardy.

"How can I help?" Hornsby asked.

So it was that on one day in the spring of 1993, Allen Iverson was nowhere to be found—which concerned quite a few people in the 'hood. Jamil Blackmon remembers calling Ra and Arnie and E: "You guys seen 'Chuck?" he asked.

"We all thought he was with you," they said.

Instead, he was visiting Bruce Hornsby. Bailey picked him up and drove him to Colonial Williamsburg. Iverson's eyes widened when they had to pass through a set of wrought-iron gates, complete with a security check, to enter the Hornsby compound. "This is like living in a castle," Iverson said.

For Iverson, the visit was a chance to see the life of somebody who had made it. Hornsby, after all, had just won a Grammy and was well compensated for his musical talent. Seeing Hornsby, Bailey reasoned, could reignite in Allen his desire to overcome all the obstacles—both in his past and looming in his future—and achieve his dream. In addition, it was a chance to see how (though no one would ever call Bruce Hornsby a rapper) someone who had made it big had kept it real. After all, Hornsby still lived where he grew up and still hung out with many of the guys he'd gone to high school with.

For Hornsby, it was a chance to play one-on-one against the best basketball player he'd ever face, a certain future pro. He'd played high-school ball, the only white on a team of blacks, and he stayed in shape by playing hoops on the road. As a piano player, however, Hornsby had to guard against any injury to his hands. So he'd come up with what he called his "Piano Hands Rules." Each player would get one shot each time they got the ball, and any rebound would be an automatic change of possession.

At Hornsby's house, Iverson gawked at the Grammy and played "Chopsticks" on Hornsby's baby grand. Then they went to a local gym to play ball. Iverson would later joke about Hornsby's "funky" jumpshot, with his elbow sticking out at an odd angle. Still, the shot went in. Just before they started playing, a nervous Bailey reminded Iverson: "Don't hurt his hands."

Iverson played tentatively as a result and didn't like the Piano Hands Rules. He'd take one shot, and whether it was good or not, he had to automatically play defense. He couldn't get a rhythm going. Hornsby could, though—and he won. The two started a friendship that continues to this day. Hornsby not only kept in touch while Iverson was incarcerated, he was among many celebrities who surreptitiously helped foot the bill for the private-school completion of Iverson's high-school education when he got out.

When Bailey dropped Iverson off at home later that day, he leaned over to him. "Listen," he said melodramatically. "I'll never ever tell anybody this happened. Because the worst thing that can happen to an athlete is that people find out that somebody in a band beat you."

Later that night, Iverson approached the corner where Jamil Blackmon hung. "'Chuck, where you been?"

"I spent the day with Bruce Hornsby," he said matter-of-factly.

Blackmon scrunched up his face in puzzlement. "Bruce Hornsby and the muthafuckin' *Range*? *That* Bruce Hornsby?" he asked.

"Yeah."

Blackmon, ever the mentor, inched closer. "Listen, nigga, that's cool and all, but don't go advertising in the 'hood that you been hanging with Bruce Hornsby and the muthafuckin' Range, okay?"

As the trial approached, Iverson grew more and more fatalistic. It was as though he already knew this wasn't going to turn out all right. He cut a photo out of the newspaper of a black man in handcuffs being carted off to jail. He cut off the man's head and, in its place, simply wrote "Allen Iverson."

When Mike Bailey mentioned in passing something about playing in the summer league so they could repeat their victory in his senior year, Iverson looked down and paused. "Coach, I'm not going to play next year."

"Why not?"

"I just think I'd be better off going to another school," Iverson said, still looking down. "So that's what I'm gonna do. Go to a different school."

Bailey was stunned and, at first, a bit hurt. "Okay, Allen," he said. "I'd love to have you back, but we can play without you, if that's how you feel."

It wasn't until later that Bailey realized what his star was doing. Of course he wanted to play next year, and play for Bethel. He wasn't unhappy. He'd love nothing more than to make it back-to-back titles in both sports. No, what Allen Iverson was doing was preparing his coach for his absence. Somehow, the kid knew this trial would be a big deal. And that it wouldn't end well. Looming in the near future was not only the trial, but a widespread backlash against the sports star, the fury of which no one fully anticipated. Except, perhaps, Allen Iverson himself.

chapter | 4

THE SOLDIER

this is a soldier's head, because i feel like my life
has been a war and i've been a soldier in it.

Most observers saw the bowling-alley incident not as a harbinger of social change or as a case study in the chasm between the races, but as little more than an unfortunate fight between a bunch of kids. The assumption was that, since these were kids without prior records and two of them—Iverson and Melvin Stephens—were juveniles, all they'd get would be a slap on the wrist.

But that didn't happen. The juveniles wouldn't be tried as juveniles. The charge would be a serious one—and all the more menacing for being so obscure. Clearly, the prosecutors were going to make an example out of the star athlete who might or might not have done the wrong thing, but who most certainly was in the wrong place at the wrong time.

Just days before his trial commenced in the courtroom of Judge Nelson Overton, Allen Iverson made a big mistake. He kicked ass on a basketball court. There was nothing new in that; only this time he was doing so in Indianapolis, where he was dominating Nike's All-American Basketball Festival. *USA Today* called him "the jewel" of the 125 college prospects on display during the five-day tournament, despite the charges he was facing. "Every school in the country wants him," Bob Gibbons, the tournament's player selection chairman, told the newspaper. "If he was John Dillinger, they'd take him."

Iverson's mistake came *after* his on-court domination, when he agreed to let Nike fly him back from the camp for the trial's Friday opening, and then fly him back to Indianapolis the next day for an all-star game. The move only buttressed the prosecutors' portrayal of Iverson as an arrogant, coddled athlete who was finally going to be held accountable. It was a perspective that may or may not have resonated with Overton, a white-skinned, gray-haired, no-nonsense Peninsula lifer who peered out at his packed courtroom over half–reading glasses perched on the bridge of his nose. To those in Iverson's corner, Overton was no impartial jurist. He was part of the Hampton establishment, having graduated from Hampton High and Virginia Military Institute.

Prosecutor Colleen Killilea delivered a blistering closing argument. "Mr. Iverson had two choices—either stay and participate, or get out," she said. "He stayed and participated, and became a member of the mob. He made the wrong choice . . . We don't care how good a basketball player Mr. Iverson is, or how well liked he is by his coach or Mr.

Williams. The fact is, he acted like a criminal that night." Killilea pointed out that two white women and a white man were injured during the fracas, in which she said black people "started hitting whatever white people got in their way." Then, in a reference to Nike's efforts on Iverson's behalf, she closed by playing on the company's famous credo. "Now," she told the judge, "it's our turn to 'just do it.' "

In his summation, Iverson's attorney, Herb Kelly, argued that prosecutors had misapplied the law in the charges against his client. Iverson couldn't be convicted, he argued, because no mob existed—at least not as the word is defined by law. Iverson and his friends were at Circle Lanes that night to bowl, not brawl. "There is no common purpose when people come running from everywhere because of the words *fight, fight, fight,*" Kelly said.

Nelson Overton wasn't having it. At 9:34 on the morning of July 12, 1993, he found Allen Iverson guilty of three felony counts of maiming by mob. (Iverson had opted for a bench, rather than jury, trial, but would later claim that Kelly never presented him with a choice.) When Overton pronounced his judgment, Iverson stood there, blank-faced, as the judge explained that the now convicted felon could remain in his mother's custody until sentencing in September. Iverson would be unable to leave home after 8 P.M. unless he was coming to or from work or school. His whole future was now up in the air. Would colleges continue to recruit? Would he be able to play his senior season at Bethel or, for that matter, anywhere?

Reaction to the verdict was tellingly split. Most local whites applauded; most blacks suspected something dirty was afoot. Still, at that point, the outrage was muted, confined to living rooms and barbershops on the Peninsula. Most continued to think—hope, really—that Overton would be lenient come sentencing time, even though state guidelines called for a punishment of eleven years and ten months for the three convictions.

Like Iverson, Michael Simmons and Samuel Wynn were convicted of felonies. Less than ten days after Iverson's conviction, the fourth defendant, Iverson's teammate Melvin Stephens, became the only one of the "Hampton Four" to go to trial before a jury. Stephens's first trial ended in a hung jury and his second one resulted in three misdemeanor convictions. According to the trial testimony, Stephens led the charge of those coming to Iverson's aid and threw a chair, even though he said himself that he didn't hear any racial slurs directed at Iverson. In short, though the testimony seemed to indicate that Stephens was more of an instigator than Iverson, the jury reduced the charges to misdemeanors. Later, Iverson would sue his lawyer for never discussing with him the merits of opting for a jury trial.

Daily Press columnist Jim Spencer had a different view. He argued that Stephens had benefited not because a jury brought perspective and common sense, but because his lawyer played the race card. In a July 21 column, Spencer, himself a white man, opened with an incendiary lead: "You honky punk, you redneck pig, you hillbilly cracker, you wimpy, fat, overprotected, rhythmless, short-striding, low-jumping, no-basketball-playing, small-handed, clumsy white boy. Are words like these enough to justify a riot?"

Spencer went on to claim that Stephens's trial produced "an outrageous defense for mob violence," going on to berate Stephens's lawyer, Jimmy Ellenson, for suggesting that "a white person calling a black person a nigger produces fighting words that justify whatever happens." Spencer wrote that "each time Ellenson talked about how the fight was justified by a racist comment, [black spectators] muttered agreement like a church congregation listening to a sermon. Too bad they didn't consider the flip side—how they would feel if a lawyer said it was okay for a gang of white folks to indiscriminately beat up blacks at a bowling alley because one of them referred to a white guy as a cracker."

The column struck a nerve. Soon Spencer would be seen in the black community as the voice of the white oppressor. No doubt Spencer did speak for many whites who saw fit to morally equate terms like "nigger" and "cracker," as though blacks and whites shared a common history. To blacks, nothing could compare with the violence implicit in the epithet "nigger"; for a white man to deny them that wound was seen as racist in and of itself. (Besides, none other than the Supreme Court of the United States had long ago established the precedent for "fighting words"— words that would lead an otherwise reasonable man to violence, making Spencer's argument more an attempt to stir emotions than enlighten.)

On September 8, the combustible case burst into flames upon Iverson's sentencing. Before Overton sentenced him, Iverson chose to address the court. He stood and, in a soft, hoarse, inflectionless voice, said, "I would like to apologize to my family and friends and the community if I caused them any embarrassment. And I think I've got my chance now to talk, so I did feel bad for what happened to the people that night at the bowling alley. I wouldn't want that to happen to anybody in that situation."

Simmons and Wynn declined to address the court. Their attorney, Buddy Fox, spoke for them and for many when he argued that the charges were too severe. "What's been lost in this entire matter is perspective," Fox said, pointing out that no guns or knives were used and that there was no evidence of any sort of drug use. Simmons was sentenced to five years and Wynn to three.

When Overton sentenced Iverson to five years—five per felony count, with ten years suspended—a chorus of gasps filled the air. While Iverson stood, stoic, staring straight ahead, and deputies moved to handcuff him and remove him from court, Ann sagged and sobbed behind her baby in the first row of the spectator section. Mike and Janet Bailey hung on to each other, each fearing the other's collapse. Boo Williams paced the court's corridor, venting, as Allen was led off to the Hampton city jail, the same place where, less than four years before, he'd visited his stepfather and gone home barefoot, having left Michael Freeman with his own pair of pristine sneakers. Just like that, he was gone, seemingly doomed to be another statistic in a country where more black men go to prison than to college.

In a courthouse stairwell, Gary Moore cornered a local newspaper reporter. "This is your fault!" he raged. "This is on you!"

Meantime, on the courthouse steps, the months of simmering racial animus detonated. In the weeks leading up to the sentencing, as outrage over Spencer's column combined with the frustration that, in an alleged race riot, only four young African-American men had been charged, a group had formed. Called SWIS, after the first letter of each defendant's last name, its two hundred members collected two thousand signatures on a petition asking Overton for leniency.

After the sentencing, the group's members ratcheted up the rhetoric and railed at Overton. "We're beginning to see Klansmen in robes of another color," said Joyce Hobson, an African-American teacher at Hampton High and one of SWIS's founders.

"I'm outraged," said Linda Mines. "Drug dealers get less than that.

Murderers get less than that. People with guns and knives get less than that."

"It's a high-tech lynching without a rope," fulminated Marilyn Strother.

Up until now, Mike Bailey had been prohibited from speaking publicly about the case by his school. On the courthouse steps, though, he made a terse, anguished statement to the media. "We didn't lose a tremendous high-school athlete today, we didn't lose a member of our student body," he said. "We lost a friend." Days later, Allen's girlfriend, Tawanna Turner, would make a special trip to Bethel High to tell the coach how much Allen appreciated his comments. "He knows you could have talked about losing a player and it meant a lot that you talked about losing him as a person," she said. "It meant a lot because it was from the heart."

Immediately following the sentencing, the media maelstrom began. Tom Brokaw, *Sports Illustrated, USA Today,* and the *Washington Post* all swept in, their cameras capturing the countless African-Americans wearing FREE IVERSON T-shirts and the JUSTICE FOR BUBBACHUCK graffiti that appeared, seemingly overnight. Benjamin Chavis, then executive director of the National Association for the Advancement of Colored People, and the Reverend Jesse Jackson both weighed in in support of SWIS.

SWIS printed up and distributed flyers calling for an economic boycott. Protesters were urged to write the word "injustice" in red marker on all dollar bills spent in Hampton. SWIS called for an immediate boycott of Circle Lanes and for an immediate cancellation of all subscriptions to the *Daily Press.* A petition seeking the recall of the commonwealth attorney began making the rounds. Most controversially, SWIS called on churches to come up with "Educational Alternatives for School Attendance," whereby students who, in protest, chose not to attend school would "learn about the historical struggle for freedom as experienced by Americans from the Pilgrims to the Haitians."

On Tuesday, September 14, a *Daily Press* editorial took on the protesters. "We believe Iverson's case was handled fairly and appropriately," the paper wrote. "Now, the legal system is under fire because it has provided Iverson a lesson in consequences . . . Incredibly, there is even some talk of pulling children out of school."

The same day, SWIS had scheduled a rally in support of Iverson at the Bethel African Methodist Episcopal Church, which had a seating capacity of four hundred. At the eleventh hour, the venue was changed to the larger Queen Street Baptist Church to handle the overflow crowd; despite sweltering heat, protesters turned out, filling the sanctuary and its balcony and milling about on the street outside. Joyce Hobson, the Hampton High teacher, told the crowd that she had received a reprimanding letter from her principal about her vocal support for the Hampton Four. "There is one thing that will squelch my voice—and that's a bullet," she defiantly announced, to roaring approval.

But the loudest cheers came when Paul Gillis, a regional NAACP representative, singled out columnist Jim Spencer, who stood alongside the church wall—one of the few white faces in attendance.

"I don't need Jim Spencer telling me what's wrong with black America," Gillis shouted. "I'm sick and tired of listening to white folks telling me what's wrong with my people." The crowd rose en masse, clapping and fist-pumping, cheering and pointing derisively at Spencer.

The same day, a group of black pastors held a press conference in support of SWIS. Calling the conviction and sentencing a "judicial lynching," the Reverend Marcellus Harris Jr. declared that "our community is determined and convinced we have a Rosa Parks–type vehicle here. And we're not going to give up this issue. Nothing short of justice will be satisfactory to us."

Whites were outraged at the parallel between Rosa Parks and Iverson. In fact, those who invoked the civil rights heroine didn't mean to morally equate Iverson with her; by talking about a Rosa Parks "vehicle"—someone they could *ride*—they were, perhaps ill-advisedly, invoking Parks in the context of a catalyst for change. But the two sides, the two races, were long past the point of hearing each other. "Rosa Parks didn't hurt anyone," the *Daily Press* editorialized. "Iverson is a troubled young man who hit a woman with a chair during a brawl. To compare the two is an insult to Rosa Parks."

As time passed, SWIS continued to protest. There were rallies in the streets, where protesters chanted "No Justice, No Peace!" and "Free the Hampton Four!"

The controversy showed no sign of abating. Few, if any, white people seemed to understand the depth of pain felt by area blacks. "It was the biggest travesty ever," Butch Harper, onetime neighbor of the Iverson brood, recalls today. "When that judge gave him five years, I'll tell you what, Joe Louis lost a fight, Martin Luther King Jr. got killed, Muhammad Ali was stripped of his championship. And Allen Iverson was going to jail."

And through it all, the by-now eighteen-year-old prodigy, who had come to symbolize so much to so many of his own people, was working in the kitchen at the Newport News City Farm, where he'd been transferred in the days following his sentencing. There, every night, he'd very consciously remind himself to keep the faith that, one day, his hoops dream would become reality.

The roughly 250 inmates at the Newport News City Farm, a minimum-security prison, worked on road crews or on the sprawling grounds of the facility. They could be seen tending to livestock or cutting grass, a white picket fence the only thing separating them from visitors. But the most famous of the City Farm inmates didn't make it out into the fields too often. Mostly, Allen Iverson drew kitchen detail, where he worked in the prison's bakery.

When he did get to go outside, he'd see them. His boys. There they'd be, on the other side of that fence, keeping their almost daily vigil. There was Ra and Arnie and Marlon and E, all the guys who, in his absence, were looking out for Ann and Ieisha and Brandy. When bills needed to get paid—those guys did it, no matter how they had to come up with the cash. Oftentimes, his teammates would be out there, too, trying to catch a glimpse, show their support. But he tried to keep his back to them and never made eye contact, not once. Oh, he wanted to; he wanted to break down, to show how much it meant to him, their presence and their tributes—he'd heard that his teammates were traveling to away games with his empty uniform. But he didn't want anyone to see him like this, caged.

There was no cell block at the City Farm. Iverson lived in a dorm with fifteen other kitchen workers. The younger guys in the prison population were the rowdy ones. They were the ones eager to test this new inmate, the star. But the older guys were guys like Michael Freeman, and they took the infamous inmate under their wing. Iverson was used to having older mentors on the streets: Gary Moore, Tony Clark, Jamil Blackmon, even Arnie Steele. At City Farm, the older guys walked with Iverson to the cafeteria through the part of the prison called "The Jungle." That's where the younger, harder guys were, the guys who'd call things out to him, who talked about taking him on. But it was just talk—he knew that from Michael Freeman, who had counseled him to avoid making eye contact with those who would try to rattle him, to always keep walking.

Throughout his time at City Farm, Iverson was a model prisoner. He was up at 5 A.M. and off to the kitchen, where he'd work with the bakers, making bread, biscuits, and pastries. Then he got two hours for recreation. There was an old, broken-down basketball rim and a deflated ball. "I'd worry about him playing basketball," recalls Billy Payne, the City Farm's warden at the time. "Those boys played rough." Eventually, Iverson started playing one-on-one with a former Iowa football player, in the dark after long days in the bakery.

But Iverson was depressed at first. He didn't comb or wash his hair, stopped ironing his clothes. And then Ann came to visit. All she had to do was say one thing: "Baby, it hurts me to see you like this. You gotta stay strong, for me," she pleaded, and he started taking care of himself, started reminding himself every night that he wouldn't give in or give up. People were depending on him.

On weekends, when she could get a ride or otherwise scrounge up money to make the twenty-minute trip by car or bus to the Farm, Ann would bring Brandy and Ieisha. Often, others on Allen's visitors list would also converge. Tawanna would always be there, as would the Baileys. When the weather was nice that fall, they'd all sit outside, Tawanna and Allen huddled together on a bench, holding hands. She was pretty, a light-skinned girl with delicate features who seemed shy and unassuming. But she was strong—"To this day, she's in charge," says Janet Bailey affectionately—and fiercely devoted to the boy who had taken her to his prom. "He was no Don Juan in high school," Mike Bailey recalls.

Now that her boyfriend was incarcerated, even she was experiencing some of the backlash fanning out across the region. Tawanna's own mother, according to Blackmon, gave her a hard time about standing by her man, arguing that he'd "never amount to nothing." Still, she was there, every visiting day. The Baileys heard the same kind of sentiments. One fellow teacher asked Mike Bailey, "Why are you doing so much for him? Don't you know he's just a ghetto kid?"

Another visitor around this time was Larry Woodward, a lawyer in the prestigious local firm of Shuttleworth, Rudolf and Giordano. Woody, as he was known, would be handling Allen's appeal. His firm's senior partner, Tom Shuttleworth, was politically connected. The walls of Shuttleworth's Virginia Beach office were filled with photos of him beside the likes of Colin Powell, former president George Bush, and democratic strategist James Carville. Together, he and Woodward began lobbying then Virginia governor Douglas Wilder—the first and only African-American governor in the nation—to grant their new client clemency. They were joined by Bruce Hornsby, who happened to be a longtime friend of Wilder's chief of staff.

Meantime, tutor Sue Lambiotte couldn't shake the idea of this promising youngster, with all his mental energy and artistic talent, languishing in prison. She hated to think that all those naysayers were right, like the one teacher who predicted, when Iverson was sixteen, that "he will never play a day of college ball." Her husband, Butch, was friendly with City Farm manager Billy Payne. Through Payne, they set up once-a-week tutoring sessions with Allen in a room smaller than her closet at home. They started out working on basic math and English skills.

An agreement was reached with the Richard Milburn High School, a private, alternative school for troubled students, to oversee Iverson's remaining high-school course work. Milburn was costly, however; among those chipping in to foot the bill for Iverson were Hornsby, Spike Lee (who had been sending Iverson books on Malcolm X while in jail), Bill Cosby, and Michael Jordan. Once the tuition was paid, Lambiotte and Iverson began working on math and sociology, the first of the six classes he needed to complete his senior year.

And then, in December, two things happened. Ann went on a pilgrimage to Georgetown's John Thompson, making a heartfelt plea on behalf of her son. And Woody came through. It was only fitting, after all the racial division, that the nation's only African-American governor was coming to Iverson's rescue.

chapter 5

FEAR NO ONE

A screaming skull with a red line through it—
FEAR NO ONE. That's me, man. You won't
catch me looking like this guy—scared.

T hey were only four simple words, but they were said with so much conviction, so much raspy emotion, that they closed the sale. Ann Iverson looked directly at John Thompson and said, simply, "Please help my baby."

They were in Thompson's office on the campus of Georgetown University. Just outside the closed door sat Jamil Blackmon, Butch Harper, and Boo Williams, the catalyst for the meeting. Blackmon and Harper were nervous; Williams, given his long association with Thompson, was more confident that, after Ann and Thompson emerged and they all piled into their rented van to head back to Newport News, there'd be some celebrating going on.

As November had given way to December, Woody's reports of a possible clemency deal grew more and more optimistic. With the looming possibility of Iverson's release, Williams started shopping him to prominent basketball programs across the country.

There were not a lot of takers. All those coaches who had salivated over the eleventh-grade phenom were unwilling to consider offering a scholarship now that he was a convicted felon; the PR risk was too great. "It's too racial and too controversial," one well-known coach said. Williams quickly surmised that he needed to target coaches who had enough clout within their university to, in his words, "get the kid past their presidents." Two names came to Williams's mind: Georgetown's Thompson and Temple University's John Chaney, both champions, and taskmasters, of the disadvantaged black athlete.

Williams called Thompson first and found the baritone-voiced bear of a coach well schooled in the particulars of Iverson's case. Thompson, Williams thought, would be just what Iverson needed. Throughout his illustrious coaching career, Thompson had been a protector and loyal champion of his players, often deflecting scrutiny from the likes of Patrick Ewing and Alonzo Mourning by strategically steering controversy *his* way.

Williams had known Thompson for years, ever since their mutual friend Sonny Vaccaro had helped build Nike into the sneaker company of all sneaker companies back in the early eighties. Nike sponsored Williams's summer program, just as it did Thompson's team. In fact, Thompson sat on Nike's board of directors, and there were those who felt that the sneaker company was a silent partner in Mourning's Georgetown recruitment, given that it was the common denominator between Thompson, Williams, and Vaccaro (who happened to be in Hampton the weekend that Mourning ended the suspense and committed to Thompson).

Additionally, Williams knew Thompson was street-smart, a big plus when dealing with Iverson. Thompson had once confronted a drug dealer who had gotten a little too close to Mourning for his liking. He'd coached and, when he needed to, jettisoned his share of players with rap sheets, like 1984's Michael Graham, he of the menacing shaved head, long before it was in vogue. Thompson simply wouldn't be played. Which signaled to Williams that if Thompson had come under criticism in the past for seeming absurdly overprotective of his more renegade players, he was also quite capable, if need be, of kicking Iverson's behind with his size fifteens.

Thompson, for his part, told Williams he'd only consider taking on Iverson if Ann personally asked him to. So Ann made the call, and here she was, making her pitch, despite Allen's own misgivings about Thompson. At the time, Iverson's friend and high-school rival Joe Smith was starring at the University of Maryland; that's where Iverson wanted to be, with Joe, doing it Newport News–style in the acclaimed Atlantic Coast Conference. Thompson, six feet ten inches himself, onetime backup to Bill Russell, had produced Ewing, Mourning, and Dikembe Mutombo, and his current team featured Othella Harrington. He was a big man's coach, Iverson argued, and a control freak to boot. He ran a heavily choreographed offense and had never given a point guard the freedom to improvise—a skill that was at the heart of Iverson's game.

Beggars couldn't be choosers, Williams responded. Even though his program had had some down years of late, Thompson was one of the few coaches with enough power at his own university to get Iverson a scholarship. Besides, Williams pointed out, Thompson knew the game. Once he saw what Iverson was capable of, he'd be foolish not to let him run. And John Thompson was anything but foolish.

Thompson was intrigued by Iverson, who was probably the most talented guard he'd ever have the chance to coach. Just as significant, he was touched by Ann's plea. "I saw the love of a mother for her son," Thompson would later recall. They hugged; Ann beamed as she strode from Thompson's office, arm in arm with the behemoth coach. Thompson outlined for Williams and the others the game plan: if Iverson was released, he pledged to send his academic coordinator, Mary Fenlon, to the Peninsula in a few months to check on the progress being made with Sue

Lambiotte. If Fenlon reported back that Iverson could do college-level work and if he scored over 700 on the SATs, he'd become a Georgetown Hoya.

Just as Williams had predicted, the ride back home was a blast. Ann turned up the volume when Sister Sledge started sermonizing that "We Are Family," and Ann started shimmying right there in her seat, throwing in the occasional thanks heavenward between the bumps and grinds. She'd never lost the faith. And now she was surer than ever. God was still looking out for her and her baby.

O h, my goodness!"
Ann Iverson's shriek could be heard from the sidewalk outside 3710 Victoria Boulevard when the car pulled up. She swung open her front door and there, just beyond the phalanx of TV cameras and newspaper reporters, was Woody and Tom Shuttleworth getting out of the car, and then, finally, Ann's smiling baby. There he was, free after three and a half months in jail, wearing a green-and-gold sweatshirt—the Bethel team colors.

It was Thursday, December 30, and Ann Iverson had gotten her Christmas present five days late, when Governor Doug Wilder ordered Iverson released. In what even a Wilder aide described as an "extraordinary" move, the governor had become convinced that Iverson had been treated unfairly. "While there is not sufficient evidence at the present time for me to grant the extraordinary relief inherent in a traditional pardon, there is sufficient doubt to merit that Allen Iverson be granted limited freedom and the opportunity to continue his education," Wilder said in a statement released by his office. A source in Wilder's office, the *Daily Press* reported, said that Iverson wrote a letter to Wilder in which he admitted wrongdoing and asked for a second chance. Wilder granted his wish, but attached conditions to the clemency. Iverson would have to complete his high-school studies, not play organized sports (the better to focus on academics), and abide by a curfew (10:30 on weeknights, midnight on weekends).

When she heard the news, SWIS's Joyce Hobson was in the car, fifteen minutes from home. "I screamed the whole way home," she breathlessly told the *Daily Press.* Like Hobson, an entire community breathed a sigh of relief. But another clenched a collective fist.

At the time he released Iverson, Doug Wilder was one of more than eight thousand African-American elected officials in local, state, and federal government throughout the United States. That number was up from fewer than three hundred twenty-five years earlier. In reality, much of that upsurge took place in the nine years after Jesse Jackson's first run for the presidency, in 1984. Another boost came following Jackson's subsequent run in 1988, when he garnered 7 million votes in the Democratic primary and gave birth to a generation of black officeholders.

Doug Wilder was part of that movement. But, as with any movement, it had its backlash, as could be seen in the aftermath of the Iverson clemency, when many whites cried foul. How predictable, they complained: a black governor bails out a black criminal. The *Daily Press* editorialized that "those who believe Iverson was treated appropriately by the criminal justice system—and that includes us—may wonder about the governor's motives." An accompanying news story suggested that Wilder, preparing to challenge Senator Chuck Robb in a statewide primary, was trying to "bolster his support in the black community." (At the time, most political observers believed Wilder needed to demonstrate an ability to cut into Robb's white support, so it was unclear how granting clemency to a convicted black celebrity could be politically beneficial.)

Sue Lambiotte found herself living in the midst of the backlash every day. Allen, now free, would begin his studies with her, six hours a day on Mondays and Thursdays and four on Tuesday, Wednesdays, and Fridays, at her Kumon Math and Reading Center. She opened the center in 1992, providing individualized instruction for students (often athletes) from kindergarten to college. Allen's work would technically be completed under the auspices of the Milburn School, but Lambiotte was in charge of the one-on-one instruction at her center, which was located, ironically, in well-to-do, lily-white Poquoson, where anti-Iverson sentiment reigned. More than once, working late, she'd receive threatening phone calls, with a voice telling her, "Your center isn't going to be there tomorrow," or calling her the most vile of names. She'd call her husband, Butch, and he'd come get her. But the next morning, she'd be back at the center, preparing for the moment when Bubba came striding in, invariably late, often with half-finished homework, but there nonetheless, ready to work.

K nowing when, in Sue Lambiotte's words, to "drop the hammer" is the toughest part of being a teacher. How forgiving of a student's failings ought you to be? Where is the line between discipline and granting opportunity? When does being a teacher morph into being a co-conspirator in a student's spree of irresponsibility?

Lambiotte, a tall, regal, patient woman with the singsong voice of a Southern belle, wrestled with all these questions during the frantic ten-month period, beginning in December 1993, that she worked with Allen Iverson. Actually, as she will tell you, "wrestled" is too weak a word; it was, she says, her central agony those months, when she'd lie awake at night and wonder whether she was doing the right thing for the student she had called Bubba ever since that trip to Kansas with Boo's team some seven years earlier. As a tutor to athletes, she'd heard the rap for years. Not only that they're coddled and irresponsible, but that they've been surrounded by an enabling crew of academics, tutors, teachers, principals, and universities who, bit by bit, sacrifice classroom standards because a kid can run or jump or shoot a ball. In the long run, no service was done to such students, she knew. Maybe if they were made to pay the price early, they'd become better citizens down the line.

From the start, Sue Lambiotte had a different definition of "success" for Allen Iverson than many of those surrounding the phenom. For them, succeeding meant the riches of the NBA. For her, it meant college. They would talk about his talent, and it was clear they were referencing his blinding speed and on-court moves. When Lambiotte discussed his talent, she was talking of his artistic flair or his critical-thinking skills, the way he'd vociferously argue a unique point of view when he became passionate about an issue. "What a tragedy it would be if this boy never got to college," she'd tell Butch.

But riling Iverson to passion—there was the rub. Iverson would come to the center, sit down to work, and his cell phone would ring. He'd answer and start chatting.

"Bubba!" Lambiotte would screech.

"Oh, yeah, sorry," he'd say, hanging up.

Other times, he'd sit there, impassive. "Bubba!" she'd prod him. "I know you're thinking something in there. Just say it!"

She searched for ways to reach him. She and Butch took him to a museum, but he lost interest halfway through. How to engage him? Bubba had told her once that he cut all those classes in high school because it was just so boring, the same routine, day after day. At the City Farm, he loved working in the kitchen—at least that was action, banging those pots and pans together. This was worse; forced to sit in a classroom each day felt more constricting than actually being in prison.

Lambiotte decided she had to tailor the curriculum to her student's particular quirks. She divided her lesson plan up into fifteen-minute units, so Allen's attention was never in danger of waning. They'd spend fifteen minutes working on, say, his paper on Malcolm X (three rewrites until he wove his own analysis throughout the biographical information), the next fifteen on a geometric proof, and, finally, fifteen on artwork—as a reward. When he was engaged, Lambiotte rarely had a better or more insightful student, as when, for sociology, he wrote a paper creating an entire civilization. In his dreamworld, it turns out, women did most of the work—the men occasionally hunted for food, but mostly they'd lovingly play with the children.

Still, there were mornings he would arrive at the center having completed only two of the previous night's five homework assignments. When she'd express her disappointment, he'd say, "But, Mrs. Lambiotte, look how much I *did* do!" To him, she realized, he was working harder at school than ever. Lambiotte begged Ann not to let Allen out of the house until he completed his homework each night, but it didn't often work out that way. One of his buddies would come around and off Bubba would go.

"Mrs. Lambiotte, I think I have trouble saying no to some of the guys," Allen would say. Lambiotte arranged for a teacher to work on SAT preparation with him, and in one exercise, Allen was called on to match human character traits to different animals. He scanned the list of animals and smiled. "I'm a beaver—the one who is always jumping around, tail flapping, here, there," he said. "I'm just like that. So's my mom, which is why we fight so much."

Despite such moments of self-awareness, Iverson was disengaged more often than not. At one point, Lambiotte had had enough. Bubba hadn't shown up again and she decided to quit. But, still, she had doubts. Was this the time to drop the hammer? She decided she needed to seek the advice of someone more experienced in dealing with disadvantaged black athletes. She called John Thompson and told him she was ready to throw in the towel.

"As you know, I'm a spokesman for the disadvantaged young black man," Thompson told her after hearing her frustrations. "And I believe that, for the group, special considerations ought to be made, like with the culturally biased SAT. But in individual cases, I'm all for holding kids to standards. If he's not dotting his *i*'s and crossing his *t*'s, and if you feel you've done all you can do, if your best judgment is to cut him loose, I support you in that."

Lambiotte had half expected to hear a plea on Allen's behalf from his prospective coach: how this may be the youngster's last chance, how he has had it pretty hard growing up. Allen, after all, may have represented Thompson's coaching future at the time. Instead, she got a high-minded dose of empathy from him, one educator to another. With Thompson feeling her pain, she decided to stick it out with Allen. Her son, Clay, laughed when she recounted her conversation with the coach and her subsequent decision not to resign. "Mom, you are so gullible," he said. "He played you like a violin!" To this day, Sue Lambiotte wonders if she was manipulated by the wily, street-smart coach. If so, she's thankful for it.

As Thompson promised, Georgetown academic adviser Mary Fenlon visited the center. Lambiotte laid out on a big conference table all of Allen's work, and Fenlon spent twenty minutes going over each assignment, showing no reaction. Finally, her eyes peered up over her Ben Franklin glasses and she uttered the phrase that Sue Lambiotte needed to hear. "I think we have a diamond in the rough here," Fenlon said.

Life at Victoria Boulevard was getting harder and harder. Michael Freeman was in and out of jail. When he was around, his drug dealing wasn't making ends meet. Allen once saw him collapse into a chair at the kitchen table after a hard day at the "office," his shoulders slumped as though life itself had left his body. He dropped his head into his hands and began sobbing.

One day Allen showed up late to study with Lambiotte. There was nothing new in that; on this day, though, he was also dressed better than usual, in pressed pants and a button-down shirt. He'd just come from the courthouse, where Freeman had had yet another hearing on drug charges. Freeman was heading back to jail, but, Allen told his teacher, they spoke before the man he called Dad was taken away.

"You're the man now," Freeman told him. "You've got to take care of your mother and sisters."

To Allen, it was a challenge to start earning some money. Lambiotte didn't have to ask how. They'd been over this territory before, she and

Allen. They were constantly arguing over Allen's view that, if you're making money for your family and the only way you can do it is by selling drugs, then that's what you do. It's a sacrifice he saw Michael Freeman make.

"Bubba," Lambiotte said. "What's wrong with working at McDonald's?"

"You can't raise no family working at McDonald's," he replied.

Still, Lambiotte echoed the advice Allen was hearing from all his friends—even the ones who dealt drugs. And it was advice, by all accounts, he followed. "Bubba," she said. "You looking for short-term money isn't a way to help your mother and sisters. The best thing you can do for them is to get this academic stuff done right, get to college, and build a future, for you and them."

Meantime, the sewer system under the house on Victoria Boulevard had structural flaws and the plumbing problems were worsening. The carpet had turned black and clumps of mold were sprouting up. The toxic smell gave everyone constant headaches. Finally, one day, Blackmon came over and couldn't bear the stench. Lifting his shirt to shield his nose, he took Juicy up on her longtime request. "Y'all can't live like this," he told the Iversons. "Come on and live with me."

So Ann, Allen, Brandy, and Ieisha squeezed into Blackmon's place in the Central Park apartment complex on Marcella Drive, where he had a three-bedroom with two roommates, Ellis and Scott. Sometimes, Ann would borrow one of their cars to run an errand and be gone for a matter of days. Allen's friends would come over and hang out: Arnie, Ra, Marlon, Gary Moore. "They'd sit around and talk ghetto shit," Blackmon recalls. "You know, bitches, weed, getting drunk. What else were they gonna talk about? Clinton's health-care plan?"

Iverson didn't go out much, because of the curfew and the fact that anywhere he went, there was likely to be some Iverson detractor looking to start something with him in order to scuttle his future, once and for all. He'd play pickup games at Bethel High after dinner; Coach Koz would usually be on the other team and Allen would blow by him like he wasn't even there. Often Tawanna would come by and they'd spend the night watching TV or catch an early movie. He saw *Pulp Fiction*, which catapulted onto his list of all-time great flicks, right up there with *Scarface* and *Dead Presidents*. The Samuel L. Jackson character was a particular favorite because here was the embodiment of cool. A *righteous* hit man, Bible in one hand, Glock in the other, doing what he had to do, administering his own brand of Justice.

It was in Blackmon's laundry room that Iverson started fretting about developing a basketball persona. He was hoping to make it to the legendary Rucker Park at 155th Street in Harlem sometime that summer. The best playground ballers in the country played there, street legends who, for one reason or another, hadn't made it in college or pro ball. They all had their own if-only stories, tales of how their talents got pulled off track, whether because of drugs, bad grades, or an inability to temper their wildly improvisational street games to the regimented style of organized basketball. Like other prodigies—Mike Tyson's encyclopedic knowledge of boxing history comes to mind—Allen was well versed in who was doing the craziest shit up in Harlem. They were showmen, guys with funny nicknames who would play to the crowd on sweltering summer nights, guys like "Half-Man, Half-Amazing," or "Skip to My Lou," a legendary ball handler.

"Man, I need a cool nickname," Iverson said while Blackmon folded laundry.

"Chuck, you're 'The Answer,'" Blackmon said. "'Cause you're the answer to all the NBA's woes."

"The Answer," Allen said, instantly brightening. "I like that."

Blackmon kept theorizing. "I mean, everybody's in love with Mike, everybody wants to be Mike," he said, referring to Jordan, who had left basketball to pursue a short-lived minor-league baseball career. "But Mike ain't around. So you're the answer, now."

As Blackmon talked, Iverson got more and more hyped, so much so that one of Blackmon's roommates gave him a lift over to the army-and-navy store in Yorktown, where he got his first tattoo—THE ANSWER—on his left biceps.

He didn't make it to the Rucker that summer. Instead, in early August, he orchestrated his own coming-out party. Georgetown was fielding a team in the Kenner Summer League, held at McDonough Gym on the university's campus. He was determined to play.

"Are you sure, Bubba?" Lambiotte asked. "It's been a year and a half since you've played organized ball. This summer league is comprised of college players and pros who are in shape. You may not have your legs to compete against them."

He smiled knowingly. "Mrs. Lambiotte, my team is going to win the championship."

Poor kid, Lambiotte thought. He's about to learn the hard way.

If word of Iverson's plan to play got out, Lambiotte and Boo Williams knew that the cozy gym confines would be packed and the media attention would be jarring. Allen didn't need that kind of pressure—especially when nobody knew how he was going to play. So they enlisted the help of a friend who had an old Dodge pickup, because no one would suspect that Allen Iverson was being driven around in a beat-up truck. And Lambiotte had friends in nearby Alexandria, so that's where Allen would spend the night.

On August 5, 1994, roughly 750 people were in the stands of the 2,400-seat gym. Iverson, playing with his future Georgetown teammate Jerome Williams, hit an early three-pointer. When the public-address announcer intoned, "Allen Iverson," a murmur swept the crowd. When, seconds later, Iverson stole a pass and outraced everyone down the court for a slam dunk, the murmur became bleacher-stomping applause. Throughout his career, Iverson had always thrived in dramatic moments of his own making; this was certainly one. He played the entire first half in one speed: overdrive. He scored 30 points in the half alone and added 10 more after halftime.

By the next night, word was out. Over three thousand people packed the gym. It was standing room only, but even those with obstructed views weren't disappointed. Just twenty-seven seconds into the game, Iverson threw down a windmill dunk. He hit his first seven shots, nailing back-to-back NBA three-pointers after his first dunk. On an inbounds play, he took off from just inside the foul line and caught an alley-oop pass high above the rim before slamming it down with a backboard-rattling jam. All eyes were on him, and he always seemed to be wherever the ball was, scoring 33 points, including 6 three-pointers.

The next night, he led his team onto the floor for the tournament championship. Outside, security guards turned fans away. Inside, some four thousand screaming fans, including his future NBA teammate Dikembe Mutombo, watched Iverson prove he was no fluke. He scored

To illustrate "propaganda" in social studies, an eighteen-year-old Iverson rendered how others were seeing him through portrayals in the media: the angel and the devil.

High school graduation day, 1994. In a class of one, Iverson was valedictorian.

26 points and his team won, 72–66. Just as he'd predicted to Sue Lambiotte, he led his team to the championship. "I think he's a great player," marveled Adonal Foyle, the opposing team's center who would go on to star at Colgate and later play for Golden State in the NBA.

As soon as the final buzzer went off, security swooped onto the court and hustled Iverson out a side exit. He wouldn't even get the chance to accept the championship trophy or his MVP award. Instead, he was rushed through the building's bowels, through a series of seemingly secret tunnels, and ushered outside, where the Dodge pickup waited. He was whisked away to avoid the media—Thompson prohibits his freshmen from giving interviews—and any would-be troublemakers. On the way back to Newport News, Lambiotte looked at him in wonder. How did he know? she asked herself. How did he know?

Even as she marveled at his athletic accomplishment, Lambiotte knew she couldn't let up on him. They were so close to completing his high-school studies. By the end of the summer, Iverson finished work on his last two courses: U.S. government and psychology. He'd taken the SAT and qualified to be eligible come the fall for his freshman year of basketball, and now he was about to seal the deal with a high-school diploma. Lambiotte had a cap and gown fitted for him and invited his family, friends, and the coordinator of the Wilburn School to her center for a graduation ceremony honoring the Class of '94, a class of one. The night before graduation, Lambiotte's son, Clay, said, "Have you thought about the fact that Allen is his class valedictorian?"

Lambiotte howled in laughter. Finally, revenge would be hers. After all the times he'd made her pull at her hair, tomorrow she'd spring on him, on the spot, that he was expected to make a valedictory speech.

When the time came, a shy but moved Allen Iverson spoke softly. "I just want everybody to know how much I appreciate what y'all did," he said, looking at Ann, his sisters, and his boys. "I know I didn't always make it easy, but I want all y'all to know how much this here means to me. And how I'm gonna make all y'all proud at Georgetown."

Seeing her pupil in his cap and gown, holding that piece of paper, Lambiotte finally felt relief. Now, she thought to herself, if he stumbles and breaks both ankles, at least he'll have exposure to good instruction and ideas; now I know his talent won't be wasted. Knowing Bubba was headed to Georgetown, Sue Lambiotte slept well that night.

THE BULLDOG

This was my second tattoo. I had the
bulldog put on my arm when I decided to go to
georgetown, where the mascot is a bulldog.

Among sports columnists, the *Washington Post*'s Thomas Boswell was an all-star. His pieces about the intricacies of baseball had already become legend by the time Allen Iverson was poised to debut as a collegiate basketball player. But baseball was not Boswell's only forte; he had also been a basketball lifer, having spent much of his career in shoe-box-size gyms just to check out the hype about *the* next phenom.

Boswell had seen can't-miss high-schoolers like Moses Malone, Alonzo Mourning, Ralph Sampson, and Patrick Ewing. He'd seen an eighth grader named Adrian Dantley who was already being targeted for the pros. He'd seen Lew Alcindor, a lanky scoring machine with unheard-of skills, well before he became a household name.

In early November of 1994, Boswell was sitting along press row at Georgetown's McDonough Auditorium prior to the Hoyas' exhibition game against the Fort Hood Tankers, an army-base squad of bruising, grown men. It was to be Allen Iverson's first appearance in a Georgetown uniform. When John Thompson's players took their places for the introductions, Boswell leaned over to then *Post* beat writer J. A. Adande. "Which one is Iverson?" he asked.

"The one on the end," Adande replied.

"You mean the little guy in the droopy shorts with the skinny legs?" Boswell asked.

"The first second he gets the ball, you'll know who he is."

Sure enough, on the first play, Boswell's jaw dropped. "My God," he said. "He's a blur."

Iverson soared and dazzled his way to 24 points in the first eight minutes. By halftime, he had 28 points and 4 assists in thirteen minutes. He hit jumpers, threw no-look passes, and drove to the basket, either making the shot or getting fouled. And he hit 16 of his 17 first-half free throws. He'd go on to total 36 points and 5 assists. "Now I have two memories on my first-impression top shelf," Boswell wrote the next day. "The man who became Kareem Abdul-Jabbar, and Allen Iverson. Ewing is third."

Late in the first half, Fort Hood center Brian Pitts, who stood six-eight and weighed 275 pounds, set a pick near midcourt on Iverson's blind side. Iverson ran full force into the behemoth, whose elbows had been up too high for Thompson's liking. Some in the crowd gasped; Iverson comically ricocheted off the ground, bouncing back up onto his feet. If he was shaken, he did a good job of shielding it, bursting into a big smile as Thompson came charging onto the court.

"Don't hurt my boy!" the coach screamed at Pitts, restrained by the refs. "You can't take him out like that!"

It was confirmation that Thompson knew just what he had in Iverson. And it was a foreshadowing of the lengths to which Thompson would go in order to give Iverson the sense that his coach was in his corner—unconditionally. The first time Thompson had met Iverson, they spoke about the bowling-alley incident. Thompson was characteristically blunt. "If you think I'm going to pass judgment on the judge and tell you how terrible the judicial system is, you're crazy," the coach said.

But, Thompson said, sitting in judgment of Iverson was the judge's job—not Thompson's. "I'm not blaming you," he said. "There's a difference between understanding how something can happen and condoning it. All of us have done something at sixteen or seventeen that we're glad we weren't caught doing."

It was straight talk that, in effect, said to Iverson: *When you screw up, I understand, because I've been there. But that doesn't mean I'm not going to demand better from you.*

Thompson's teams had long had a tough, rebellious image; Georgetown jerseys in the 1980s had become a staple of inner-city style. But Thompson was known as a disciplinarian. When Iverson showed up for college wearing an earring, Thompson told him to remove it. His players were prohibited from wearing big gold chains and from experimenting with wild hairstyles. They were required to dress in a suit and tie when traveling to and from games.

"A man that's in college that doesn't have a suit has no projection for his future," Thompson would later say, when asked about his dress-code rules. "Don't tell me the poverty story. You can go to Goodwill and get a suit. But you need to own a suit if you expect to run something, if you expect to own something, if you expect to administer something. That's my responsibility as a teacher."

Thompson taught by bellowing, but also through humor. Later, Iverson would regale others with stories of how the bulky coach, in attempting to prod his big men to move their feet on defense, might serve up an example of light-footedness by breaking into a jig or two-step, with a sly

"I know I look like a fool" smile on his lips. Then there was the way Thompson would feign anger before affectionately playing off Iverson's reputation. "Iverson, you little shit!" he'd bellow throughout the gym, silencing the team, before breaking into a smile and putting his arm around his point guard. "I've had some criminals in my time, but you take the cake." Iverson and his teammates would laugh at Thompson's ribbing.

On the court, as Boo Williams had predicted, Iverson had no reason to worry about Thompson restricting his style of play. Thompson told his prized recruit from day one that he was granting him unprecedented freedom. The ball would be in his hands and he would be off to the races. Thompson's great teams of the past had played a scrambling, pressing defense. Their offenses, however, tended to be plodding and dull and there were those who wondered if the times hadn't passed Thompson by. The previous year's team, after all, was a merely respectable 19–12. Thompson hadn't been to a Final Four since Ewing's time, in 1985. He had even been unable to take his team that far when Alonzo Mourning and Dikembe Mutombo played together on the same Hoyas team.

This year's team, Thompson said, would break from the past. "Georgetown will run this year for one reason: Allen Iverson," he said. Of course, the new style was, first and foremost, a basketball decision. But Thompson also took into account Iverson's needs psychologically. Here was someone who had already been denied his freedom. "Think about what's happened in that child's life," Thompson explained. "The last thing he needs is structure. He needs to be free as a bird. He needs to fly."

Almost half of the 1994–95 Hoyas were freshmen or transfers. Three starters returned from the previous year, including center Othella Harrington, who had scored a team-high 14.7 points and grabbed a team-high 8 rebounds per game. Also back were senior forward Don Reid, who would be Iverson's roommate and a steadying force, and senior guard George Butler, whom Thompson would kick off the team at midseason for academic reasons. Transfer six-foot nine-inch forward Jerome Williams was expected to contribute as well.

The season began with a daunting challenge. In the inaugural Martin Luther King Jr. Classic Tournament in Memphis, they faced the defending national champion Arkansas Razorbacks, led by Corliss Williamson—no stranger to Iverson, thanks to their AAU days. Come game time,

Thompson's new up-tempo style played right into the hands of Arkansas's experienced, athletic team. Iverson, who had scored 39 points in Georgetown's second exhibition game, was held to just 19 points on 5-for-18 shooting. He played out of control at times, committing eight turnovers. But he showed a dogged spirit, continuing to drive the ball to the basket, his moves often drawing gasps from the crowd. After the 97–79 drubbing, Nolan Richardson was a believer despite Iverson's mediocre statistics.

"I've never seen anything like that," the coach said. "I've seen three calf shows, nine horse ropings—I even saw Elvis once. But I've never seen a guard do what he can do with the basketball. I saw him go through traps of ours nobody's ever gone through. He's awesome. Wait till he starts playing. He's always on the attack. That boy's going to make that team so good it'll be unreal."

Richardson's words were prescient. The Hoyas started winning and Iverson's twisting, acrobatic shots started falling. In early December, he scored 30 points in a win over Providence College, becoming just the second player under Thompson to ever score 30 or more points in back-to-back games. The Hoyas were soon 7–1 and ranked twelfth in the nation, and Iverson was averaging 21.5 points per game.

But Iverson's scoring—and Thompson's toleration of his star's shooting—was having an adverse effect on Othella Harrington. In his career, the big man was nearly a 16-points-per-game scorer. So far, he was barely getting five shots a game and averaging just over a third of his career numbers. But the team was winning, in part because Iverson couldn't be stopped.

Meantime, media fascination with Iverson rose to new heights. As he did with all freshman, Thompson prohibited his star from giving interviews in his first semester at school. Come January, however, and owing to an overwhelming number of press inquiries, Thompson stood by Iverson's side one day at practice and allowed the player to answer basketball-only questions. Media outlets from all over the East Coast descended on the pair.

"I talked to Coach before I came here and he told me he was going to let me play my game, let me run up and down the court, and he's done that," Iverson said. "I don't feel like I'm playing like I want to right now, but I'm learning. A lot of times, I get caught up in the hype in a game, and I get out of control sometimes. That's the thing Coach tells me the most about, patience."

"Have you been impressed by Allen, Coach?" asked one writer.

Though Thompson looked at his questioner upon replying, the response seemed aimed at Iverson—as a coded reassurance that the coach had the player's best interests at heart. "If you've been in this business for a while, you're not here to be impressed with people," Thompson said. "You're here to attempt to help mold them and get them prepared for the next stage of their life. That's what education is about. Allen has done what I've asked him to do, and when he has not done it, we've sat down and talked about it, and that hasn't been frequently at all. He's been extremely easy to work with."

By late January, the Hoyas were ranked tenth in the nation with only two losses, to then number-one-ranked Arkansas and number-two-rated Connecticut. Iverson made his first trip to his future home, to face Villanova in Philadelphia's Spectrum. The Villanova Wildcats upset the Hoyas, 66–60, in large part because Iverson could only play ten minutes on a sprained ankle. But Thompson was more upset by the reception his star had gotten than by the score.

The Philadelphia crowd rode Iverson all night long. One sign called Georgetown CONVICT U. Another read: IVERSON: THE NEXT JORDAN, only JORDAN was crossed out and O.J. written above it. "I will not continue to play under these circumstances," Thompson told Villanova officials. "I am not letting that child play in that atmosphere."

Security guards confiscated the signs, though the catcalling continued, which was nothing new—it was just louder in Philly. In Pittsburgh, a singsong "jailbird" chant started when Iverson was on the line; when he sank a free throw, quieting his taunters, he looked right at the student section and smiled.

Though the Hoyas dropped the game to Villanova, Harrington broke out of his doldrums, scoring 21 points and grabbing 11 rebounds. Of course, his inspired play—largely in the injured Iverson's absence—fueled doubts about Iverson's game that would linger for some time in the pros as well. Yes, he was a great scorer, the thinking went. But will he ever slow down long enough to accommodate a teammate? Could others flourish alongside him? Or, in the interest of his creative pursuits, were others stifled?

Off the court, Iverson took to college life, though his past was never far away. In fact, the day before leaving for Georgetown, he visited

Freeman in the Hampton city jail, where his stepfather was once again incarcerated. "I'm going to leave after two years and go pro and take care of you," Iverson promised.

At school, in the dorm room he shared with Don Reid, Iverson plastered the walls with clippings chronicling his high-school championships and with photos of Method Man, Redman, and the rest of the Wu-Tang Clan. Wu-Tang was, after all, an inspiration. Here were guys who had hung out back in the day all making it—together. Iverson was, in his mind, authoring the same kind of script for Cru Thik. At the dawn of the school year, however, the future of Cru Thik seemed imperiled when "E" was arrested and charged with maiming in a shooting death that occurred during the summer when a stray bullet killed a Newport News woman. A shaken Iverson went off to Georgetown worried for his friend. He'd finally gotten *his* freedom—and now "E" was going to have to go away? Early in Iverson's first semester, though, the charges against "E" were dropped after witnesses refused to testify against him.

From then on, "E" joined Arnie, Ra, and some of the others who always seemed to be down in Washington. On weekends, Blackmon would come to town. Once or twice, Michael Jackson—Thrilla—visited.

"You need anything?" Iverson would ask Jackson, who was attending Hampton University.

"Man, you're a college student just like I'm a college student—how you gonna take care of me?" Jackson would say.

Iverson had access to an apartment in Bethesda, Maryland. It belonged to some friends of David Falk, Thompson's agent. The Cru Thik members would often stay in Bethesda and mess around in the apartment's recording studio. Meantime, tension developed among those around Iverson. Blackmon started referring to himself as "Mr. Cellophane," because he felt he was being looked right through. When Arnie was around, 'Chuck wouldn't give Blackmon the time of day. Still, Blackmon hired a tutor for Iverson (someone who Blackmon now claims wrote papers for Iverson). As Iverson quickly emerged as the most exciting college basketball player in the country, the jockeying for position around him intensified.

It's an old story, really. The late sportswriter Mark Kram, who covered Muhammad Ali in his prime, saw it in the sixties, the way those around Ali fought for his ear and his approval and his attention. "You always had to read the body language of the entourage to figure out who was up and who was down on a particular day," Kram once recalled. "They competed against one another."

Midway through his freshman year, Iverson became a father when Tawanna gave birth to Tiaura. Tawanna was back in Hampton, living with her mother, taking care of the baby. Allen would visit when he could, often showing up outside Michael Jackson's window at two in the morning after an evening at home with Tawanna and the baby. He'd throw rocks at Jackson's window until his friend would come downstairs and they'd sit on a curb and talk into the wee hours.

Around the same time Tiaura was born, Iverson had contact with his biological father for the first time since he was an infant. When Iverson had been arrested at seventeen, Allen Broughton saw his son, all grown now, on TV, handcuffed and being led off to jail. He tracked Ann down through NBC, which had aired the story he'd seen. The TV station passed his number along to Woody, who gave it to Ann. She called her ex-boyfriend, who asked if there was anything he could do. No, she told him, the lawyers were handling it. But the two kept in touch, and when Allen went off to Georgetown, Broughton said he wanted to have a relationship with his son.

"You can't go to him like he's a kid," she warned. "He been through a lot. So when you talk to him, talk to him correctly. Be straight up." She gave Broughton her son's phone number in the dorm.

All told, the two men had about ten phone conversations; the stilted tone of the first call never really abated. "How are you doing?" Broughton asked.

"Fine."

"Are you upset with me about the past?" Broughton asked.

"My ma told me it was hard back then."

"I wish I could have been there for you."

"It's no problem."

Broughton had read the interviews about how Allen called Michael Freeman Daddy. That didn't bother him so much as the parts where Allen credited Freeman for teaching him basketball. Well, he may have taught Allen to play ball, but, Broughton thought, everything Allen did on the court came from my genes. After all, Allen Broughton had played ball all his life and everybody who grew up with him did double takes when they saw Iverson play, so similar was Iverson's style to Broughton's.

Iverson was always polite, but terse and resistant to Broughton's plans. Broughton targeted a series of dates to visit Georgetown, see a game, and meet his son, but Allen demurred every time. "I'm really busy," he said.

Broughton was still hoping to visit his son late in Allen's sophomore season when his girlfriend of ten years, Chrystal Owens, broke up with him. He told her she would not live to see her thirty-first birthday in four days. Two days later, while she was ironing her work uniform, Broughton, drunk, stabbed her six times, twice in the arm and four times in the stomach. He'd await trial for two years before being sentenced to nine years in prison in 1998. From jail, he has tried to send letters to Ann and to Allen, tried to convince them he's not after anything other than a relationship with his famous son, but to no avail. He hasn't heard from either of them since.

In mid-February, the Hoyas had another shot at the now number-one-ranked team in the country, Ray Allen's Connecticut Huskies. Georgetown was ahead by 8 points with nine minutes to go when Connecticut unveiled a pressing, trapping defense designed to discombobulate Iverson. Georgetown turned the ball over four times in five possessions, blew its lead, and lost the game, 91–85. Iverson notched 29 points, 8 rebounds, and 9 assists, along with a move that would go on his permanent highlight reel, a no-look hook shot while in traffic that kissed the glass and went in.

Despite the fact that Harrington and Iverson were still unable to have good games at the same time, Thompson was as tolerant as ever of his prodigy after the loss. "He's a child who gives you a bucket of milk and then kicks it all over you," Thompson said, smiling. The problem was that Iverson and Harrington played at vastly different speeds. Unlike Iverson, Harrington worked best in a patient, slow-down offense, with support players willing to work the ball inside to him. Often, by the time he'd set up underneath the basket, Iverson would already have launched a shot. "[Allen's] just starting to realize that fast is good, but not always fast," Thompson said. Shortly thereafter, in an upset over Syracuse, Iverson and Harrington played well together for the first time. Harrington had a season-high 27 points and Iverson scored 21, on 9-of-18 shooting—the first time he'd hit at least half his shots in six weeks. Iverson, shooting just below 40 percent on the season, wasn't a bad shooter. He just took too many wild shots, yet they were taken with Thompson's approval. The coach was not about to inhibit his star.

The Hoyas finished the regular season 18–8 and Iverson, who averaged 19.8 points per game in eighteen conference games and set a league record with 64 steals, was named Big East Rookie of the Year and Defensive Player of the Year. In his dorm, he received a phone call offering congratulations: "You may be beating up on those college boys, but what are you going to do about this forty-year-old piano player?" Bruce Hornsby asked.

In the NCAA Tournament, Thompson's team went to Tallahassee, Florida, to face Xavier in the Southeast Regional first round. The relationship between Thompson and Iverson had ebbed and flowed; Iverson had never received such tough love. Thompson often singled him out in front of the team, though usually using humor, not rage, to ride his star.

On the eve of the game against Xavier, though, the relationship between player and coach entered a new phase. Iverson was summoned to Coach's hotel room for a one-on-one meeting. Usually Coach didn't ask to see you mano-a-mano if you weren't in the doghouse. But Thompson had something else in mind.

"I want to let you know something I haven't told you all year," Thompson told his nervous star. "That I'm very proud of you. Regardless of what happens, I wanted to let you know that. I'm going to get on you and curse you out, but I'm proud of how you've handled yourself and the pressure you've withstood." Iverson stood in stunned silence for a moment, before shakily extending his hand.

"I think the kids are more comfortable with me when I'm fussing and yelling at them," Thompson said later, laughing as he recalled the moment. "He was probably thinking, 'What the hell's wrong with Coach? He's being nice to me today.'"

The Hoyas beat Xavier and advanced to the Sweet Sixteen round, where they ran up against Dean Smith's University of North Carolina Tar Heels. Led by Jerry Stackhouse and Rasheed Wallace, the Tar Heels were the favored team. The game was played in Birmingham, Alabama—not exactly Iverson country. But by game's end, Iverson would have the crowd on his side.

In the first half, it looked like the kid was all hype. He was nervous and sloppy; in one ten-second sequence, he badly missed three out-of-control shots in a row. He misfired on all six of his first-half attempts and Georgetown was down by as many as 16.

In the second half, though, Iverson battled back. Against Dean Smith's legendary defense, he cut loose for 21 points in fourteen minutes, bringing the Hoyas to within 4 points. Carolina withstood the furious charge, however, to win, 74–64. When Thompson took Iverson out, the crowd gave him a rousing ovation. These were not solely Georgetown fans; they were basketball fans, and they were cheering not only the eye-popping second-half performance they'd just seen (24 points, 8 rebounds), but also a stellar freshman season (20 points per game) and, perhaps, a year-long display of grace under pressure in the face of taunting crowds.

"Watch 'em next year, they ought to be something," Smith said after the game. "[Iverson] has his own solo fast break. Then he scores. He can really break a defense down."

It had been a draining season. And the off-season promised to be just as tumultuous. First, a three-judge panel of the Virginia Court of Appeals announced it was reversing Iverson's 1993 maiming-by-mob conviction and expunging his record. "Although the evidence would have been sufficient to prove individual assaultive conduct, it was insufficient to prove beyond a reasonable doubt that Iverson acted as part of a mob," the court wrote. "Iverson's confrontation with [accuser Steve] Forrest was an incident that may have precipitated a brawl, but was separate from any mob activity. No evidence proved that Iverson was a member of any mob that later formed."

When Thompson got the word, he placed two phone calls. The first was to Georgetown University president Reverend Leo O'Donovan. O'Donovan had withstood a lot of media criticism when he signed off on Iverson's enrollment. Thompson thanked him for "giving this young man an opportunity." Then he called Ann. "This is not a time to gloat," he told her. "This is a time to be happy. The important thing is for him to move on, put this behind him and do something successful with his life."

In August, Iverson went overseas for the first time in his life to compete in the World University Games. University of Illinois coach Lon Kruger took a team to Japan stockpiled with big names. Player of the Year candidate Tim Duncan of Wake Forest and Charles O'Bannon of the NCAA champion UCLA Bruins were on the team, as were Iverson's Big East rivals Kerry Kittles from Villanova and Ray Allen from UConn. The relationship between Allen and Iverson would go on to become cordial over the years, but it was anything but on this trip. Inside a hotel room, Iverson playfully threw some candy at Allen. Allen reacted too seriously for Iverson's liking: "You better stop or I'm gonna fuck you up," he said.

The battle of words escalated. Iverson ended up decking Allen right there, bloodying his teammate's nose. On the court, Iverson was just as combative, often dominating. He scored 21 points on 10-of-15 shooting to lead the U.S. team to a 105–81 quarterfinal win over Lithuania. In the gold medal game, he led all scorers with 26 points in a 141–81 rout over Japan.

By the time his sophomore year rolled around, Iverson knew his game had holes—and what he had to work on. As a freshman, he had shot a mere 39 percent from the floor and committed a turnover for every assist. "I have to be more patient," he acknowledged to friends and teammates. And he'd have to add some nuance to his game instead of just relying on overdrive all the time. Little did he know that the precise tweak his game needed would be provided by a walk-on teammate.

During warm-ups, Spike Lee stalked the Madison Square Garden floor, shooting footage through a camcorder. First he was focused on the shortest guy warming up on Georgetown's side. Then he zoomed in on the shortest guy at the other end of the floor. Lee's cinematic machinations were the first sign this would be a special night.

It was to be a much-hyped "heavyweight" battle in which both combatants weighed less than 170 pounds. It was the semifinals of the preseason National Invitational Tournament in late November 1995, and Iverson's 3–0 Georgetown Hoyas were facing the 2–0 Georgia Tech Yellow Jackets, led by freshman point-guard sensation Stephon Marbury. Marbury had been a high-school phenom on Coney Island. He'd even had a book written about him already, which chronicled his high-school hoops dream.

Less than three minutes into the game, Marbury had committed three turnovers. Though he used an assortment of spin moves and fakes to get by Iverson at times, Iverson was clearly the more experienced player. He scored 15 first-half points and 23 for the game, with 6 assists and 5 steals. Marbury ended up missing 10 of his 14 shots en route to 13 points, 8 assists, and 7 steals. The difference for Iverson was his new backcourt mate, freshman Victor Page, who scored 25 points.

After the game, Iverson talked about how he'd been working on improving his shot selection and patience. And he heaped praise on the player he would consider a rival for years to come. "He forced it a couple of times," Iverson said of Marbury. "That's just Stephon's heart. He has a big heart. He tries to do things for his teammates just like I did last year. I think it's incredible, his heart. He's a freshman, coming in with all of this notoriety, and he's backing it up."

The Hoyas would lose the NIT championship game to Arizona, despite 40 points from a battered and weary Iverson. Then the easy, early part of Georgetown's schedule kicked in, pushover games against lesser opponents. Wins over Rutgers and Duquesne followed. In a blowout win over St. Francis, Iverson soared over a six-ten forward to grab Page's missed foul shot as the ball caromed off the rim and, in one fierce motion, slam-dunked. A moment later, when he dove out-of-bounds for a loose ball, the hometown crowd gave him a standing ovation.

After beating DePaul to go 12–1, Georgetown became the nation's sixth-ranked team. This was largely due to the growth in Iverson's game. As awe-inspiring as he had been his freshman year, this season's version seemed far more developed. Through thirteen games, he was averaging 23 points, 6 assists, 4 rebounds, and 4 steals per game. Most impressive, his shooting had climbed to 53 percent. Thompson heaped the praise on. "We've never had anybody who's given more effort," the coach said. "In that respect, he reminds me of Ewing. Allen has gotten twenty stitches in his face this season diving for a loose ball—in practice."

Later, in the pros, Iverson wouldn't enjoy a reputation as a dedicated practice player. But at Georgetown, he often stayed after practice to play one-on-one against walk-on guard Dean Berry. Berry had known Iverson since the eighth grade, having played against him in AAU tournaments. Now, Iverson was clearly the better player, but one who, in Berry's estimation, got by on pure talent alone. He was so quick he never had to develop moves in order to get to the basket. He could just get there, period. But that would not be the case forever; as the level of competition rose, so, too, did the challenge to invent ways to succeed.

Berry, with his limited skills, had spent years developing his game. A cerebral player, he started studying tapes in the seventh grade of great ball handlers. Over and over again, he'd watch Tim Hardaway's crossover dribble, commonly referred to as the "UTEP Two-Step." (Hardaway, now starring for the NBA's Golden State Warriors, had gone to UTEP.) He watched Isiah Thomas's unique version of the same move. He saw John Stockton remove all the bells and whistles and confound opposing guards with it.

No matter the permutation, the crossover defied basic ball-handling tenets. Since biddy basketball, kids were taught to use the body as a shield between the ball and the defender when dribbling; this way, if a defender tried to steal the ball, he'd have to commit a foul. The crossover, on the other hand, put the ball directly in front of the defender; the ball handler, alternating the dribble between his left and right hands, would coax the defensive player into leaning one way and then change direction and dribble the other way—right in front of him. It was a risky move because the ball was exposed throughout.

Berry adopted facets of every crossover he studied. He mimicked the way Hardaway's crossover dribble barely came up off the floor, the way Hardaway stayed low to the ground. If a defender wanted to swipe the ball away, he couldn't reach it. From Thomas, Berry borrowed the quick cut. The crossover dribble needed to be fast and hard, because it accelerated the ball handler around the crossed-up, shaken defender.

The reason Iverson kept playing Berry after practice was that he couldn't stop Berry's crossover—even when he knew it was coming. He'd tell himself not to go for the fake, and he knew he was quicker than his teammate—the twelfth man on the team!—but then Berry would drop a cross on him and the next thing you knew, the walk-on was around him.

"Man," Iverson finally said, "you gotta show me that shit."

From then on, Berry taught his superstar teammate his favorite move. Iverson's deft feel for fakes combined with his natural speed soon made the move the most lethal Berry had ever seen. Iverson started adding his own in-your-face touches to it. He'd establish a rhythm to set up his man. First, he'd dribble in on the defender, the ball right out there in front of him, almost between the two men, tempting. He'd slowly move it from his left to right hand, real low, almost daring the defender to take a swipe. The defender, mildly hypnotized, would sync himself to Iverson's rhythm—lock himself into it. Then Iverson would raise up and take a high, shoulder-length dribble with his right hand; if the defender started to raise up out of his defensive crouch, too, Iverson would have him. In a flash, he'd take one hard, low dribble from right to left directly in front of his startled man; the high-to-low movement, combined with Iverson's preternatural burst of speed, had him around the defender and en route to the basket before recovery was possible.

Soon something started happening whenever Iverson crossed his man over. The crowd started buzzing and screaming and high-fiving, a reaction that, until now, had been reserved for the slam dunk. Fans started coming to games to see Iverson "break ankles" the way a previous generation of fans came to games hoping to see Michael Jordan soar through the air.

In late February, the Hoyas raised their record to 22–5 with an 81–60 upset over number three Connecticut and Ray Allen, whom many were touting as the collegiate player of the year. Iverson came out before the tip and motioned for the home crowd to get on its feet and make some noise. He scored 26 points and had 8 steals. Early in the second half, he dunked over Connecticut's Rudy Johnson; sitting courtside, NBA scouts Jerry West and Kevin McHale shook their heads, as though there were a chance their eyes had gotten it wrong.

By now, though still only a sophomore, Iverson had emerged as a team leader. He not only excited the hometown crowd, he got in his larger teammates' faces as well. And he led by example in practice—something he'd be criticized for not doing as a pro. At the end of every practice, Thompson had his team run length-of-the-floor sprints. At every practice he attended at Georgetown, Iverson never took a single sprint off, winning each one.

"I saw his leadership in our first game that year," remembers Berry. "It was against Colgate in the Preseason NIT. Early in the second half, he tried to dunk on Adonal Foyle and it was an ugly collision. He dislocated his shoulder and busted his nose. We didn't need him for the rest of this game, but he'd never hide behind an injury. He came back out. We knew it wasn't because the game was that important. We could handle Colgate. It was important for him to be there for his teammates."

Iverson's commitment in practice had everything to do with his rela-

In two seasons
as a Georgetown Hoya,
Iverson quickly became
the most exciting college
basketball player
in the nation.

tionship with Thompson, Berry and others attest. "He was like the obedient son," Berry, now a Florida businessman, says today. "They were like father and son. Allen was never late for practice, because that would be disrespectful to Coach. I'm not saying they didn't have blowups. But Coach would never go to the media with that stuff; he'd come directly to us. Things never got out of the gym and that meant everything to Allen."

Thompson also tended to be indulgent of Iverson's class-clown tendencies, as opposed to coaches in Iverson's future, like Larry Brown, who would see his wisecracking as proof that the player wasn't taking the game "seriously." Thompson, on the other hand, seemed to derive great joy from Iverson's pen-and-paper caricatures of him with a giant stomach and even bigger head. Similarly, Iverson's teammates were amused when Iverson would sneak up behind a sleeping player on a plane and lean down, his mouth just behind the slumbering teammate's ear. He'd start doing his impression of a buzzing fly until his victim, half-asleep, started swiping at the air around his head.

In the regular season finale, Iverson scored 37 points to lead Georgetown over Villanova. The Georgetown students, much to Thompson's chagrin, pleaded with Iverson to remain in school after this season by chanting, "Two more years! Two more years!" Thompson had never had a player leave early for the NBA, and he doubted Iverson would. Still, he grew angry anytime the subject was raised.

During the game, television announcer Billy Packer called Iverson a "tough monkey." Eighteen minutes after the remark, Packer apologized for saying it, but stressed that "it had absolutely nothing to do with race." Both Iverson and Thompson said after the game that they were not offended by the remark. Jesse Jackson called for the network to take action against Packer, who responded by saying, "I only apologized [during the game] to those people who have those sensibilities . . . I'm not apologizing for what I said, because what I said has no implications in my mind whatsoever to do with Allen Iverson's race. Al Capone was a tough monkey. Mike Ditka was a tough monkey. I don't think of Allen Iverson as a black player. I think of Allen Iverson as a player."

As would happen often throughout his career, Iverson was front and center in a morality play that went beyond the basketball world. The *Washington Post*'s Courtland Milloy excoriated Packer's version of his own color blindness. "The sportscaster would have us believe that he is immune to what ails the rest of America," wrote Milloy. "Where police see black, where the courts see black, where the media see black, Packer sees . . . well, tough monkeys. His response reflects the arrogance and denial that are the cornerstones of racist thinking in America today."

Meantime, as the Big East Tournament got under way, Thompson sought to put an end to the rumors of Iverson's early departure from Georgetown. The constant media speculation about his plans, Thompson felt, amounted to attempts to "solicit" him to leave school. "Allen's not going anywhere unless I tell him it's time to go," the coach said. "Tomorrow, I may tell him it's time to go. If Allen Iverson leaves, it will be because I told him to go. Quote me on that."

In the Big East championship game, the Hoyas led UConn by 11 with five minutes to go. Iverson was in foul trouble and Ray Allen had missed fourteen shots in a row. Until the crushing game winner, that is—a bank shot that bounced around the rim and finally fell through the hoop with 13.6 seconds to play. Neither Iverson nor Allen played particularly well. But Allen redeemed his subpar performance with the clutch shot.

Iverson was devastated. In the locker room after the game, Thompson went to console his star. When Iverson looked up at him, the coach could see the tears welling up. Thompson realized it was the first time he'd seen Iverson cry—remarkable, really, given Iverson's past. "I don't know as a child if I would have been able to handle what he's handled," Thompson would later say.

Iverson spent that night and many others replaying in his own head the final sequence of events, including his own fallaway jumper at the buzzer that missed. It was hardly a consolation when Iverson, with averages of 24.7 points, 5 assists, 4 rebounds, and 3.5 steals per game, was named to the Associated Press all-American first team days later.

When the NCAA Tournament began, the 26–7 Hoyas were seeded second in the East Regional. Their first two games would be played in Richmond, Virginia, just an hour from Newport News. There was Ann, arriving at halftime, sitting courtside in her Georgetown number three jersey, holding a sign reading PLAY BALL, BABY! and MOMMY LOVES YOU!

Also in the stands was now former governor Douglas Wilder, who came specifically to see the player to whom he'd given a second chance. When Ann saw Wilder, she gasped and ran toward him. Wilder looked up, squinted at the signs in her hands and at the jersey (IVERSON'S MOM, it read), and before he could speak, she'd enveloped him in a bear hug.

During the tournament, Thompson continued trying to protect Iverson. When a reporter asked the player to talk about the "second chance" he'd received after the bowling-alley incident, Thompson stepped in. "No, he can't speak about that," he said. "He came to play basketball. He's a child. Have some sensitivity toward him. Do you want me to ask you about your personal life, your family, your children, your wife?"

The Hoyas beat Mississippi Valley State, New Mexico, and Texas Tech, even though Iverson was suddenly in a shooting slump. Finally it came down to an East Regional championship showdown between Georgetown and the University of Massachusetts. UMass manhandled Iverson and wore him down. After scoring 17 points in the first half, he hit only one of ten shots in the second. As usual, there was a highlight. After crossing over defensive specialist Carmelo Travieso, six-foot eleven-inch shot blocker Marcus Camby stood between Iverson and the basket. Iverson threw down a two-handed slam over Camby that seemed to stun the defensive player. But UMass outlasted the Hoyas, 86–62, ending Iverson's sophomore season. And, maybe, his collegiate career.

Would he stay or would he go? That was the question the moment the Hoyas were ousted from the NCAA Tournament. The conventional wisdom was that he should stay in school. The *Washington Post*'s Mike Wilbon wrote, "Don't do it . . . If you're going to hit 16 of 50 shots (32 percent) and register a total of six assists and seven turnovers in the two games against Texas Tech and UMass, then how are you ready to play point guard in the NBA? Don't believe the hype, Allen."

NBA director of scouting Marty Blake pronounced Iverson "not ready." In the years to follow, countless underclassmen would declare themselves eligible for the NBA draft. But in May of 1996, it was still a rarity.

While the debate raged, few knew that Iverson's decision had been made long ago. He'd even been driving a $130,000 S600 Mercedes-Benz since early April, courtesy of an auto dealer who was a Georgetown booster. The arrangement was not permitted under NCAA rules; had Iverson intended to remain eligible, he no doubt would have refused the car. But the truth was that Iverson had always planned to come out after two years, just as he had pledged to Michael Freeman that day in the Hampton city jail before he left for his freshman year.

Iverson's decision had been made, but others loomed. After the Massachusetts game, for instance, Iverson was consoled by Spike Lee, who was wearing an Iverson jersey. Lee had offered to be his agent; Thompson had offered the services of David Falk. Iverson soon sought the opinion of Freeman, who felt one couldn't go wrong aligning oneself with the man who made Jordan.

So it was on May 1 that Iverson, Ann Iverson, Thompson, and Falk sat at a podium to announce that Allen Iverson was heading for the NBA. "My family needs me right now," Iverson said in a voice hoarse with emotion. His four-year-old sister, Ieisha, he explained, still suffered from seizures and needed medical attention. His one-year-old daughter, Tiaura, needed financial support. "I didn't like the things going on back in Hampton with my mom and my sisters' living situation."

"I'm really grateful to Coach Thompson and his staff," said Ann Iverson. "They made my little boy a man."

Despite the doubters, Thompson expressed no reservations about Iverson's impact at the next level. After all, as good as his freshman year had been, he had improved dramatically as a sophomore. His scoring went from 20.4 to 25 points per game, his shooting accuracy from 39 to 48 percent, his three-point shooting from 23 to 37 percent. He had reined in his racehorse pace to accommodate teammates like Harrington. Every time he had set his mind to doing something on a basketball court, it had gotten done. No, Thompson had no worries about Iverson's ability to flourish in the NBA.

But there were other concerns. Iverson would be leaving the safe cocoon of Thompson's team. Thompson knew firsthand of the emotional challenges facing professional athletes. John Thompson wasn't concerned about the two hours a day when Allen Iverson would be expressing himself on a basketball court. "I'm worried as hell about the other twenty-two hours," he said.

chapter | 7

CRU THIK

cru thik is the name of my crew, the guys i grew up with.
that's also what we've called our rap group. i got cru thik
in four places because that's who i represent.

T hat is one crazy white dude," Allen Iverson said, staring at the TV screen. He was hanging at Uncle Stevie's place and they were watching the NBA draft lottery on TV. A thin white guy with close-cropped hair and a goatee was jumping up and down as a panel of NBA suits looked on in astonishment. The guy even hugged David Stern, the staid and venerated league commissioner. His energy seemed to leap off the screen and into Uncle Stevie's living room.

It was Allen Iverson's—and most of the nation's—first glimpse of Pat Croce, the new president and part owner of the Philadelphia 76ers. Prior to the live airing of the lottery, Croce and the other draft team representatives had been warned against making any public displays of enthusiasm during the telecast. But Croce—like Iverson, actually—was not a man whose self-expression would be easily squelched. Croce catapulted from his seat when his team won the lottery, and thus the rights to Iverson, and started high-fiving and hugging the stunned conservative older men whom he had just beaten out. Just days later, Commissioner Stern would affectionately call Croce "stark raving mad." Maybe so. But back in Uncle Stevie's living room, Iverson had looked at his new boss letting it all hang out and realized he was witnessing something genuine.

The ensuing marriage between Allen Iverson and the Philadelphia 76ers was, at least in the minds of Iverson and Croce, the union's two protagonists, nothing short of a cosmic convergence. Throughout Iverson's adolescence, the 76ers had been Michael Freeman's team and Allen had been raised on tales of the one-on-one exploits of Dr. J, World B. Free, and Andrew Toney. His grandmother had always told him that everything happens for a reason, and just as he stayed true to the aphorism when he was in jail, now he was convinced that a bigger plan for him was in motion. After all, Freeman was incarcerated as Allen finished his sophomore, and final, year of college and declared himself eligible for the NBA. It was as though, to Iverson, the Sixers picking him first overall redeemed all the sacrifices Freeman had made for him—including the sacrificing of his own freedom, time and again. That's why, in interview after interview leading up to draft night, Allen proclaimed his desire to be a Sixer. And that's why Philadelphia would be the only team he would visit and work out for prior to the draft.

Besides, it had to be more than just coincidence that the 76ers, long a league doormat, were setting out to turn things around, just as he'd turned things around in his own life. They had a new arena, new management, and—perhaps most important of all—new ownership.

The public face of that ownership was the ebullient, charismatic Croce, whose ascent in Philadelphia was well known. At forty-one, he was the town's preeminent rags-to-riches story. A street kid from a white, working-class part of Philly, Croce spent his adolescence partying and raising hell in local taprooms. Like Iverson, he was tattooed, sporting a colorful pirate ship on his left forearm. Like Iverson, he cultivated an outer toughness that in part compensated for a thin, wiry build. A black belt in karate, he had been tossed from his first college for hospitalizing his dorm's resident adviser.

As the eighties dawned, Croce went back to school to study athletic training and physical therapy and was among the first to anticipate the nation's oncoming fitness craze—or, rather, its consequences. People, he realized, were going to start hurting themselves. He became trainer to the Philadelphia business elite. In the basement of a ritzy Main Line mansion, he taught karate to a college kid named Jay Snider. Snider's father, Ed, owned the local hockey team, the Philadelphia Flyers.

In that house, he first heard the word "entrepreneur" and realized that that was what he wanted to be. "He was just always around, watching and asking questions," Ed Snider recalls. "The kid had a lot of moxie. You had to like him instantaneously."

The senior Snider began dispatching Croce to soothe the body aches of his friends and colleagues, among them Chuck Barris, host and creator of TV's *The Gong Show*. Soon Croce became the Flyers' and Sixers' strength-and-conditioning coach; in the process, he created a high profile for himself as trainer to stars like Mike Schmidt, Julius Erving, and Charles Barkley. He began hosting a high-energy radio show during which he'd hang up on callers if they didn't begin by shouting his by-now-famous tag line: "I feel great!"

To many, Croce was little more than an amusingly hyper media personality. Behind the scenes, though, he began building an empire. He opened a string of fitness centers, offering the average Joe the same type of intense workouts and rehabs that made pros like Barkley hurl in front of a crowded, gawking gym. Along the way, T-shirts starting appearing: I SURVIVED PAT CROCE. He even transformed members of the media into something approximating good condition (for them), virtually ensuring that nary a negative word would be written or spoken about him.

In 1993, Croce sold his forty fitness centers for $40 million to a company that then merged with rehab giant NovaCare, and he began setting his sights on the next big thing. Wouldn't it be cool, he thought, to embark on a different type of rehab project? By the 1995–96 season, the once-proud Philadelphia 76ers franchise was floundering. Under head coach and general manager John Lucas, they'd won only eighteen games that season. Croce began pestering then owner Harold Katz about selling. Later, Katz would say he only sold because "Pat Croce called me fifty times, until I said yes."

In April of 1996, Croce catalyzed a deal that established Ed Snider, Comcast Corporation (owned by Ralph Roberts and his son Brian), and himself as partners. Croce became president of the Sixers with 10 percent ownership of the team and 2.5 percent of the overall $500 million deal. (Snider became chairman of the newly formed Comcast-Spectacor, under the aegis of which Comcast's new sports-and-entertainment acquisitions would be run: the Sixers, the Flyers, the then-named brand-new Corestates Center arena and its predecessor, the Corestates Spectrum.) The boisterous, backslapping Croce would report to the reserved Snider, who had a reputation for cutthroat business practices. At the press conference to announce the deal, Croce took to the podium and erupted in an ear-piercing Tarzan yell before shouting "I feel great!"

Croce immediately embarked upon his reclamation project. Soon Philadelphians were treated to a local commercial for Sixers season tickets in which Croce, perched perilously atop the new arena, shouted his motto into the heavens. His first substantive move was to hire a general manager who could oversee the remaking of the basketball team and who would not squander the precious first pick in the draft, as past Sixers regimes had done. Along with a Snider lieutenant, Croce interviewed a host of candidates before settling on Brad Greenberg, a forty-two-year-old coaching and player personnel veteran. For eight years, Greenberg had been director of player personnel for the Portland Trail Blazers, responsible for the talent evaluations that went into forming a roster that made it to the NBA Finals just three years earlier.

Croce, a detail freak, was impressed by Greenberg's preparation for their interview. Unlike many of the other candidates, Greenberg came equipped with preliminary scouting reports of the top players and he didn't hedge when asked whom he'd pick with the number one choice. Iverson, he said, had "ridiculous skills" and possessed what he called the "wow factor." "He's the kind of player that makes you say 'wow!' and look at whoever's next to you and say, 'Did I really just see that?'" he remarked. He'd still do his due diligence on other players, Greenberg said, and he'd be open to the possibility that, in a workout, one of them might blow him away and change his mind, but if forced to choose now, he'd pick the player who would be the toughest to guard at the NBA level. That would be Iverson.

So it was that, during the weeks leading up to the NBA draft, Greenberg and Croce arranged for their first meeting with Iverson. Croce got to the lobby of the Embassy Suites hotel near the Philadelphia airport before Greenberg and took a look around. He didn't see a basketball player waiting for him, as had been the plan. He inquired at the front desk and the clerk nodded to the lobby's far corner, where a baby-faced kid sat in big, baggy sweats with headphones on, slumped down, head thrown back, eyes closed, mouth open.

"*That's* Allen Iverson?" Croce said, before making his way over and shaking the ballplayer awake. "Allen Iverson? I'm Pat Croce!" he said, loudly, jarring the kid.

They moved to a small table, where they were soon met by Greenberg. Iverson quickly got the sense that Croce wasn't just another suit by the way he refused to tiptoe around issues surrounding Iverson's troubled past. "I've got to know about that bowling-alley scene," Croce told him. "'Cause that's the baggage you carry around with you, that's what everyone's going to throw in your face."

Iverson volunteered his version of events, how he'd been called "nigger" and then was rushed out of the bowling alley when all hell broke loose. Croce sat still for a moment, before inching forward in his chair.

"You mean to tell me," he said, "that a guy called you a nigger and you didn't hit him?"

"That's right."

Croce paused. "Well, then you're a fuckin' punk."

Iverson flinched and lurched forward in his chair, chest puffed out. "I'm tellin' you, man—I couldn't," he said, in a forceful tone, making solid eye contact. "I ain't stupid, man."

Looking back, Croce would target the moment as the real beginning of their relationship. He'd challenged the kid, sending the message that there'd be no bullshit between them. And the kid responded in kind, by looking him in the eye.

Greenberg brought up the subjects of drugs, his mother, and his friends. "I respect my mom, I love my mom," Iverson said. "I've heard rumors all my life about my mom and drugs and it hurts me. She says she doesn't do them and I believe her." Of his friends, Iverson said, "I liked to hang around older guys 'cause guys my age were doing some bad things—worse things than the older guys I hung around with." He mentioned Arnie Steele and Marlon Moore as two of the guys who would come with him to Philly. He reassured Croce and Greenberg that if he did something stupid or wrong, it wouldn't be because of his friends. "If I fuck up, it's going to be because I fucked up," Iverson said. "Not because some guy told me to fuck up."

Greenberg worked Iverson out that afternoon and saw nothing to dissuade him that this was his guy. But Greenberg's work was just beginning. He brought in other potential picks as well. He and Croce had dinner with Stephon Marbury; during his workout, he paused for a moment to throw up—before resuming play. They also hosted Marcus Camby, Iverson's collegiate rival Ray Allen, and the most intriguing draftee, eighteen-year-old local high-schooler Kobe Bryant. None, Greenberg thought, came off as real as Iverson did.

Bryant had starred at nearby Lower Merion High School; just a year earlier, he had been invited to a Sixers practice by then coach John Lucas and spanked the Sixers' go-to man, Jerry Stackhouse, in a game of one-on-one. Bryant was a phenomenal talent, but Greenberg knew the Sixers needed a star right away. Already, Greenberg could tell that Bryant possessed a star's ego from the way the teen strolled through the Sixers' workout facility—indoors—wearing expensive shades all the while.

Compared with Iverson, Marbury seemed overly polished, schooled by his agent to talk in sportspeak clichés. The conventional wisdom was that Marbury was a purer point guard than Iverson, someone who, like point guards of old, would sacrifice his own scoring for the good of his team. Iverson, the thinking went, was not that sort of player. Indeed, come draft night, when Marbury was selected by Minnesota with the number four pick, he drew a distinction between himself and Iverson: "Iverson is a scorer in a point guard's body," he said. "I make other players better."

Greenberg sensed it was a more complicated issue. In their conversations, Marbury kept referring to his prospective team as "my team," as though he were interviewing for the position of owner. Iverson, on the other hand, talked about how he'd do whatever it took to win, including whatever it took to make his teammates better. (Ironically, after a few years in the league, Marbury's reputation would come full circle, and especially after his trade to Phoenix for Jason Kidd in 2001, Greenberg's view of him as a me-first type of point guard would become widely shared.)

Meantime, Greenberg continued looking into Iverson's background. He interviewed John Thompson, who told him Iverson didn't like school, was not a thug, had some "'hood friends," but was "coachable, football-tough, and liked by his teammates."

University of Illinois's Lon Kruger, who coached Iverson in the World University Games, called him the "most talented point guard I've ever seen" and dubbed him "high maintenance." The one time he pulled him from a game, Iverson retreated into himself for a day. "His instincts are to pout a little," Kruger said. "He's as competitive in a good way as anyone I've ever seen. He could struggle in dealing with his teammates if they aren't competitive enough."

A private eye hired by the Sixers reported back that Iverson's home life had been erratic, that he frequently came to school dressed in dirty clothes, and that "sources and interviews reveal that Iverson's mother and her associates have been involved with drugs at Iverson's place of residence."

The Sixers also subjected Iverson to a battery of psychological tests. The psychologist's report found that Kruger was on the right track when he called him "high maintenance." Terming Iverson a "restless type of personality . . . who continues to harbor a great deal of anger and frustration," the psychologist diagnosed that, under prolonged stress, he "can often revert to being sullen, defiant, and feeling misunderstood. . . . He's a loyal guy, wants to belong," wrote the psychologist. "He needs direction and guidance, but needs an arm around him also. Fully confident on the court, [but] off the court is a mistrusting place. He has blind spots to his behavior that aren't good . . . more a case of not knowing the appropriate behaviors than being disrespectful of others." The psychologist recommended that, in dealing with Iverson, authority always had to be carefully balanced with sensitivity, and that he could use a "positive locker-room role model."

Just days before the draft, Greenberg was close to making his final decision. Iverson just had too much talent to pass on. He and Sixers assistant coach Maurice Cheeks, a legendary point guard, talked often about Iverson's "freakish skills," as Greenberg put it. In the NBA, when a player dribbles by his man, the next move is almost always to either shoot or pass—defensive players are so quick to react, there's always a second defender lurking nearby to come to the aid of his beaten teammate. But Iverson was the exception to the rule; he'd go by his man, and then the next, and then the next. He'd find a way not only to get to the basket, but to score—or "finish" in basketball parlance—often over the outstretched arms of seven-footers. "He's got a Ph.D. in little-man tactics to score," Greenberg told Cheeks. Together, they'd marvel at Iverson's technique in changing directions while dribbling, how he'd push off his outside leg to make the sharpest, quickest of cuts. Or how he'd subtly raise up while dribbling in on his man, elongating his posture, a hesitation move that a defender would invariably mimic—allowing for that split-second opening for Iverson to blow on by. "Maybe it's a football thing," Greenberg theorized, "the way he can fake a guy out to avoid being tackled, and now he applies the same change of direction and change-of-pace moves on the basketball court."

There was no question, then, as to talent. But Greenberg wanted to see one more thing. He'd just hired his head coach, Johnny Davis, who had been an assistant in Portland. Before settling on Iverson, he wanted to confirm Thompson's view that he would be coachable. He called David Falk and told him the Sixers were prepared to make Iverson the number one pick, provided Falk got his client to come to Philly for one last workout. This time, it would be done surreptitiously—there'd be no press conference. "I want to see him go all out," Greenberg said. "If I see what I hope to see from him, he'll be our pick."

Falk was ecstatic; he was working on a $50 million endorsement deal for Iverson with Reebok that had a higher chance of coming to fruition if Iverson was the top pick, especially in a major market like Philadelphia. The next day, Iverson met Davis, and Greenberg told him he wanted to see "all game shots—no tippy-toe shots." It was a test of his character, not his game. The coach and general manager wanted to see how he would respond to their wanting more from him. Would he give them more? How bad did he want to be the number one pick? They weren't disappointed. One thing Iverson always possessed was a seeming reservoir of energy; he spent the workout in constant motion.

That night, Cheeks and Greenberg took the twenty-one-year-old to dinner at the Italian restaurant inside the Korman Suites hotel, just a few blocks from Cheeks's center-city Philadelphia apartment. In stark contrast to his seemingly sullen, monosyllabic interview style, Iverson exhibited a Croce-like level of enthusiasm as he soaked up Cheeks's wisdom about the NBA game.

"Who is your favorite point guard?" Cheeks asked him.

"Oh, Gary Payton," Iverson replied.

"Why?"

"Because he's tough," Iverson said. "And when a guy scores on him, he comes right back on him."

Cheeks, renowned for his selfless play during a career of setting up scorers like Julius Erving and Moses Malone, smiled. "Is that what you do when a guy scores on you?"

Iverson smiled, bragging now. "Yeah, I go right back at him."

Cheeks paused. "Well, as a point guard, if a guy goes at you and scores, do you think it's always the best thing for your team for you to go right back at him?"

Now Iverson, suddenly unsure of his position, looked back and forth between Greenberg and Cheeks. Cheeks filled in the silence. "All I'm saying is, there are four other guys with you. If you get caught up in your own private game with your man, what about your guys?"

Iverson smiled. "So who do you like?" he asked, part question, part challenge.

"John Stockton," Cheeks replied without hesitation.

"John Stockton?" Iverson asked, his face scrunching up in surprise. Stockton could play, no doubt, but there damn sure wasn't anybody on the playgrounds emulating the game of the player with the shortest shorts in the league.

"Yeah, John Stockton," Cheeks said. "You want to talk about tough? He never misses a game. And he's been the best screener on Utah's team for years. That boy can play. He knows the game."

Watching the exchange, seeing Iverson's eagerness to soak up knowledge, Greenberg made up his mind. That night, he reviewed all his scouting reports and interview notes one final time. There was Kruger, talking about Iverson's "extra gears." And Duke coach Mike Krzyzewski saying Iverson "has the heart of a lion." He penned his final player evaluation report, which would be shown to Croce and Ed Snider before the Sixers made their decision. "There aren't many players in professional basketball that are this competitive," Greenberg wrote. "Similar to Jordan in that respect. He doesn't have Jordan's discipline nor the fundamentals that Jordan had when he left college. If he could develop in those areas then he could approach being a Jordan type in a six-foot package. I can't predict that for him because the environment Allen experienced prior to entering the pros suffers by comparison to Jordan. However, the mere fact that I bring up Jordan in some sort of comparison tells a lot about his talent level."

Later, in retrospect, the choice of Iverson would seem to have been a no-brainer. But at the time, there was considerable risk, owing to what Croce called Iverson's "baggage"—the controversial past, the dysfunctional upbringing, the shady friends. But this was the NBA, where you rolled the dice on talent.

Draft night was at New Jersey's Meadowlands. When David Stern leaned into a microphone and intoned that "with the first pick of the 1996 draft, the Philadelphia 76ers select Allen Iverson, Georgetown University," the Iverson clan burst into a paroxysm of celebration. There was Arnie, Marlon, and Ra surrounding their fellow member of Cru Thik—who was wearing a suit. When once asked what he had been thinking on the night he was drafted into the NBA in 1984, Charles Barkley replied: "I thought, 'I ain't poor no more.' " Now the same thought likely occurred not only to Iverson, who would soon sign a three-year, $9 million contract, but also to a whole contingent of Iverson supporters. They were with him, as he liked to say, "from day one," and they were with him on draft night, whooping and hollering as the evening wore on. And right in the middle of the celebratory tumult was Ann, who, moments after her baby was selected, shocked NBA front-office personnel by loudly proclaiming, "We are going to par-tay tonight! I am getting *fucked* up tonight!"

The Allen Iverson era had dawned.

The NBA in 1996 was at a cultural crossroads. Michael Jordan had not only remade the league, he'd redefined tried-and-true sports marketing notions. Before Jordan, stars of individual sports such as John McEnroe had led the way in endorsement income. But Jordan's impact went beyond the bottom line. He debuted in the 1980s and immediately altered pop-culture style trends, ushering in the shaved-head look, hoop earrings, and sleek, tapered suits; it all added up to a level of seemingly color-blind crossover acceptance at a time, not coincidentally, when *The Cosby Show* was the number-one-rated sitcom in both white and black living rooms.

Throughout the first half of the nineties, the search was on for the next Jordan, for an icon-in-waiting who would advance Jordan's athletic, business, and cultural legacies. Every year, it seemed, a new candidate would be anointed Jordan's "Air Apparent." There was the upper-middle-class Grant Hill, by way of Duke University. There was Anfernee "Penny" Hardaway, a Nike endorser. There was Harold Minor—nicknamed "Baby Jordan" for his leaping ability. (There was only one problem: he couldn't quite play.) And there was Iverson's new teammate on the 76ers, Jerry Stackhouse, who came into the league with an above-the-rim game, a University of North Carolina pedigree, and a big marketing push from Nike competitor Fila.

All had, like countless others, signed on to the popular Gatorade-marketed mantra at the time. They all were trying to be "Like Mike." All, that is, except this new kid, the upstart Iverson, who didn't seem interested in repackaging himself in order to garner white, suburban acceptance. Shortly after Iverson's entry into the league, it became clear that he represented an epochal moment, the dawn of a new era for the black athlete. Something more in-your-face, more consciously authentic than the Jordan model, an image that owed more to hip-hop than to Motown.

Before Iverson even played his first NBA game, proof of his groundbreaking impact surfaced. Prior to Iverson's first pro training camp, Falk, the visionary who altered the landscape of professional sports by matching Nike with Jordan, worked out a ten-year, $50 million endorsement deal for Iverson with Nike competitor Reebok. Iverson chose Reebok in part for their canny approach to what would be his signature shoe. Called "The Question"—a play on Iverson's nickname—the $100 shoe would hit stores by January. In his second year, the company would change the product's name to "The Answer."

Cleverly, Falk encouraged Reebok not to market Iverson as though he were Jordan. Iverson himself insisted on marketing imagery that, instead of transforming and mythologizing him, merely reflected the way he saw himself. For a profile in *The New York Times Magazine,* Falk allowed writer Lynn Hirschberg to sit in on a strategizing session with Team Reebok:

"We're here to talk about who Allen is," Falk begins. "The single most important thing is to manage his image. It gets so diffuse. Every company wants to be Fellini and control the guy's image. It cannibalizes the guy's appeal and it confuses the audience."

Everyone agrees, and Iverson sits quietly, listening. "How do you feel about that?" Falk asks Iverson. He thinks a minute. "I would be more into it," he replies slowly, "if I could be myself."... "Would you say speed and innovation work for you?" Falk asks Iverson. There is a long silence. "I would say creativity," Iverson says, finally. Everyone nods.

From Reebok's perspective, the alliance with Iverson gave the company a leg up in the race to win over an emerging demographic, the hip-hop kids. The athletic shoe market was a $7 billion industry and 40 percent of it belonged to mighty Nike. Reebok, though number two, had fallen on hard times, its market share slipping a full percentage point to 20 in the year prior to Iverson's signing. In the months following Iverson's deal, however, investor confidence in the company's future rose. Reebok stock climbed from $26 per share to $38. Iverson was seen as the key to turning Reebok into a hip, cutting-edge brand.

Reebok's executive charged with managing the Iverson line would be Henry "Que" Gaskins, a thirty-one-year-old Washington, D.C., native who had been a buyer for Saks Fifth Avenue after getting a master's in business administration from the Kellogg Graduate School of Management at Northwestern University. Gaskins, a black man who dressed in stylishly baggy clothes and would soon wear his hair in cornrows, moved to the Philly area to manage the Iverson account. Some saw his role as that of glorified baby-sitter; indeed, he admitted, there was some of that.

But Gaskins had seen firsthand some of the missteps his company had taken in the marketing of its other star endorser, Shaquille O'Neal. Shaq was a huge name, yet his shoes weren't selling. Indeed, Gaskins knew that the shoes of big men rarely sold as well as those of smaller, quicker players. Children idolize athletes who remind them of the way they see themselves in their dreams: nimble, rising, untouchable. Jordan, in the mind's eye, invariably floats; Shaq, as great as he is, remains earthbound, a stone leviathan. It is difficult to even picture him in motion.

Iverson would be just the opposite. It would be impossible to imagine him at rest. Shaq, moreover, under the business tutelage of his then agent Leonard Armato, was starring in kids movies and his image was even reproduced on Saturday-morning cartoons. Gaskins knew that a new urban youth culture was emerging, a demo with money to burn. Just as they were spending it on rappers such as Tupac Shakur and Biggie Smalls, so, too, would they flock to a ballplayer who represented antiestablishment mores. Being dubbed the anti-Jordan in the sports pages surely posed a risk, but it was a risk that only applied to that insular world. In the culture at large, there was a market for someone like Iverson.

Gaskins made his case time and again to his superiors at the lily-white multinational corporation, and to Iverson himself, who didn't seem too charged up by strategic talk of his "positioning." The athlete's sole demand was that the company not try to change him, and he got no disagreement on that front from Gaskins.

This was new territory in professional sports, so naturally the 76ers had concerns. "We knew Reebok wasn't doing one of those corporate marketing plans with Allen," recalls 76ers general manager Brad Greenberg. "It was going to be more of a hip-hop theme, geared to younger kids and urban kids. Reebok endorsed his being this sort of anticorporate guy. I understood that, but in some ways it was a bit contrary to the direction we hoped he'd go. There were posters of him with his jeans down to his ass, without his shirt on, flexing his skinny muscles. But they had a plan and Que was a bright guy, so it wasn't really an issue."

As training camp approached, word reached Greenberg that Iverson's street credibility—which Gaskins was so enthused about—might be more risky than anyone had thought. Greenberg learned that gunshots had been fired at Iverson's Mercedes-Benz outside a party back in Hampton. Iverson was inside the party at the time, but two of his friends, Michael Powell and Alex Rhoden, were in the car. Powell, a closer friend to Arnie Steele than to Iverson, had two felony convictions on his record, cocaine possession in 1990 and possession of a weapon by a felon in 1992. Powell and Rhoden were unhurt in the incident, but Greenberg sat Iverson down the moment Iverson arrived for training camp.

"If they can shoot at your car, that might be a message," Greenberg said; Iverson assured him the incident was just one of those wrong-place, wrong-time things. After receiving assurances that neither he nor his friends were involved in anything that could warrant such violent message sending, Greenberg felt relieved. Enough of the off-court stuff; it was time to concentrate on basketball.

Well, almost. The Sixers played a couple of exhibition games against the Knicks at the Nassau Coliseum on Long Island. Iverson's friends took rooms at the same hotel as the team, and, over three days, they ran up thousands of dollars in room service and phone charges. "How long can these guys stay on the phone? How much room service can they eat?" Greenberg wondered when he was shown the bill, which he paid, deducting the amount from Iverson's next paycheck.

Just prior to tip-off of the first preseason game, Greenberg noticed that the only people not standing for the national anthem were Iverson's friends. It wasn't that they were trying to make a political statement. As his team psychologist had predicted about Iverson—and now Greenberg realized the same applied to his friends—they were sometimes oblivious to commonly accepted standards of appropriate behavior. It led to the first of many conversations with Iverson, during which Sixers officials from Croce to Greenberg to Coach Davis tried to get him to see that his friends' conduct reflected upon how people viewed him. "It ain't up to me to tell them how to act," Iverson would say whenever he was approached with news that one of his friends had, say, left a car in a handicapped parking spot or gotten in the face of an arena usher. Getting Iverson to come around on this point might be more of a battle than getting him to dominate on the court. As his rookie season dawned, all the distractions notwithstanding, there was no quarreling with Allen Iverson on the court.

Two hours before the Answer's NBA debut, Pat Croce stood in the concourse of his brand-new building, playing host. As fans rushed in, the new owner would extend his hand for shaking or raise his arm for high fives. Much has been written about the surliness of the Philadelphia fan, but this scene would consistently repeat itself over the next five years. As if his feel-great gregariousness were contagious, Croce would be swarmed by well-wishers dressed in Sixers garb—and, more often than not, in Iverson number three replica jerseys.

On this night, the crowd parted around Croce when, as if to classic funk background music, Ann Iverson approached. Croce had yet to meet the mother of his new franchise player, but he'd heard from his staff that she was, in his words, "a trip." ("Honey," she'd later say, "I ain't no trip. I'm a damn *journey*.") Now here she came, parting the crowd as though she were starring in her own movie, wearing a big fur coat, jeans, an Iverson jersey that read IVERSON'S MOM on its back, and, of course, her trademark ruby-red lipstick.

"Mr. Pat! Mr. Pat!" she called, not walking so much as sashaying toward him. "You gotta come see my new Jag-Wire! You gotta see the Jag-Wire my baby bought me!"

Before Croce could respond, she was upon him, bear-hugging. Croce, a hugger himself, instantly sensed he'd found someone who could match his frenetic zest for life, who shared his legendary penchant for celebrating the moment. She took his hand and led him past the turnstiles and the onrushing crowd to the entrance, where ticket holders were still streaming in; there, parked right outside, in the middle of the crowd and fifty yards from the nearest parking lot, was a shiny red Jaguar. Just as he'd promised so many years ago, Ann Iverson's baby had gotten her that candy-red Jag.

"Ann!" Croce said, laughing. "You can't leave that there!"

"Mr. Pat, I need to ask you something," she said, somber now. "You think you can give my baby an advance on his paycheck? My baby don't got nothing in his refrigerator."

"No wonder!" Croce said, throwing his arm around the bubbling ball of energy before him while nodding at her new ride. "There's where the money went!"

Ann laughed, and threw her arm around her new friend. "You gotta make sure my baby eats, Mr. Pat," she said. "He got nothing in his refrigerator. I'm counting on you now."

Meantime, down on the basketball floor, the team that warmed up was an immensely talented one that nonetheless had aficionados doubting whether it could actually win. First-year coach Johnny Davis had his challenges. In addition to the well-hyped rookie Iverson, he had shooting guard Stackhouse, who had led all rookies the year before in scoring (over 19 per game), but whose game had some surprising holes, given his North Carolina roots. A tremendous athlete, he wasn't a consistent shooter, he often seemed disinterested on defense, and he had a tough time dribbling the ball, as evidenced by his league-leading total of turnovers the previous season. Stackhouse needed the ball; how would he mesh with Iverson, who likewise was accustomed to being "The Man" with the ball in his hands?

One forward spot belonged to Clarence Weatherspoon, a solid, if uninspiring, small forward capable of putting up respectable numbers. Mercurial veteran Derrick Coleman was the power forward as well as the big question mark. NBA observers had long agreed that Coleman was one of the league's most talented players. He could shoot, rebound, pass, and possessed a stellar basketball IQ. His career to date, however, had been a disappointment. He hadn't consistently led his teams to winning records. The conventional wisdom: he had an attitude problem. While with his previous team, the New Jersey Nets, he'd been portrayed as a ho-hum player skating by on talent. In New Jersey, he'd once feigned enthusiasm in an interview by declaring "whoop-dee-damn-do," and at the start of one season, he even offered to write a check then and there in the amount of a season's worth of fines for violating the team's dress code.

Most coaches tolerated Coleman because, when healthy, he was a legitimate 20-point, 10-rebound producer. But on the eve of this season, he sent a disturbing signal when he rejected Davis's offer to be a team captain. Croce, given his holistic-health-care roots, worried: Sure, Coleman could put up good numbers, but what kind of influence would he be on Iverson, who, the team psychologist had said, was in need of positive veteran teammates?

In front of a sellout crowd of more than twenty thousand fans, including John Thompson, Ann, and thirty Iverson loyalists from back home in Virginia, Iverson's first game foreshadowed much of the coming season. There were breathtaking plays that seemed to portend endless possibilities, followed by playground-style turnovers. In the second quarter, Iverson took a Coleman outlet pass, raced the length of the floor, and lofted an alley-oop to Stackhouse, who threw down a reverse slam to thunderous applause. Minutes later, Iverson and Stackhouse broke out on a two-on-one against Milwaukee's Johnny Newman; where most point guards would set up their shooting mate, Iverson instead faked the pass and took off, soaring for a dunk that inspired Philadelphia's TV color commentator Steve Mix to exclaim, "Oh! Oh, my!"

At other times, Iverson would bring the ball up court and look to Coleman in the post; if he was covered, Iverson would fake out his man and launch a long jumper—none of his teammates having so much as touched the ball.

But that's not what the crowd was buzzing about. Who *was* this hustling blur of a little man—this kid—who seemed to be scoring at will? Iverson would end up hitting 12 of 19 shots for 30 points, while dishing out 6 assists. But his inexperience showed when, with his team nursing a 98–96 lead with just over three minutes to play, he committed a foolish foul away from the basket, giving the Bucks two free throws. Compounding the error, he pursued referee Mike Mathis, who was known for his oversensitivity, asking over and over, "What'd I do? What'd I do?" It wasn't what he said so much as how he said it: demonstrative, in-your-face. Mathis, certain he was being "shown up" by a rookie, blew the whistle and called a technical foul; Milwaukee would never trail again. To make matters worse, Iverson's collegiate nemesis, Ray Allen, also a rookie, nailed a three-pointer to seal the win.

After the game, a jostling media pack surrounded Iverson at his locker. He was upbeat about the NBA game and characteristically confident. "There are no zones, no junk defenses," he said. "In the NBA, it's just you and your man. I feel I can score on anybody."

Watching the media swarm around his new teammate, Sixers big man Scott Williams, who had played on the championship Bulls team with Michael Jordan, recognized that something special was in the making. He'd spent many nights earlier in his career watching Jordan in wide-eyed wonder, but there was something just as awe inspiring going on here. "He's got a Ford motor up his butt," Williams marveled while looking at his point guard.

The next game, Williams's former team awaited. In retrospect, Iverson would claim that his rookie season changed irrevocably after he first squared off against Michael Jordan.

There was a lot of love on that other bench. That's what winning could do, Allen Iverson knew. He was watching his opponents celebrate the hoisting of yet another championship banner to the rafters of Chicago Stadium prior to the start of his second NBA game. Iverson had heard all about how Scottie Pippen and Dennis Rodman didn't talk to each other; he'd heard the tales of how demanding and insensitive Jordan could be as a teammate. But, staring over at the mighty Chicago Bulls, winners of a record seventy-two games the season before en route to another NBA title, he saw that winning cured all ills. On a losing team, personality issues were "dissension." On a winning one, they were constructive friction.

The game wasn't close. Jordan scored an effortless 27; the Bulls won, 115–86. It was over quickly. Iverson was nervous at first and committed all five of his turnovers in the decisive first half; his passes bounced off teammates' hands and his shots clanked off the rim. He'd end up scoring only 15 points on 4-of-13 shooting.

Still, even when the outcome was no longer in doubt, Iverson played at only one speed: blinding. Even on the receiving end of a blowout, he chirped away at the superior opposition, his mouth moving almost as fast as his feet. Once garbage time came, Jordan and Bulls guard Ron Harper retired to the bench, laughing at the arrogant newcomer.

Afterward, the battle extended to the postgame interviews. None other than Dennis Rodman fumed about the rookie's irreverent on-court behavior. "I don't like too many of these young players, but I like him the least," Rodman said. "You've got to respect the game and the players you're playing against. He doesn't respect people. He thinks he's God. He thinks the court is his street, his playground, and he can do anything he wants and say anything he wants."

"He just has to learn to be quiet," Harper said, making sure to praise Iverson for his play, if not his style. "I thought I could play defense. Now I don't know."

During the game, both Rodman and Pippen razzed Iverson about taking too many of his team's shots. A previous generation of black athlete would have been schooled in turning the other cheek. But Iverson, who came of age in a generation that saw such Jackie Robinson–like restraint as tantamount to selling out, responded with a blistering comeback: "I don't care what Scottie Pippen says," he said. "Scottie Pippen doesn't know what goes on in my family, so it doesn't mean anything to me. Rodman, I don't pay him no mind. His whole game is about trying to throw you off."

His comments wouldn't have sparked any controversy whatsoever had it not been for Jordan's simultaneous remarks in the home-team locker room. According to Jordan, he tried to console Iverson on the court when Rodman and Pippen were picking on him. "At one point, I mentioned to Iverson, he was going to have to respect us," Jordan said. "If you don't respect anyone else in this league you have to respect us. He said he doesn't have to respect anybody."

And so the media had its story—one that would dominate the league for months to come. Allen Iverson had dissed Michael Jordan. For those who knew Iverson, it was absurd to think that he didn't respect Jordan; this was a kid, after all, who had once painted Jordan's portrait on his bedroom door and tried to take the door with him when it came time to move. Iverson tried time and again to explain that he was simply speaking of matters *on the court* when he said he didn't have to respect Jordan. He'd seen too many players fear Jordan on the court, and he knew Jordan thrived on intimidating the opposition. To Iverson, his statement was an announcement of his own competitive fires, something that should have been applauded, not jeered. David Falk, agent to both men, elaborated: "Allen idolizes Michael, and because he's aware that he idolizes him, he doesn't want his respect for Michael to interfere with his ability to compete against him."

Nonetheless, for purposes of the soap-opera-like daily sports narrative, Iverson was the perfect bad-boy foil to Jordan's good guy. The story line was set: Sinner versus Saint. Over the next few months, Iverson would find himself branded as the preeminent symbol of a generation of athletes seen as too selfish, too spoiled, too cocky for their own good. Iverson saw the maelstrom for what it was, the natural by-product of a generational handoff. He said as much after the game against the Bulls, when he reacted to the suddenly swirling controversy by saying, "I think the younger guys want to show that we belong up there. We want to make our mark, too."

Indeed, the names were different and the times had changed, but like so many media plots, the story felt vaguely familiar. In the seventies, a seemingly ghetto fabulous character named Dr. J came into the league wearing an Afro and big gold chains and displaying a high-flying playground style. The old guard looked on in disdain. None other than legendary Celtic coach Red Auerbach remarked that "Julius Erving is a nice kid, but he's not a great player." Similarly, in the eighties, Jordan showed up for his first all-star game not in an Armani suit and Kenneth Cole shoes, but in baggy jeans and a backward baseball cap. Back then, he was the irreverent, arrogant newcomer who needed to be taught a lesson; veteran players, led by Isiah Thomas, even froze him out—refusing to pass him the ball—during the 1985 all-star game.

Even as Jordan grew, he wasn't always deserving of the automatic halo the sports press bestowed. As Sam Smith spelled out in his book *The Jordan Rules,* Jordan was the kind of superstar who reduced teammates to tears, blew off team meetings to play golf, took it upon himself to cancel practices, and checked his statistics with the official scorer during games.

One NBA coach said that when Bulls coach Phil Jackson closed practice to the media, it was so no one would find out just how often Jordan didn't bother showing up. So while Iverson was portrayed as somehow antithetical to Jordan, the truth was that, in both their strengths and flaws, in their competitiveness, egocentrism, and brilliance, Jordan and Iverson were more alike than different.

Early in his career, Jordan heard some of the same criticisms Iverson was now facing, though they were never voiced quite so vituperatively. Jordan's first three seasons were losing ones; experts compared him to established stars like Earvin "Magic" Johnson and Larry Bird and wondered if, like them, he'd ever make his teammates better. But thanks to his ingratiating crossover style, the criticism never reached the crescendo of condemnation Iverson encountered in his rookie year.

Despite the distraction of more media attention than he'd anticipated, Iverson led the Sixers to their best start in years. They finished November with seven wins and eight losses, not bad for a team that had won all of eighteen games the entire previous season. Iverson led the team and was among the league leaders in scoring (21.8 points), assists (6.4), and steals (2.67). But he also led the league in turnovers, committing 5.3 per game.

Part of the high turnover rate was attributable to unprecedented attention from the referees. With the crossover, Iverson had done for the dribble what Dr. J did for the dunk—turn it into a fan-friendly spectacle and a weapon of on-court intimidation. In his first game against the Knicks at Madison Square Garden, for instance, he scored 35 points as not one but *two* opposing point guards fouled out trying to stop him. Charlie Ward committed six fouls in twenty-nine minutes, and his backup, journeyman Scott Brooks, fouled out in all of fifteen minutes. On one play, Iverson dribbled the ball from side to side in front of Brooks, teasing him, before faking one way, luring Brooks into a reaction. Iverson was off in the opposite direction once Brooks merely flinched; the defender stumbled and fell, the crowd gasped, and Iverson scored.

At this point, Iverson was clearly the impetus behind a league memo that called for a crackdown not only on Iverson's type of long, droopy shorts, but also on his style of dribbling. In truth, his crossover dribble did flirt with being a carry; the word went forth that the refs would be calling palming more often. Iverson's high hesitation dribble on the crossover was suddenly being called illegal, sometimes two or three times a game.

The Sixers weren't a deep team, and injuries started to mount. The team went into a tailspin. Coleman fractured his pinkie finger and was out for weeks; while recovering, he fell badly out of shape. Backup players Don McLean and Lucious Harris likewise went down. Meantime, on the court, the turnovers mounted. League-wide, Iverson and Stackhouse were number one and number two, respectively, in giveaways. They were also, potentially, the most explosive backcourt in the league. But Iverson and Stackhouse were both learning on the job, in front of a particularly demanding fan base that saw their raw talents and couldn't figure out why it was taking so long for them to put it all together. But they were the youngest backcourt in the league; had both stayed in school, Stackhouse would have been only a senior and Iverson a junior.

Complicating the problem was that both came with their own loyal amen corners, entourages composed of friends and family who saw it as their role to let their guy know that *he*—and not that other dude—was really the Sixers' go-to man. Columnist Peter Vecsey reported that, outside the team's practice facility, Iverson's three-man posse "got into an impromptu rumble" with Stackhouse's. In his trademark acerbic style, Vecsey wrote that the respective entourages had been "forced to mill around together outside [the facility] and casually mull over whose homeboy deserves more money, minutes, magazine clips (as in shots, I think) and pub . . . Naturally, it was time to choose up sides, three-on-three. Call your own felony. Suddenly fists and feet were flying and landing everywhere."

Coach Johnny Davis was in danger of losing his team. They'd not only lost seventeen of eighteen, but Coleman had blown off some practices, and Iverson was increasingly tardy at team meetings and practices—just as Croce had feared. And now, in a sign of just how much the NBA was changing, Croce and Greenberg had to deal with a possible altercation that didn't involve their players, but their players' *friends.*

Both Iverson and Stackhouse denied the report, and the Sixers soon said that Vecsey apologized for the column. (Today Vecsey says—rather implausibly—that he doesn't recall whether his report was accurate or not: "Do you remember everything you wrote six years ago?" he said in 2002.) By the time the new year rolled around, whether their friends got into it was beside the point. Stackhouse and Iverson came to blows during a practice—not an unheard-of occurrence among teammates. Ostensibly, the scrap was over Iverson's failure to pass Stackhouse the ball.

But their problems weren't personal. A temporary flare-up of tempers notwithstanding, Iverson and Stackhouse liked each other and even hung out together. Later in the season, when the team visited Charlotte, Stackhouse's mother would prepare an artery-hardening home-cooked meal for her son's backcourt mate.

Instead, the Sixers' chemistry ills could be traced to a confluence of factors. There was the youth and inexperience of Iverson and Stackhouse, plus the ego-distorting refrain each heard from his respective cheering section. Plus, both men had grown up poor and black; at least one former NBA star says that, often, the call to put your team before your own interests can run afoul of a lifetime of learned every-man-for-himself survival skills. "Only people who have something can afford to be unselfish, unless you're a saint," writes former NBA star Chet Walker in his memoir, *Long Time Coming.* "In the ghetto, you often must take what you can before someone takes it away."

Then there were the lessons prodigies like Iverson and Stackhouse learned from the league itself. It doesn't take long for players to get the message that individual statistics like shots and minutes played are to be fought for. Even relative newcomers like Iverson and Stackhouse heard the stories about the players who followed their coach's advice and concentrated just on passing, defense, and setting screens; the same player, come contract time, would be denied a raise or altogether cut loose because, the general manager would say, "you only averaged six points a game." It is a cutthroat league and players like Iverson and Stackhouse—whose outsized egos were exactly what had gotten them to the highest level of their profession in the first place—were tacitly encouraged to get theirs, to look out for number one. It's why Bulls coach Phil Jackson was fond of saying that the hardest thing to do in coaching is to get players to "sacrifice the me for the we."

The Sixers limped into the all-star break with a desultory 12–34 record. Iverson traveled to Cleveland to play in the all-star rookie game. It had been a trying first half of his rookie season. Little did he know it would only get worse, and soon. He was about to walk into a media buzz saw.

The 1996–97 season marked the fiftieth year of the NBA, and in keeping with David Stern's flair for marketing the league brand, the all-star game would honor the fifty greatest players in league history. There, assembled on one floor, would be Wilt Chamberlain, Bill Russell, Kareem Abdul-Jabbar, Michael Jordan, Magic Johnson, Larry Bird, Oscar Robertson, Jerry West—and forty-two other legends.

However, it would be a player who wasn't even in the all-star game— let alone among the fifty greats—who would steal the headlines. On some level, given that every generation tends to wring its hands over the next (think of the onetime hippie baby boomers who today deride their hip-hop offspring), the ensuing media squall ought to have been predictable. Here you had the greats of yesteryear, convened for the first and only time. And here came the sudden symbol of the new NBA—*their* NBA. And he was dressed to make a statement.

Iverson had decided to go to Cleveland for his rookie game appearance sporting a new style: cornrows. (In his case, the onetime look was really more like mini-cornrows, because his Afro hadn't yet grown out enough.) Black male rappers like Snoop Dogg were wearing their hair in braids, and the style was catching on—though not among professional athletes, where the Jordan-inspired shaved head still predominated. Athletes' agents, still wedded to the crossover model of marketing, wouldn't countenance cornrows, which were seen as too in-your-face, too black. Iverson may not have known specifics about the style's Afrocentric roots—cornrows were worn during ceremonies in the time of the Third Dynasty Egyptian ruler Akhethoptep—but he knew it was not the traditional way African-Americans sought to assimilate.

So when Iverson arrived in Cleveland with his hair braided, it was a shock to the NBA's old guard—every member of which just happened to also be in town. The *New York Times* reported that it didn't go over well with the veterans: "Rookies making fashion statements do not often sit well with veteran players, who privately mocked [Iverson's] new hairdo behind his back."

The older players let the rookie have it, and the media was all too happy to play courier in a war of words between the generations. "Allen Iverson plays the game like a runaway train," said Hall of Famer Elvin Hayes. "The bottom line is what your team does, and his team is not doing anything."

"The mugging and the trash-talking of today was not part of the game when I played," agreed old-timer Jerry Lucas. "In some ways, we're going in the wrong direction."

Without singling out Iverson, Magic Johnson expressed concern for—and maybe some financial envy of—the new generation. "They are not making the kind of money they are making because of what they have done," he said. "They are making it because of what we did."

"Somehow, blackness became equated with how thuggish you look and how tough you act," said Isiah Thomas. "When we were growing up, it was okay to wear a suit and tie and to respect people."

The most vocal critic of Iverson and the hip-hoppers was, ironically, Charles Barkley, who, just seven years earlier, had declared himself "a nineties nigga." (Indeed, one columnist referred to Barkley during all-star weekend as "the conscience of the game"; within the next year, said conscience would hurl a heckler through a plate-glass barroom window.) "Iverson has to understand that Michael Jordan and I had shoes before he had his shoes," Barkley said. "He's not the greatest, just the latest . . . Allen Iverson doesn't know anything. Grant Hill listened to us and took the criticism."

Suddenly the always-controversial Barkley had morphed into Paul Lynde from *Bye Bye Birdie*—gnashing his teeth over "these kids today." Why was Barkley so fired up? "Because we, the veterans, have an obligation to be caretakers," he said.

Rather than taking care of the game, the concerned players turned the fans against one player. When a mini-cornrowed Iverson took to the Gund Arena floor for the rookie game, the Cleveland fans serenaded him with thunderous boos. As always, rather than give in under the weight of fan disapproval, Iverson used it as fuel. He'd always believed that his heart was more important than his skills, that the emotion of his game *was* a talent. He came out with something to prove, scoring 19 points, dishing out 9 assists, and leading the East to a 96–91 win. Fellow rookie Kobe Bryant led all scorers with 31 points, but it was Iverson who was named MVP—an announcement that prompted yet more booing, even as Iverson made his way over to legendary coach Red Auerbach, who had coached Iverson's college coach on the Celtics years ago and who today directed the West squad. "It's a pleasure to meet Coach Thompson's coach," Iverson said, extending his hand.

Afterward, in the media room, Iverson said he was stunned by the reception he'd received. "Maybe people felt Kobe should have won the MVP," he theorized after the game. "I've never had people boo me for playing hard."

While being questioned by the media, Iverson clutched his two-piece MVP trophy, a glass star atop a marble base. "Here, hold this," he said,

In 1997 Iverson was one of the first players in the NBA to wear his hair in cornrows.

handing the trophy to Sixers PR man Bill Bonsiewicz, who promptly juggled and dropped it, shattering the top piece.

"Bill, my ma is going to kill you," Iverson deadpanned, before breaking out in laughter.

As if on cue, Ann Iverson came barging into the interview room, calling out, "Where's my baby?"

"Ma," Iverson called, "Bill broke your trophy!"

Iverson was still laughing at his team's PR man when Bonsiewicz introduced the star to his parents, who lived nearby. The next night, the Sixers played the Cavaliers on the very same floor. Iverson, still carrying a grudge against the Cleveland fans, lit up the home team, but the Sixers lost. Afterward, on the team plane back to Philly, Bonsiewicz sat near the back, frozen in trepidation, as Iverson got up from his first-class seat and made his way down the aisle, looking pissed. "Bill," Iverson whispered, taking the seat next to him, looking down. "You've got a great family. Don't ever take that for granted." He kept his voice low, Bonsiewicz would later realize, because he was guarding his tough-guy image. And it made sense to Bonsiewicz that someone who had already been on the receiving end of such judgment and denunciation would erect a self-protective wall of machismo. Iverson said what he had to say. Without looking the PR man in the eye, he brought his headphones up to his ears from around his neck and loped off, back up the aisle, lost in his internal world.

As Iverson's rookie season continued, so did the media pile-on. Mike Wise of the *New York Times* wrote that "Iverson has gone from being hailed as an emerging young player to being an emerging young pain in the neck, a 20-year-old who appears to be somewhat out of control on the court, and perhaps off it."

An Associated Press piece called him "a punk. A trash-talker. A ball hog. A brash kid who even dissed Michael Jordan early this season." Sportswriter Lisa Olson opined that Iverson "is impertinent and cocky and thinks legends like Larry Bird and Magic Johnson are just characters in a Sega video basketball game. Because he believes the game of hoops didn't really, truly begin until he arrived."

Come April, Iverson went on a historic scoring tear. If he didn't win Rookie of the Year honors, it would be because voters took off-court issues into consideration. He scored 40 or more points in an NBA record five straight games, beating Wilt Chamberlain's thirty-seven-year-old record. The Sixers lost all five, which had aficionados throughout the league saying their "I told you so's." The kid could score, they'd say, but he can't win.

Still, it was an amazing streak—something Jordan had never done, not even in his first three seasons when *his* team was losing. Iverson burned Atlanta for 40, Cleveland for 50, and Milwaukee for 44. At home against the Bulls, he would serve notice that, like it or not, a changing of *the* guard was in the offing. He scored 44, but it was just one of those baskets that will forever be remembered. It was the culmination of his long-ago prophecy, when a scrawny runt of a kid in Newport News proclaimed, "I can take Mike."

This time, he really did take Mike. Just in front of the Bulls bench, Clarence Weatherspoon had the ball on the wing, with Jordan on him. He handed it off to Iverson and Phil Jackson barked out, "Michael! Get up on him!"

Jordan jumped up above Weatherspoon's screen as Iverson dribbled the ball slowly to and fro before him. The crowd buzzed: this is what they paid to see, a one-on-one showdown between the two most creative players in the game. It all happened so quickly. "I wanted to see if he'd bite on a little cross," Iverson would later say, explaining the first part of the move, a mini-crossover to the left. Jordan did, in fact, bite, and Iverson hesitated for a split second, letting Jordan set his feet again. Jordan may have regained his balance, but Iverson knew he had him, because Jordan would be expecting the same tempo as the mini-cross. Iverson started to go left again, in almost an instant replay of the move Jordan had just recovered from; same pace, same cadence. Only this time, thinking that this was *the* move, Jordan lurched that way, to his right, and it was all over. Iverson switched gears and crossed to his right while Jordan, struggling to react, stumbled. Leaving Jordan in his dust, Iverson raised up at the right elbow and drained an open jumper.

The roar from the Philadelphia crowd was more deafening than anything anyone had ever heard before—louder than the cheers that ever greeted Dr. J's soaring flight patterns or Charles Barkley's length-of-the-floor rumbles. In the owner's box, Pat Croce leaped to his feet, arms raised, screaming, and felt fans grabbing at his shirt from behind; turns out, in his gleeful abandon, he was dangerously close to falling out of the box. "It felt like a moment that really meant something," Croce would later say. "That we were there to witness this passing of the NBA torch. Michael wasn't ready to give it up, so Bubba just took it from him!"

Still, there were nonbelievers. The Sixers finished the season winning just twenty-two games, only four more than the year before Iverson's arrival. Croce had had a rough rookie year as an NBA owner, once donning a goalie mask to face a handful of impatient season-ticket holders. He saw a lack of team discipline that he knew he never would have tolerated in his former life, when he was running the fitness and rehab facilities. Players wouldn't practice, or they'd show up late. He had signed off on the hiring of a rookie coach to direct a high-maintenance rookie, and it was, in retrospect, a recipe for disaster. We should have hired a veteran, experienced coach, he realized. The day after the season ended, Croce announced the firing of Davis and—to the surprise of some—Greenberg. Croce's senior partner Ed Snider thought Greenberg, who had hit a home run drafting Iverson but who struck out in hiring Davis, could be retained; Croce wanted a fresh start. In a rare move from a sports-team owner—or from anyone in public life, for that matter—Croce took full responsibility for the disappointing season, apologized to the fans, and vowed to not screw up again.

The season ended on at least one positive note, however. Buzz had it that Iverson was about to be named Rookie of the Year, though there were still some vocal detractors. Barkley, calling Iverson "me, myself, and Iverson," announced that Vancouver's Shareef Abdur-Rahim should be named Rookie of the Year. "Iverson is the playground Rookie of the Year," Barkley said. Kevin McHale, Minnesota's director of basketball operations, lobbied for his player, Marbury, saying that rewarding Iverson for his me-first play "tells young kids to come into the league and just put up numbers and you will get rewarded." (Of course, Marbury had the luxury of playing with superstar-in-waiting Kevin Garnett; Iverson had been given the green light by Davis because Davis had more confidence in a forced Iverson shot than in an open jumper by almost anybody else on his team.)

McHale's fears were realized when the Sixers got word from the league that Iverson was its Rookie of the Year on a Wednesday, six days before the award would be announced. Once the season had ended, though, Iverson had headed back to Virginia. Croce had a pager number for him, but the pages were unreturned on Thursday, Friday, and through the weekend. He didn't know if Iverson knew he'd won the award, let alone whether he'd be attending the press conference to announce it. At seven on Monday morning, the day before the press conference, Croce dispatched Bonsiewicz on a plane to Norfolk, Virginia, giving his employee a toothbrush and a scrap of paper with some phone numbers that *might* still be good for Iverson's relatives. "This'll be fun," the ever-upbeat Croce told his skeptical employee. "Operation Find AI."

Thanks to the boxing ties of Sixers vice president Dave Coskey, Croce had arranged for Bonsiewicz to be met at the airport by Peter Joiner, boxer Pernell Whitaker's bodyguard. Joiner, known as PJ, sported a sparkling gold tooth and drove a black Mercedes. For the next hour, while an amused PJ looked on, the six-foot-four and white Bonsiewicz, wearing a suit, knocked on doors, holding out his card. One door led to another, led to another. At one house, eight cars were parked in the driveway. Sounded like a party was going on. "He just left," someone said, before slamming the door.

Bonsiewicz called Croce. "Pat, it's crazy here," he said. "We're never going to find him."

Just then, Bonsiewicz's call waiting beeped.

"Bill! You down here?" Iverson said. "People are calling me from all over the place, telling me some white dude named Bill is looking for me!"

Bonsiewicz explained he was there to bring Allen back for his press conference, which riled up the Rookie of the Year. "You think I can't get to my own damned press conference?" he said.

"You don't even know when it is, do you?" Bonsiewicz challenged him. "One o'clock!"

"Wrong—it's noon!"

"Well, they can't start the damned thing without me!"

Finally, Iverson agreed to fly back to Philly in the morning with his mother and Bonsiewicz, who asked Iverson to recommend a hotel. "Go to the Days Inn, tell 'em you're Bill," Iverson said.

"I'm Bill," Bonsiewicz said upon arrival, "and I—"

"Bubba called." The clerk cut him off. "You're all set."

Relieved, Bonsiewicz got to bed early. But his phone rang at 4 A.M. It was Iverson's friend Arnie. "Be downstairs in half an hour," he told the groggy PR man. "We've got to find A.I."

Arnie picked up Bonsiewicz and they went over to Ann's house. At some point in the night, turns out, Ann and Allen got separated. Here it was, five in the morning and there were people strewn throughout the house, some watching the big-screen TV, some cooking breakfast. Like her son, Ann required little or no sleep at night; her "normal" regimen was to stay out all night and sleep till four or five in the afternoon. ("The

Iversons are like vampires: they come out after midnight, drinking Cristal," once quipped a member of the Sixers team.) Bonsiewicz got the feeling that no one in the house had slept a wink all night as he listened to Ann make phone calls, trying to track down her son.

Finally, a little after 6 A.M., Ann screamed, "I got him!" and they were all bustling out the front door, into the limo Ann had rented. They stopped at the Omni Hotel, where Bubbachuck stood, smiling, until he saw Bonsiewicz, and then he put on a face of mock anger. "I can't believe you thought I'd miss my own damned press conference, man," he said.

Once they landed in Philly, Bonsiewicz told Iverson breakfast was waiting at the arena. "I'm going home to change, man," Iverson said. Bonsiewicz's heart dropped; after all this, he couldn't go back to the office without him, could he? He called Croce to ask what he should do. "What are you worried about?" Croce said. "I trust Bubba. He'll be here."

A couple of hours later, the press was silent—maybe even a bit frightened—when Iverson walked in, followed by a procession of his stone-faced boys. All of them, including Allen, wore white Reebok warm-up jackets and white skullcaps pulled tightly over their heads. In fact, in the months to come, the league wouldn't publicize photos of Iverson receiving his award because of the skullcap. ("It looks like something people wear in prison," NBA deputy commissioner Russ Granik would tell Croce. "It's made by Reebok!" Croce would say, putting a few in the mail to him.)

But none of that mattered to Ann Iverson. Her son was about to be named the best of his class, and she waltzed in, beaming, and took her place at the podium, for Allen was giving this award to his ma.

Croce presented the trophy. "Now the world knows what we in Philadelphia have known," he said. "That Allen Iverson is one of the most exciting, most dynamic, most fearless players in the NBA."

Iverson talked humbly about how much he owed to his mother, and then he was gone, off to enjoy the summer months. He'd just decided to turn down his friend Spike Lee's offer to audition for, and most likely star in, a basketball flick Lee would be directing, *He Got Game.* Rebuffed by Iverson, Lee would ultimately give the role to Ray Allen.

Iverson's reason for turning down the movie?

"Man, this is my first summer with money," he told Lee. "I ain't working. Me and my crew, we gonna enjoy having money."

God's

Finest

BAD

让

this is chinese for "respect." i feel that w
deserves a lot of respect—being from there, s
there, and staying true to everybod

NEWZ

Throughout his short life, Allen Iverson has often balanced dueling worlds. Sports in America, after all, is the province of middle-class values, a world where media, coaches, and even parents place higher standards of behavior upon athletes than they do on any other type of entertainer. Unlike rappers, actors, or even sports broadcasters, athletes are "role models."

Iverson is, by necessity, in that world, but not of it. He intuited early on that almost anytime a sports role model took center stage, the result was a thinly veiled commercial script; role models existed to sell kids sneakers and junk food.

The anti-Jordan would not play that game. He'd hawk the Reeboks, of course, but not if it meant—as he made clear to the company in their first meeting—he couldn't be who he was, someone who hailed from a parallel world. He was from the streets, where adopting the safe, middle-class mores foisted upon so many young black athletes could get one killed or—worse, perhaps, given his fatalism—disrespected.

No, Iverson would walk that fine line, keeping one foot in the rarefied air of the NBA, at the pinnacle of America's commodity culture, and the other in the asphalt streets that produced him. It wasn't a conscious decision so much as an implicit declaration of who he was.

Perhaps no twenty-four-hour period spoke more eloquently of Iverson's delicate balancing act than that which began on May 1, 1997, when he accepted the Rookie of the Year award. During that ceremony, even while his hip-hop garb so turned off the NBA's powers-that-be, Iverson seemed—weirdly enough—an exemplar of family values.

"Now it's her award," Iverson said, giving the trophy to Ann. "Without her, none of this would have happened. She gave me the heart that I have. She made me believe since I was young that I could do anything that I wanted to do. I dedicate the award to my mom."

Nor did he stop there. Iverson extended his tribute to other women in his life. "There was a space in my heart [all season] filled by my little sisters," he said of Brandy and Ieisha. "All of the different things I did on the court were for my sisters back home, watching on TV."

Less than twenty-four hours later, however, he was in a less wholesome setting, front and center in a scenario that wouldn't quite have middle-class fans dabbing at their eyes. Wearing a stylish gray suit and a collarless black shirt, Iverson raised his right hand and swore to tell the whole truth and nothing but, before taking the stand to testify for Michael Freeman, who was, for the fourth time in his life, facing felony charges.

On April 5, 1996, the man known as House Mouse on the streets of Newport News had been arrested and charged with possession with intent to distribute cocaine. Again. Freeman had been released from jail four months prior and was living at 704 Delaware Avenue, with his three brothers, their mother, and their uncle. When the house was raided by police, Freeman and his brothers were in the kitchen, with scales and sandwich baggies on the table in front of them. He had over a thousand dollars in cash in his front pocket, along with a plastic bag containing three grams of cocaine.

Freeman would testify that it was his brothers, not him, doing the dealing, that his brother Wayne had given him a folded-up stack of bills to hold. Wayne, for his part, told the same story on the stand. Both men testified that, unbeknownst to Michael, there was a bag of coke in the center of the wad of cash. Freeman's probation officer testified that Freeman had previously sought permission to move from the residence, because his brothers were dealing drugs. Permission was denied. And his brothers kept on dealing. "I ain't nobody to them," Freeman explained.

The defense—Iverson's lawyers Tom Shuttleworth and Larry Woodward—argued that Michael Freeman wouldn't have had to sell drugs in April of 1996 because he was fully aware that, in a matter of months, he would never have to make money illegally again. "I wrote him when I was in school and told him, you know, everything that I had planned on doing," Iverson testified. "Um, I asked him for advice on what agent I should get and things like that, but I just let him know that I was going to leave . . . and I told him that I was going to take care of him and take him with me to Philly or to wherever I went."

Iverson testified that, after his last season at Georgetown had ended, many of these conversations about their future took place when he visited Freeman at the Delaware Avenue house, where Freeman was confined by electronic monitoring as per the conditions of his parole.

"This is how Iverson lived his life as he was finishing up his career at Georgetown," wrote Iverson's former critic, the *Daily Press*'s Jim Spencer. "He was in and out of a Hampton crack house several times."

Shortly after Freeman was found guilty, Iverson slipped out a court-room side door.

As Allen Iverson evaded the phalanx of reporters outside the Hampton Circuit Court, Pat Croce was also trying to fly below the media's radar.

Unlike so many team owners, Croce didn't present himself as an expert when it came to the *X*s and *O*s of his sport. No, he was a manager of people who lived his life in accordance with a never-ending supply of bumper-sticker-like aphorisms, such as "You can delegate authority, but you can't delegate responsibility." It was this thinking that caused him to apologize to Philadelphia after his rookie season of ownership, when he fired Davis and, over the objections of his senior partner, Ed Snider, general manager Brad Greenberg.

But that bold move had left him more vulnerable than ever. "I can't play, coach, or select talent—yet I'm the team now," he bemoaned to friends and colleagues. "I've got no one."

If he was going down, he figured, he'd go down trusting his gut. And his gut told him that he needed a marquee name, someone to rejuvenate the basketball side of his organization's operations. He'd liked Johnny Davis personally, but quickly recognized that the current generation of players had little respect for coaches who, in the players' parlance, had no "juice"—whose reputation didn't precede them.

He needed someone whose résumé would capture Iverson's imagination. First, he began stalking the youthful and energetic University of Kentucky coach, Rick Pitino. As Pitino led his team on a march to the NCAA Tournament championship, Croce had lavish gifts awaiting the coach in every hotel room along the way. The two had lunch in Kentucky; another of Croce's axioms is to "listen between the lines," and his ears perked up when he heard Pitino wax less than enthusiastic about Iverson's one-on-one style and Coleman's dour on-court demeanor. He asked the coach point-blank: "If you come back to the NBA"—Pitino had coached the Knicks earlier in his career—"would it be in Philadelphia?" Pitino gave it some thought before deciding that, if he returned to the NBA, he'd rather coach in Boston, where he had roots. (That's where he ended up, signing a lucrative ten-year deal as president and coach.)

Croce decided to think even bigger. Phil Jackson, leading the Bulls to yet another title, was in the last year of his deal. His contract allowed teams not in the play-offs to speak to him about their coaching vacancies. When Croce got him on the phone, the two spoke for ninety minutes. Unlike Pitino, Jackson loved the talent level of the 76ers. He believed they just needed a catalyst to turn themselves into a team. As Jackson went on, using terms like "empowerment" and "responsibility," Croce thought he'd found a kindred spirit, someone in line with his own careful tough-love approach to Iverson's tender psyche. With the Bulls, Jackson had gotten Jordan to buy into his system; Croce knew how much Iverson wanted to win—it was all he talked about—and that Jackson's championship rings, combined with Jordan's endorsement of the coach's unconventional, Zen-inspired techniques, would earn Iverson's loyalty. "There would be instant respect," Croce said.

But there was a catch. Jackson was only going to leave the Bulls if management—with whom he had often feuded—broke up the team and jettisoned Jordan, who was looking for a big payday. If owner Jerry Reinsdorf signed Jordan, Jackson would re-sign, too. But none of this could be resolved until after the Bulls' championship run in late June. Croce kept calling Jackson during the NBA Finals to see if anything had changed. No, Jackson told him. He was still in limbo. (Ultimately, Reinsdorf would sign Jordan to a $30 million contract for one year and bring Jackson back, as well.)

If Croce rolled the dice and waited, he could be out of luck. Indiana Pacers coach Larry Brown was rumored to be thinking of resigning, and five other teams were in the market for a head coach; Brown had a reputation for rejuvenating NBA teams. He was also known for his wanderlust and for being high maintenance.

"Good luck," Pacers owner Herb Simon said sardonically, when Croce called for Brown's agent's phone number.

"Good luck," echoed Pacers general manager Donnie Walsh.

When Croce finally got Brown on the phone, he heard moaning and groaning in the background. "Coach, are you at a gym?" he asked.

"No," Brown replied. "I'm in a hospital delivery room. My wife is giving birth."

Brown sounded remarkably, even strangely, calm. "Well, enjoy the moment," Croce said. "But tell me—is it a boy or girl?"

"It's a girl," Brown said.

Within minutes, Croce was on the phone to his favorite florist, telling her he wanted Mrs. Brown's delivery room to "look like a Mafia funeral parlor." Sixty-two pounds of flowers were soon on their way, and Brown was soon inked to a five-year, $20 million contract.

When Croce called Iverson on his cell phone to tell him the news, his star was underwhelmed. He'd played against Brown's Pacers, but knew little of the coach's background. He knew Brown had been a point guard himself—a long, long time ago—and that he'd never coached a team to an NBA title. And he knew through the NBA grapevine that Brown's team had rebelled against him during the season just past.

From Brown's point of view, he recognized the talent of Iverson and Stackhouse, but felt they "played like strangers." Privately, he wasn't looking forward to coaching Iverson. "I wanted nothing to do with him," he would later recall.

At first blush, no two men could be more different. Brown was a fifty-six-year-old Jewish man, raised on Long Island, who had spent a lifetime suppressing emotions behind a blank stare and a monotone that made Al Gore seem charismatic. He considered himself, first and foremost, a teacher; indeed, with his emphasis on the game's fundamentals, he seemed to have stepped right off the screen from the movie *Hoosiers;* he'd often fantasized about giving up the pro game to coach at the high-school level. He deemed his curriculum as nothing short of his sport's Holy Grail. He spoke of "playing the right way," and his pedigree showed he had the lineage to back up his basketball fundamentalism. He had played for the legendary Dean Smith at the University of North Carolina, who played for Hank Iba at Kansas, who played for none other than Dr. James Naismith, the inventor of the game.

When they heard Brown invoke his "playing the right way" mantra, the Pacers, particularly the talented young hip-hopper Jalen Rose, came to see it as the inflexible preachings of an old-school coach. He said "right way"; they *heard* "my way." But Brown viewed himself as the trustee of sacred basketball truths passed down from the game's fathers.

In Brown's view of the game, team trumps all. At North Carolina, bench players under Smith were required to stand and applaud when a teammate came out of the game. Similarly, when Brown watched video footage of his team or others, he'd often rewind the tape to focus on those who weren't even playing, trying to see who on the bench appeared supportive of his teammates.

On the court, Brown's style was to emphasize defense and rebounding; if a team helped one another when defending, he reasoned, they were more likely to share the ball on offense. He disdained many of the game's modern manifestations. He hated the three-point shot because it rewarded bad shot selection. The purpose of Dr. Naismith's game, after all, was to take the highest-possible percentage shot. The three-pointer was a low-percentage shot, yet the NBA now provided incentive to take it. Consequently, he was one of the last holdouts against the three-point specialist. Jackson had brilliantly paired Jordan with a series of long-range bombers who could hardly be called all-around players. Guys like John Paxson, Steve Kerr, B. J. Armstrong, and Craig Hodges might have been defensive liabilities, but they were deadeye shooters, particularly when set up by a constantly double- or triple-teamed Jordan. Brown wasn't having it; if you couldn't play defense for him, you didn't play.

Brown's practices consisted of the same high-school-type drills, day after day. Ad nauseam, his players practiced basic "L" cuts and the most minute nuances that go into the setting of picks. Other coaches tried to keep their players engaged by mixing up their regimen; some, like Jackson, spent almost as much time coaxing commitment out of their players' psyches as they did drawing up plays. Brown, however, was a throwback. "I coach execution, not effort," he said.

No one had ever doubted Brown's basketball acumen, but he was not known as a stable bet. He'd had eight head-coaching jobs in twenty-four years, once even quitting as coach of the New Jersey Nets on the eve of the play-offs. He was often referred to as a basketball nomad, someone who, despite outward appearances, made emotional decisions. He fell in and out of love with his jobs, with women (his marriage to the twenty-eight-year-old Shelly Brown was his third), and with players. As coach of the Denver Nuggets, he traded Bobby Jones to Philadelphia for George McGinnis; after McGinnis's first practice, he tried to rescind the deal.

On the surface, it appeared that Brown and the anti-Jordan would have little in common. There was Iverson, so focused on maintaining his identity, on taking his posse with him on this strange trip of a life. And there was Brown, who picked up stakes time and again, who not only had no posse, but who seemed to reinvent himself at every stop. In time, both men would reveal their similarities to each other; both had spent their lives fatherless, alternately in pursuit of, and recoiling from, male authority figures, and both shared a highly sensitive artistic temperament, quick to wound, slow to forgive. All this would become clear, in time. But shortly after Brown was named Iverson's coach, Tim Roye, the radio voice of the Golden State Warriors, put it best: "My money is on December," he said. "That's when *Sports Illustrated* will run the piece on Larry and Allen, feuding, under the headline CITY OF BROTHERLY LOVE?"

Que Gaskins knew from day one that Allen Iverson had the love and adulation of those who were, like the ballplayer, from the streets. After all, Iverson had burst onto the national scene bearing unmatched street credibility, the first African-American sports star to step onto our playing fields *from* jail—where he'd been unjustly incarcerated, to boot. Kids could relate to him, to his size, his style, his toughness, his loyalties; when the media chastised him for his choice of friends, they recognized it for what it was: The media don't want him to be around people like us, they thought. From Harlem to North Philly, Newport News to Watts, it was as though they recognized Iverson from their very own block.

Gaskins understood all that. But how to explain this? How to explain the packed, screaming, gyrating crowd on five levels of a mall in Chile, all jockeying for a glimpse of the American ballplayer? Iverson, eyes wide, looked at Gaskins. "This shit's crazy, man," he said.

It was summer, and they were on a three-week Reebok promotional tour of South America. Ann Iverson and Gaskins's wife, Cindy, along with representatives of the NBA, Reebok, and David Falk's office, were all part of the entourage. Whether in Chile, Brazil, or Santo Domingo, Iverson-mania reigned.

"Man, I got crazy love like this all around the world?" a stunned Iverson asked Gaskins.

At one point, when a crowd inside a mall pushed up dangerously close, the group made an about-face and started running away; Cindy Gaskins stumbled, and laughing, Iverson and Que rushed back toward the storming crowd to help her. They barely avoided being trampled.

"That's when Allen's mind opened to what an international presence he was," Gaskins recalls today. It also led Gaskins to be the first to identify Iverson's potentially unique crossover appeal. He realized that Iverson could be a prime example of what he liked to call "fusion marketing." Fusionism, according to Gaskins, was the science of connecting brands and consumers globally. It was shortsighted, he argued, to think of the Iverson brand consumer as an inner-city African-American back in the States. The cheering crowds throughout South America proved to Gaskins that Iverson's attitude, style, and way of playing—his whole persona—appealed across traditional lines of geography and demography. "The essence to Fusionism is summed up in a quote from the book *The Social Life of Information:* 'The way forward is paradoxically not to look ahead but to look around,'" Gaskins would later write. "Fusionism is way more than just skin color. It's about attitude. It's about a liberated mind-set. It's about the elimination of cultural boundaries and stereotypes."

Though others accompanied them on the tour, Gaskins and Iverson bonded on their journey. Gaskins would speak breathlessly of his spiritually based marketing theories. Iverson, more grounded in street-level realities, would affectionately kid him about being "the dumbest smart person I know." Other times, they'd watch videotapes of Eddie Murphy movies, Murphy being one of Iverson's favorite comedic actors. Gaskins not only sat through some thirty viewings of *Trading Places,* he was also entertained by Iverson's dead-on impressions of Murphy in the lead role.

From the beginning of their relationship, Gaskins saw himself as much more than a corporate watchdog for Iverson. Others in the industry snickered that he was a baby-sitter, but Gaskins viewed himself as a role model. He quickly saw that Iverson learns by experience, not by being lectured to. So he felt his best course of action was to conduct himself in a way Iverson could respect—and hopefully emulate. While Iverson's friends initially looked warily at this corporate interloper, Gaskins steadfastly resisted telling Reebok anything of their star endorser's doings beyond what headquarters absolutely needed to know. He saw the various and difficult demands placed upon the young star by those around him and insisted on pulling his own weight.

Most important, he took Iverson into his new home, just outside nearby Wilmington, Delaware. Iverson had already seen that Gaskins brought his stunning wife, Cindy, and their two young children wherever he went. Others seeking Iverson's acceptance tended to boast of how "hard" they were, of how many hardships they'd had to overcome; though Gaskins hailed from the tough inner-city streets of southeast Washington, D.C., he was determined to set an example of what the future could be. The first time Iverson came over, he looked at Gaskins and spoke in a hoarse, heartfelt voice. "You know how lucky you are, man?" Iverson said, looking around the comfortable suburban home. "I really respect the way you show love for your family."

Neither Iverson nor Gaskins cut their hair during their eye-opening trip. Despite the backlash engendered by his hairstyle statement during all-star weekend, Iverson was not cowed. "I'm gonna let my shit grow out and start the season with cornrows," he said.

"Man," Gaskins said. "You do that, and they gonna eat you alive."

"Whatchu mean, 'eat me alive'?" Iverson said.

"I'm telling you, you don't want to do this," Gaskins said.

"Whatchu mean? *You* can't do it 'cause you work at Reebok."

"Reebok don't care about stuff like that."

"Yeah, right."

Now Gaskins felt challenged. His mother, who ran a highly praised tutoring program for neighborhood kids back in D.C., had always told him that there are many different images of success—and that it was up to him to create his own image. Along with Allen, he could make a statement: Success, and traditional values, can come in different looking packages. "Tell you what," he said, smiling as he imagined the reaction his plan would get back in the corporate world. "You grow your hair, I'll grow mine."

They shook on it, and it was settled. Iverson would follow up on his all-star weekend buzz and be the first athlete to buck the NBA's style status quo. He and his mentor would braid away.

B ubba, you're killing us."

That was the first thing Pat Croce said to Allen Iverson as the two men broke from their hug. It was déjà vu all over again. Here was Iverson, in a suit, in a conference room in the Hampton County Courthouse, facing charges.

In early August, the news broke that Iverson had run afoul of the law once again. His 1996 Mercedes was pulled over on Interstate 64 in Virginia at 1:30 in the morning, doing ninety-three miles per hour in a sixty-five-mile-per-hour zone. Iverson was in the passenger seat; thirty-two-year-old Maduro Earl Hill was driving, and Damon Darnell Stewart, twenty-five, was in the backseat.

The state trooper smelled marijuana as he approached the driver's-side window. Iverson leaned over from the passenger seat. "Officer," he said, "I got a gun in the car."

The .45-caliber Glock was on the floor in front of Iverson's seat. The officer, Michael Pierce, considered it concealed; Iverson balked. "It's right out in plain view," he argued. (In Virginia, it was illegal to carry a *concealed* gun, even if it was registered.)

Iverson was released on $2,000 bail; now, in a deal Woody reached with prosecutors, he would plead no contest to a concealed-weapons charge in exchange for avoiding prosecution on a misdemeanor marijuana-possession charge. The sentence would be three years' probation. But first he ducked into the court's anteroom and Croce's outstretched arms.

"You know I love you, Bubba, but you're killing us," Croce said. Like Gaskins, Croce knew firsthand that patronizing lectures don't work with Iverson. Instead, he began talking about his own life and his own hard lessons. He reminded Iverson of some of the buddies he'd introduced him to at the arena, the guys from his rambunctious youth who now came to watch the games with him from the owner's box. They were no-nonsense tough guys with names like Meat and T-Bone who rode Harleys and had lived lives. "They're *my* posse, Bubba," Croce said. "Only there were times I couldn't hang around with one or two of them, because they wouldn't stop powdering their noses. They'd bring me down. When they got their shit together, I welcomed them back."

But that's just the thing, Iverson explained—these guys weren't even his friends. He hardly knew them. He had just written some lyrics at a party, and as was his custom when inspiration hit, he was rapping aloud in front of anyone and everyone, a group of relative strangers. Someone said they had access to a recording studio in Richmond. Next thing you know, he was giving up the keys to his Benz to someone who knew the way. "I can't believe I did something so stupid," Iverson said now, looking at Croce, but speaking so softly he just may have been addressing himself.

As would often be the case, he'd provided his critics with ammunition; the widespread rookie-year bashing of his friends resumed. The irony was, of course, that had Gary Moore or Ra or Arnie or Marlon been around, they'd have never let him drive off with perfect strangers. But the pundits weighed in. "The 'hood and the arena don't always mix," wrote *Philadelphia Inquirer* columnist Tim Dwyer. "Iverson may be suffering from a case of blind loyalty to the 'hood."

Michael Wilbon's tone in the *Washington Post* was mimicked in papers and on broadcasts throughout the country. "There's no sense in preaching to Allen Iverson anymore, because all the indications are he ain't listening," he wrote. "Entourages didn't do a lot for rappers Tupac Shakur and Biggie Smalls, did they?"

Iverson's old friend Jim Spencer went so far as to suggest that new coach Larry Brown ought to "bench Iverson . . . until he found some more savory friends."

For his part, Iverson continued the pattern. He used the off-court controversy for fuel the next time he hit the hardwood. He didn't have to wait long. The day after his plea bargain, he was en route back to Philly, determined to wow his fans at a charity game.

The Baker League was an institution in Philadelphia, as was its longtime organizer, Sonny Hill. Hill was a widely respected community leader who had spent years using basketball leagues to mentor area youth; one of Croce's first moves as president of the 76ers was to make Hill his "executive adviser." During games, Croce would greet fans at one entrance while Hill glad-handed at the other. Now Hill had arranged for a group of 76ers to play in an exhibition against the traveling team Mel Rhome, which featured a number of ex–NBA players, including Rick Mahorn, who had gone to high school with Ann Iverson.

All day long, rumors were rampant that Iverson would show for Sonny's game. Hints were made on Power 99, Philly's hip-hop station, and on WIP, the all-sports talker. But Iverson had already gained a reputation as a no-show. He'd recently blown off an advertised appearance with Stackhouse to model their team's new uniforms for the crowd at an area mall. Come game time at Temple University's McGonigle Hall in North Philadelphia, two thousand fans awaited the possibility of the Answer's arrival and the buzz was palpable: Would he or wouldn't he show?

Croce, in jeans and a polo shirt, stood at one baseline, near Hill. Larry Brown sat in the stands, impassive as ever. Then, at 7:27, three minutes before tip-off, a roar went up from the entrance opposite where Croce stood. The cheers carried across the arena as Iverson, with his flair for the dramatic, came bounding onto the court. He hugged Stackhouse and then lingered in an embrace with Hill, who, as was his wont, whispered sagacious words in Iverson's ear. "I knew I'd be around people that love me," Iverson would say later, when asked why he'd showed.

But first he got busy on the court. In front of his new coach, he scored 47 points, dished out 7 assists, and swiped 2 steals. He was quicker, more determined, feistier than anyone else on the court. He fed off the close, intimate crowd, often slapping hands with kids sitting courtside. He was all emotion, smiling widely when he'd come frustratingly close to a steal, cursing when a touch foul was whistled against him. The crowd, likewise, oohed and aahed at his every move. All, that is, but Brown, who sat there, stoic.

Inbounding the ball a couple of times, Iverson was literally a matter of feet from Brown. Their eyes, however, wouldn't meet. It was as though both men were studiously avoiding each other.

With a little over a minute to go, and the game safely put away, Iverson ran off the court—as swiftly as he'd charged onto it. In the locker room, he briefly answered reporters' questions while putting on some $300,000 in jewelry and donning a Washington Redskins jersey. Then he was out the door, hustled into the passenger seat of a black Mercedes, while legions of kids gave chase down a rain-slick city street. Inside the arena, Larry Brown sat in the stands, exchanging pleasantries with Croce and Hill. He and his star had been in the same room for two hours, often just a matter of feet apart from one another. And neither man had thought, or could bring himself, to so much as say hello.

When the elevator opened in the lobby of Atlanta's Swiss Hotel, a cluster of young black men strode into the room. Terry Royster sized them up. None seemed tall enough to be an NBA stud. No, this couldn't be Allen Iverson and his boys.

Royster didn't follow basketball. He'd never heard of Iverson, but in the days leading up to this tryout assignment, scores of friends had filled him in on this character, who was, he was given to understand, not only the best thing since Jordan, but also the toughest, hardest dude in sports. Iverson's latest brush with the law convinced the star, and those around

Under the boards, Iverson likes to say, he is the "littlest man with the biggest heart."

him, of the need for a bodyguard. Who knows? Had there been someone being paid to watch his back that night in early August, maybe Iverson would never have embarked on his ill-fated trip to Richmond.

Royster had been handling security for a spate of South Beach clubs in Miami when, at David Falk's instruction, the bodyguard for Alonzo Mourning had contacted him. At six feet four inches and with a black belt in jujitsu, the thirty-seven-year-old Royster had protected the likes of Janet Jackson and Lionel Ritchie. Now he was in the lobby of an Atlanta hotel, home base for a wild weekend of parties starring everyone who was anyone in the hip-hop underworld. He was waiting for this Iverson character to show up.

"You my bodyguard?" the shortest of the group to come off the elevator said to him. Could this be him? This little guy? Royster started laughing; having heard how hard Iverson was, he was expecting a cross between Mike Tyson and Suge Knight. They shook hands while Iverson's boys—Ra, Arnie, Marlon, "E," Gold—looked him up and down. Another interloper.

First, Royster accompanied Cru Thik to a music-industry party and basketball game between Puff Daddy's Bad Boy Entertainment and Jumaine DuPri's Atlanta-based So So Def Records. Iverson refereed and hit it off with the best baller there—Mase, of Bad Boy. Mason Betha had played high-school ball at Manhattan Center High School, where he had scored over 30 points against Stephon Marbury in a play-off game. His high-school teammates included Richie Parker—a phenom whose career had been curtailed because of sexual-abuse charges—Cameron Giles, and Tim Gittens. Giles is now better known as the rapper Cam'ron and Gittens as "Headache," the New York City playground legend. (Fans at Rucker Park would throw Tylenol onto the court when Headache played.) Other well-known rappers showed they could play as well, including Busta Rhymes and Jadakiss, who would later star with Iverson in a Reebok commercial.

That night, Puffy threw a party at Echo's in Atlanta. Iverson found a spot atop the railing by the bar, and he settled back to watch the crowd while drinking Rémy Martin. So far, Royster had seen nothing to warrant Iverson's hard-bitten street reputation. In fact, the bodyguard was struck by just how laid-back the star was. At clubs, such would often be the case;

Iverson would get a drink and hang, surrounded by his boys. He'd neither socialize nor dance. If he weren't a star, he would hardly be noticed.

On this night, Royster detected the makings of a fight from clear across the room. In a matter of seconds, the rumble started to approach Cru Thik. Chairs were being tossed through the air; Royster reached up and grabbed Iverson from off the landing—the Rémy Martin spilled all over Iverson's white shirt—and started knocking people out of the way in a mad dash for the exit. Once outside, Iverson was livid. "Look what you done to my shirt!" he shouted. "Now I'm gonna smell like Rémy Martin all night!"

The rest of the night, Iverson wouldn't speak to Royster. Instead, he'd address his friends with asides meant for Royster's ears. "Can y'all believe what this nigga did to my shirt?" he'd say, over and over again.

"Dude," Royster finally said, "I kinda almost saved your life. Forget the shirt already."

No such luck. When he first saw Royster the next day, Iverson said, "Try not to spill anything on my shirt today." The talk of the weekend was the predicament Stephon Marbury found himself in. He was afraid to leave his hotel room—something Iverson couldn't quite comprehend. Turns out, Marbury had hit on the girlfriend of a notorious drug dealer. The dealer had already twice slapped Marbury in public, once at a club and once in the hotel lobby. Puff Daddy tried to settle matters by suggesting that Marbury and the dealer go at it for real, mano-a-mano.

"That's some bullshit right there," Iverson protested to his friends after Puffy's proposed settlement. Iverson recalled Puffy's treatment of Marbury a year earlier, when Iverson and Marbury had joined many of the Bad Boys' players for a night of partying just after they'd been drafted into the NBA. Marbury had some of his friends from Coney Island with him; when he poured them some champagne that Puffy was paying for, Puffy turned on the young star. "You pay for that?" he yelled. "You lucky I'm letting *you* drink my Cristal, let alone your punk-ass friends!"

"That was wrong," Iverson recalled now. "We were just drafted, we didn't have no money, and we were celebrating. So Steph pours a glass for his man. And this nigga, who was showing us off like we his little toys, just flipped on him."

Iverson asked Royster to see if he could help Marbury. Royster approached the dealer, whose defiant tone immediately softened when Royster mentioned that he was working for Allen Iverson. "I didn't know he was a friend of Mr. Iverson's," the dealer said, backing off. Royster could barely contain his laughter; even though Iverson had been nothing but cold toward him, he could see that the player was, in his words, "as sweet as apple pie." But because of his past in jail, not to mention his hip-hop look, Iverson's street reputation was right up there with gangbangers you didn't want to mess with.

Maybe it was Royster's rescue of Marbury. Or maybe it was Royster's good-natured reaction when Ra—the most gregarious of those in Cru Thik—started teasing the bodyguard for wearing slacks and shoes. "Look at them Sears pants!" Ra cracked. "Look at that shirt. He dress like a preacher!" Iverson, who still hadn't had a meaningful conversation with Royster, nonetheless signed off on the idea that he needed a permanent bodyguard. Royster would be moving to Philly to be by Iverson's side when his second professional season began.

The psychodrama that would grip Philadelphia, and much of professional basketball, for the next five years—the saga of Allen and Larry—got off to an inauspicious start. The Sixers opened the 1997–98 season at home against the Milwaukee Bucks sporting new uniforms; Croce, knowing of Iverson's artistic interests, had sought input from him in their design. But tonight Iverson wasn't wearing his uniform. He was serving his one-game suspension for the August arrest.

In his absence, it was widely anticipated that Stackhouse would shoulder the scoring burden for the home team. But Stackhouse would only play twenty minutes, hitting just one of five shots for 5 points. This after leading the team in scoring during the preseason, at 17 points per game, not to mention leading all second-year players the previous season (20.7 points per game). Larry Brown was Stackhouse's third coach in three years, and after the game, the player was visibly frustrated.

"Man, Coach keeps saying not to think about scoring," he said, taking one last look at the hang of his olive-green Donna Karan suit before leaving the locker room. "That's hard to do when you're a scorer. That's my game. My preseason numbers were misleading. Look at the Boston game. Sure, I got thirty-three points, but even that was only on eight shots. The rest were free throws."

Just a few doors away, Brown was facing the media. He didn't single out Stackhouse for criticism, but there was little doubt whom he was speaking of when he said, "There are one or two guys in that locker room who aren't buying into what we're trying to do. They say the right things, but if you're not going to guard somebody, you're not going to play for me." In the first half, Stackhouse had gotten lit up by the Bucks' Ray Allen.

Given Stackhouse's North Carolina pedigree, few expected him to be such an early tenant in Brown's doghouse. But Stackhouse didn't come into the league with Dean Smith's wholehearted endorsement. He had had the temerity to complain about his playing time during his freshman year at North Carolina, and though Smith loved his athleticism, he was never fully convinced that Stackhouse was his kind of "team-first" player. Perhaps that explains why, during training camp, Brown stripped Stackhouse of his team captaincy in favor of newcomer Jimmy Jackson, who played a similar go-to-the-hole style.

From his perspective, Stackhouse was playing with a backcourt mate who detracted from his game. Because Iverson wasn't a pure point guard focused on setting him up for high-percentage scoring chances, Stackhouse maintained, his own shooting suffered. In basketball jargon, he was having to create all his own shots. "Allen is really a shooting guard," he said. "He's not interested in being a distributor."

Iverson came back for game two of the young season, but it didn't matter. In fact, the Sixers lost their first five games. After losses, once the media cleared away from their lockers, Stackhouse and Iverson would sit together, commiserating. Neither had ever lost so regularly before. "It's going to get better," Stackhouse would tell his backcourt mate.

"It's got to," Iverson said. "Can't get no worse."

When Seattle visited Philadelphia, an incident during the game's waning moments signaled the changing times confronting the NBA. A fan charged onto the court toward SuperSonics star Gary Payton. Rather than turning the other cheek, Payton "kept it real": the two jawed at each other, faces pressed together, while security rushed the court. When asked later why he didn't just walk away, Payton responded, "Hey, I'm from the 'hood in Oakland. If he pulled a gun, I'd knock him out."

A new cultural moment was upon the league. It consisted of a generation of players, who, like the music they were raised on, were more in-your-face than ever before. The Sixers lost to the Sonics, 112–105. After the game, Brown didn't talk specifically of what Payton's demeanor might portend for the league. But he was fuming about his team's me-firstism, and he saw it as not unrelated to the new attitude embodied by the likes of Payton and Iverson. He spoke sarcastically of the hip-hop lexicon used by today's player—how, if you're "the man," you refer to yourself as "a baller"—and he blasted his own team to the hometown press. "We're not a team," he said, in that tight monotone that masked bubbling emotions. "As soon as things go bad, we start playing like a bunch of strangers. We look like a summer league all-star game on MTV . . . We don't play like a team. A team does little things. They get on the floor for loose balls, they block out, make an extra pass, set a screen."

Two days later, the tension of their winless start began getting to the Sixers. At practice in Houston, Stackhouse and Iverson sat next to each other on the sideline. Iverson rose to make his way to the Gatorade and Stackhouse called out, "Get me one, too."

"Do I look like Mr. Fuckin' Belvedere?" responded Iverson, walking away with his cup. Stackhouse just shook his head.

That night, however, the two were finally in sync on the court—even if it was only for one game. Against Charles Barkley's Houston Rockets, Iverson dominated. He scored 26 points and dished out 15 assists, many to Stackhouse, who hit 8 of his 13 shots. Astonishingly, the point guard who had led the NBA in turnovers as a rookie didn't commit a single giveaway the whole game. The Sixers won for the first time under Brown.

Privately, though, the Sixers knew they'd have to trade Stackhouse. Salaries were exploding throughout the league; the collective-bargaining agreement would be up at the close of the current season and contentious negotiations loomed. Owners wanted to institute a hard salary cap that would give them cost certainty. The panic reached new heights when Kevin Garnett re-signed with the Minnesota Timberwolves in a record six-year, $126 million deal. ("Call me when you're serious," Garnett had told his team when rejecting its first offer of $117 million.) There were indications that Stackhouse, who was in the final season of his three-year deal, would be seeking somewhere in the neighborhood of $70 million. More important, the new axiom in the NBA was that, to win, you needed two players who required double-teaming. It was still unclear whether Stackhouse would consistently draw two defenders.

In the meantime, Brown went public with praise for Stackhouse in an effort to boost the player's trade value. "Stackhouse has really worked on his medium-range jumper," he said. "Except for Michael Jordan, the midrange game is a lost art. I'm just happy Stack is working on that."

Still, the team was struggling, as were its two stars. The jettisoning of Stackhouse would, in effect, signal the handing off of the team to Iverson, a risky proposition. Few teams in league history, if any, had ever been built around a barely six-foot player. And was Iverson ready to be an NBA go-to man?

It was a question raised by Sixers officials after a loss in New York in mid-December. Iverson had just two assists in the game. Worse, he hooked up with Mase afterward, and the two, accompanied by members of Cru Thik and Bad Boy, spent the night in New York clubs. Iverson missed practice the next day at the New York Athletic Club; the *Philadelphia Daily News* reported that it was his third missed practice of the young season.

Pat Croce flew to Boston—the site of the Sixers' next game—in order to confront his star player. He was in a rage. He was angry and disappointed in Iverson, of course. But he was also frustrated by his coach's penchant for nonconfrontation. If Allen was missing practices, it was because he felt he *could*.

The trip to Boston turned out to be cathartic for Croce, as he had time to ponder how to reach his star. In his previous life as a physical therapist, he'd considered his talent spiritual, not technical. Anyone could learn how to administer ultrasound; Croce believed his gift was to get inside his patients' heads, to begin the healing process by showing them he cared about them. Allen, he realized, doesn't know what he doesn't know. When he blows off a practice, he doesn't mean to let me down, or Coach down, or Que down. He's just tired and hungover and—like any kid—he's going to sleep it off. Yes, the more he thought about it, the more Croce realized that he needed Allen to know how angry he was, but also how much he cared for him. He knew from therapy, as he'd later explain, that "when someone feels that someone believes in them, there's no telling what can be accomplished."

In Boston, Croce stormed into the locker room. Unlike the last time he came to Iverson's side during a turbulent time, there was no hug. Croce took Iverson into the vacant Bruins locker room and began by cursing and yelling at the player. He got up close, invading Iverson's treasured space. Peering into his eyes, Croce asked, "Do you believe I care about you?"

"Yeah," Iverson said softly, taken aback.

"DO YOU BELIEVE I CARE ABOUT YOU?" Croce shouted, the two men jaw to jaw. At first blush, it might have appeared that Croce was pulling a drill-sergeant power trip on his young charge. But then he explained himself: "C'mon," he prodded, still shouting. "I need your mind to hear your mouth say it! DO YOU BELIEVE I CARE ABOUT YOU?"

"Yes," Iverson responded, more forcefully.

"LOUDER, BUBBA!"

"YES!"

"You gotta know, Bubba, if I'm pissed like this, there's a reason," Croce said. "It's because I want you to get better. Because I care about you."

Outside the door, a handful of Sixers players milled about, a little confused and a little amused by the shouting coming from within. From Iverson's perspective, that Croce took him aside, one-on-one, made all the difference in the world. It reminded him of his relationship with his college coach; whenever John Thompson had a problem with Iverson, he'd express himself directly. "And I can take that like a man," Iverson explained. It was an approach that stood in stark contrast to the way Brown had been treating him. In fairness to Brown, coaches for ages had used the media as a conduit to get messages across to players. But Iverson was particularly sensitive to the specter of male-authority-figure betrayal; he seethed when he saw quotes in the newspaper from his coach about his play or punctuality—the substance of which Brown hadn't always communicated to him, man-to-man.

Despite the tension between Iverson and Brown, the Sixers announced a blockbuster trade in mid-December, with the team's record at 6–16. Stackhouse and center Eric Montross were shipped off to Detroit for six-foot ten-inch shot-blocking big man Theo Ratliff and six-foot five-inch guard Aaron McKie, a Philadelphia native who had starred at Temple University.

The Sixers still struggled, but Iverson began to flourish in Stackhouse's absence. In early January, he led the team over the mighty Bulls, scoring

31 points. A week before outdueling Jordan, he was named the NBA's Player of the Week. At the same time, Brown made a little-noticed move that would prove critical to the team's long-term success. He sent a second-round draft pick to Seattle for backup point guard Eric Snow, who rarely logged minutes for the Sonics because he had the misfortune of playing the same position as Gary Payton.

By the time the all-star break rolled around, Iverson was averaging over 20 points and nearly 7 assists per game. He didn't make the East's all-star squad, however, a snub that he vowed to use as motivation during the season's second half.

Allen Iverson inherited his mother's body clock. Like her, he requires little to no sleep. Also like Ann, he is naturally peripatetic. Off the court as well as on, he is meant to be in motion. So it ought to have been no surprise that he became a staple in Philadelphia's hip-hop scene, regularly appearing at clubs in the wee hours.

Not that he lived ostentatiously. Typically, Iverson's nights began at TGI Friday's on City Line Avenue, the same spot where Charles Barkley had reigned years before when he was Philadelphia's resident basketball superstar. (In fact, it was at Friday's where Barkley met his wife, Maureen.) Until the local sports-talk radio station started reporting it, Iverson would park his Bentley in one of the restaurant's handicapped spots and he and his friends would hang out, eating fried foods and drinking until near midnight. Then it was off to either some strip clubs—Studio 37 and Prince's Black Experience were among the obscure favorites—or the clubs on Philly's Delaware Avenue.

One night, Iverson and his friends, accompanied by Sixers forward Tim Thomas, headed for a CD release party for the rapper Kurupt at Gothum Night Club. In the house was alleged Philly mobster "Skinny" Joey Merlino and Luke Campbell of the pioneering rap group 2 Live Crew. Upon entering, Royster exchanged words with the bouncer. "It's never a good sign when a bouncer has an ego," he told Iverson, once Cru Thik was searched and admitted entry.

As the night wore on, the crowd grew wilder. Campbell had come accompanied by some exotic dancers, who, at his urging, peeled off their formfitting dresses and began simulating oral sex for the crowd. Shortly thereafter, the gunshots started.

Seemingly en masse, the crowd rushed for the exit. But there were people outside shooting back *into* the club. The first wave of those seeking escape made an about-face and tried rushing back in; now people were getting trampled. The shooters made their way into the club; two feet in front of Iverson, a man was hit thirteen times in his chest.

"Trust me and follow!" Royster yelled, maneuvering his way through the screaming crowd. Along with a handful of others, they found their way to a side exit and crawled under a fence. They ran for the parking lot; except the shooting was now coming back outside; the only sound filling the night air was the *ping, ping* of bullets ricocheting off cars. While Iverson sprinted, a stranger appeared alongside him, stride for stride.

"Allen, I want you to hear this tape, man!" the man said, huffing and puffing to keep pace. "When you open your record label, call me! My name is on the tape!"

Iverson didn't break stride, but he did break out in laughter. Bullets were whizzing by—and this guy was trying to sell himself! Just then, a car came speeding down the street, shooting. Everyone dove for cover, with Royster on top of Iverson, who couldn't stop laughing. "This is something out of a movie, man! This is fun," he said.

Finally, safe in the car, Iverson couldn't stop laughing about their action-adventure sequence. "Y'all see me? Dive and roll, man, dive and roll!"

When Royster picked Iverson up for practice the next day at Iverson's home in Conshohocken, a suburb of Philly, the star was, as ever, mum. Getting in the passenger seat, he teased Royster about the Tupac song "All Eyez on Me" that was playing—as always. "This nigga knows one rap song and he's always got it playing, trying to impress me," Iverson would say to his friends while Royster laughed at the ribbing. "I think he adjusts it when he's in the driveway so when I get in, I think he's cool 'cause he's listening to a rap song."

As always, they stopped at a Wawa convenience store and Royster bought Iverson a copy of the *Daily News*. Iverson took his headphones off as he read the news account of the previous night's shooting. No mention of him, which was good. Nor did it capture anywhere near how many people had been wounded. Iverson had seen bodies being thrown into cars that barely slowed down before peeling away. Though he'd been laughing the night before, it was laughter born of adrenaline and crisis.

"Man, that shit was crazy last night," he said, folding up the paper. "We are not going back to that place." (According to press reports, a patron who had been thrown out of the club shot and killed the bouncer and wounded two bystanders.)

Unlike his rookie year, when a rotating cast of Cru Thik members resided with him in the Conshohocken house, Iverson's home life was becoming more settled. At Ann's urging, the friends no longer crashed at the house every night. Instead, Iverson rented a floor at the nearby Holiday Inn, where some of the wilder parties went down. That's where Ra, Arnie, Jamil Blackmon, and the rest stayed; often, after one or the other would ring up in excess of $15,000 in room service and phone charges, the account would come due. Iverson would pay up and identify one room—say, Arnie's—as the one that could order room service. So the whole crew would crowd into Arnie's spot, gorging, until that room's bill got big enough to be called to Allen's attention.

Meantime, at the house, Aunt Jessie—Li'l Bit—came to cook for her nephew. Tawanna and Tiaura would visit every so often from Virginia. When Ann was around, there was no missing her. The first time Royster met her, he wondered if she ever stopped talking long enough to catch her breath. "You the bodyguard supposed to be watching my baby?" she said. "You better watch my baby's ass!" Without missing a beat, she was on to a totally different subject, Royster's presence no doubt having reminded her of David Falk: "And where is that bald-headed muthafucka that's supposed to be getting me all my money every month?" she vented. "How come I never see his muthafuckin' ass around here?"

Iverson was providing for his mother, her boyfriend George Jackson (known as Jack), Allen's two sisters, Jessie and her three kids, uncles Stevie and Greg and their families, not to mention all his friends—and their kids, including their babies' mothers. Each month, Falk's office would cut checks to an extended, and rotating, list. At Christmastime, Iverson took about twenty of his friends and relatives to the Coliseum Mall back in Hampton for an unprecedented shopping spree. Guys bought computers and big-screen TVs for their parents, grandparents, and significant others; Royster estimates that Iverson spent close to six figures in one day.

For a guy with a reputation for being irresponsible, Royster thought, he's the most responsible person I've ever seen. It seemed like he willingly shouldered the burden of lifting up an entire community. And yet Royster never heard Iverson complain. Once, together, they counted the number of people Iverson supported. It came to twenty-nine. "You know what?" Iverson said. "You and me are the only two people I know who've got jobs."

"That's fucked up," Royster said.

"Yeah, but think how fucked up they'd all be if it wasn't for me," Iverson responded.

The Sixers were out of the play-off hunt early in the second half of the 1997–98 season, but the season's drama was far from over. The question hanging over the team was, would Iverson re-sign during the coming summer, or would he enter his third NBA season next fall as a potential free agent the following spring?

Iverson was still wounded from what he saw as Brown's hypocrisy—Brown would use words like "family" to describe his team, and then, from Iverson's perspective, he'd take their family business public during postgame press conferences, pointing fingers that ought to be pointed in the locker room. "I'll remember everything this summer," Iverson said. "I really will think about all the things that have been said about me this year."

As so often would be the case, Brown and Iverson were talking past each other. Brown bemoaned Iverson's oversensitivity; why, he wondered, couldn't Iverson realize the difference between *criticism* and *coaching*? Iverson's complaint wasn't with the substance of what Brown had to say; it was *who* he was saying it to. When he publicly questioned Iverson's shot selection, or—a common complaint—the fact that the point guard would often take a shot before one of his teammates had touched the ball, Brown seemed to be an accomplice in what Iverson considered the cartoonish media portrayal of him as selfish and disinterested in winning.

Indeed, as Brad Greenberg had predicted before drafting Iverson, he was the most competitive basketball player this side of the almighty Jordan. Jordan's competitive fires were played up in the media as the stuff of legend; how they'd fueled his gambling jones, how he'd force his teammates to play cards until he was ahead. Those around Iverson saw the same qualities, only it was hardly ever chronicled. They saw Iverson tire of losing at pool, of seeing his name with a zero next to it on his basement scoreboard, and *will* himself into being the best pool player among his friends. They saw him, tipsy after a night of clubbing, challenge others—strangers and friends alike—to 2 A.M. dashes down deserted city streets, cell phones and pagers flying off his body, determined to prove no one could take him in a footrace, even if he'd been drinking, even if he was wearing Timberlands.

"He's just not going to be in the losing column," Royster recalls today. "I don't care what it is. Once, in Norfolk, we played two-on-two touch football on a whim. He said, 'I'll take T, and I betcha we score every time.' He tells me, 'Just run this pattern and the ball will be there every time.' And, I mean, it was—a touchdown, every time. He'd take a three-step drop and throw that thing seventy yards, and it was there, every single time. And it didn't have to be basketball or football. We once played seventy-five games of checkers in his basement, until I couldn't beat him."

The Sixers started making moves that appeared designed to heighten the chance that Iverson would remain with the team. First, they traded Clarence Weatherspoon, Jimmy Jackson, and elder statesman Terry Cummings to the Golden State Warriors for Iverson's old friend from back home, Joe Smith. Smith, the top pick in 1995, had, so far, been a disappointment as a pro. The acquisition of Smith made the Sixers the only team in the league to have three players who had once been top picks in the NBA draft: Iverson, Smith, and Derrick Coleman. Yet with all that talent, Brown hadn't yet molded his roster into a team.

Coleman, in particular, presented a dilemma. Incongruously, Brown loved him. Though Brown was known as a coach who valued practice, Coleman didn't practice often; when he did, he could be lackluster. But he had a tremendous basketball IQ and would talk basketball for hours with Brown. From Croce's perspective, however, championships are built on intangibles as much as physical talent. It didn't bode well that, when Croce rounded up every player for a trip to Philadelphia's Children's Hospital to lift the spirits of ill kids, Coleman was the only player to decline. "I don't do hospitals," he said.

Well, it's *his* soul, Croce thought, storming off. But the more he mulled it over, the more convinced he became that, in his view, a soulless player would be an impediment to winning—and a bad influence on Iverson. Coleman's contract could be bought out for $5.5 million at season's end. Until now, Croce had kept silent on matters pertaining to basketball, deferring, as was his management style, to an expert like Brown. But now he made it known: he didn't want Coleman back. He told Brown it would be his call, but that there would have to be unanimity among the basketball staff: head scout Tony DiLeo and vice president of basketball operations Billy King, Brown's onetime assistant at Indiana, would have to sign on to bringing Coleman back as well.

Meantime, Brown experimented on the court with an idea that would ultimately alter Iverson's career and the Sixers' fortunes. His team was losing to Dallas by 14 with less than six minutes to go when, seemingly on a whim, Brown paired Eric Snow at the point with Iverson at shooting guard. Iverson, relieved of the stress attached to running the team and thereby spared Brown's carping, scored 12 points, including a clutch three-pointer with 5.5 seconds left, to lead the Sixers to a 91–90 comeback win. For the remainder of the season, Brown continued the experiment, finding fifteen minutes or so per game for Iverson as a two-guard.

Iverson didn't see much in the distinction between point and shooting guards. To him, his game was his game. "I'm not a point guard or a two-guard," he said. "I'm a creator." And in the modern NBA, the lines blurred. Old-time, classic "distributor" point guards like Mo Cheeks were becoming a thing of the past. Now Michael Jordan or Scottie Pippen brought the ball up for the Bulls—was either of them the "point guard"? Hardly. They were good ball handlers who could start the offense.

Iverson may have thought Brown was unnecessarily wedded to an antiquated model, but Brown was looking for a way to get Iverson's teammates some touches. (Phil Jackson had accomplished the same goal in Chicago by running the "triangle offense," a much-lauded system of cuts and passes, at least until a game was on the line; that's when Michael took over.) In Brown's estimation, the Sixers would never become a true team until other players felt the ball in their hands more often. He also started to realize that Iverson's teammates needed to be of a special breed; that is, they had to be willing to put their own egos aside, to forfeit their own scoring, in order to play with someone who would take so many shots.

Late in the season, *Sports Illustrated* published a story on Iverson that reverberated from the Sixers' locker room to a Connecticut prison. In Connecticut, where Iverson's biological father, Allen Broughton, had taped photos of his son to his cell's walls, a guard came to see him. "You don't have anything to worry about when you get out," said the guard.

"Your son said in *Sports Illustrated* that he's gonna take care of you when you get out."

Broughton's heart leaped. Then he read the article. Iverson said, when asked about his jailed father, "Soon as he gets out, I got him. I got him forever. Whatever he needs." There was only one problem: he was speaking of Michael Freeman, the man he considers his father. Broughton, heartbroken, still claiming he wanted nothing from his son but a renewed relationship, resigned himself to the fact that he'd never get what he wanted from his famous progeny.

While Broughton agonized over one line in the *SI* piece, Iverson was incensed by a quote from another would-be father figure who often disappointed him: Brown. "To Brown the problem is modern NBA superstardom, which too often prevents a player from getting to know his teammates, prevents him from *trusting* them," wrote Rick Reilly. "When you bolt every game with a phalanx of high school buddies, bodyguards and Reebok chaperones, any teammate who is trying to bond with you has to follow along in his own car. 'The company Allen's with is Reebok, not really us,' Brown says."

Iverson read the line over and over. He'd known that Brown hadn't been warm to Gaskins, had actually kept him from the locker room on occasion. But did his coach really think he was more loyal to Reebok than to his own team? How could his own coach help the media—which had been against him since high school—assassinate his character that way?

The season ended with the Sixers posting a 31–51 record. Though it was the team's best record since the 1991–92 season, more questions plagued the organization than answers. As they headed into a perilous off-season labor dispute, the jury was still out on whether Larry Brown and Allen Iverson could peacefully coexist.

chapter | 9

LOYALTY

This is Chinese for "loyalty." Because I'd rather
be loyal to the people that were loyal to me.

The summer of 1998 became the off-season that wouldn't end when, thanks to contentious collective bargaining negotiations, NBA owners locked out the players. The upcoming season was in jeopardy.

Commissioner Stern succinctly summarized the issue facing his league: "Revenues are rising, profitability is declining, and ticket prices are going up." The main point of contention centered on the players' share of league revenues, defined as "basketball-related income." According to the league, the players were now getting over 57 percent of that income, and some thirteen teams were losing money. But the players, led by Iverson's agent, Falk, and Jordan (who was keeping mum about his retirement plans, the better to maintain his leverage in the labor talks), weren't buying it. They argued that the owners had been crying poor despite the windfall from a whopping $2.64 billion TV contract with NBC and TNT. (Barkley even chided Stern about the commissioner's $9 million annual salary: "Have *you* ever heard the words 'salary cap'?") But the owners could afford to play hardball and institute a lockout because the TV money was guaranteed—whether there was a season or not.

The issue really came down to defining league revenues. Deputy Commissioner Russ Granik maintained that "basketball-related income ... now basically includes the kitchen sink." Not quite. It didn't include the bulk of money generated by luxury seating or arena signage, for example. Comcast, the company that owns Iverson's Sixers *and* the arena they play in, assigned revenue generated by naming rights, premium seating, signage, concessions, and parking to their building—thereby protecting that money from being shared with the players. Moreover, Jordan argued that the owners were seeking givebacks from the players as relief from their own bad salary decisions. The owners had all made fortunes as capitalists, yet here they were, fighting for a salary cap, an artificial restriction on their laborers' earnings. In a way, Jordan cemented his place as the nation's premier working-class capitalist by arguing for a free market.

The negotiations were likely to directly impact Iverson. Given the precedent of the Garnett megadeal, he'd be looking at a long-term contract in excess of $100 million. But it was precisely those kind of numbers the owners were seeking to bring in line. Despite his personal stake in the issue, Iverson didn't get involved in the labor dispute. Later, he'd regret his disinterest. But the summer of 1998 found him once again basking in his off time, even if it had no end in sight.

In July, Iverson got ready to host the first Allen Iverson Summer Celebrity Classic, a weekend of activities in Hampton organized by Gary Moore to benefit the local Boys and Girls Clubs that Iverson used to attend. The decision to do something for area kids emerged from a pact he had made many years before with Gary Moore, his grade-school football coach and mentor, to remain committed to kids who grew up just as he had. "I just want these little kids, who aren't fortunate enough to have resources other kids have, to know they have someplace safe to go, you know what I'm saying?" Iverson explained.

But his good intentions were also colored by his characteristic defiance. After all that had happened to him in his hometown, there was a part of Iverson that wanted to stick it to those who had doubted him—by doing good. "I was incarcerated for something I didn't do," he said. "I could have easily been bitter and stayed out of Hampton and never done anything for the community. But I didn't. I was the bigger man in that situation . . . For what y'all did to me, I'm coming right back to the same place and I'm going to raise money for the Boys and Girls Clubs. I'm going to do something for these kids and this community, whether you like it or not."

Iverson's charity event was overshadowed by the news on the eve of the weekend that Arnie Steele and Mike Powell had been arrested in Norfolk driving Iverson's $138,000 Mercedes-Benz and charged with dealing cocaine. Iverson was not involved in the arrest, nor was he brought in for questioning. But his car was impounded and subject to Virginia drug-forfeiture laws. The Benz was history. More pressing, the arrests led to more headlines about the crowd Iverson ran with—at the precise moment when he was seeking to do something good back home. "He was pissed at Arnie at first," recalls Royster, who was with Iverson when he heard about the arrest. "But that quickly turned to being concerned for him and just wanting to make sure the guys were all right."

As the summer stretched to fall, there appeared no end in sight to the labor impasse. Iverson used the extended time to pursue another passion, rap music. Mase had blown up into a full-fledged superstar; his CD *Harlem World* had topped the charts the year before. He invited Iverson to Atlanta, where he was recording. In the studio, Iverson penned some lyrics and got behind the mike.

Iverson had always modeled his rapping style after that of "E" and Ra, the two best rappers he'd known. "E" especially had a distinct flow; he didn't rhythmically sync his voice to the beat so much as speak in a natural cadence that floated above it.

Now, as Iverson started rapping, Mase cut him short. "No, no," he said. "You gotta say it without it sounding like you just wrote it."

Mase encouraged Iverson to feel the beat. They pulled an all-nighter, taking time for only one break, during which they played hoops and hit a couple of strip clubs, before returning to the studio. They eventually emerged with Iverson contributing two verses on a single called "Pay Per View": "Yo, this is the Answer/It's a dirty, dirty, dirty dance/If we don't get the money we want, we're locked out/That's why I run with them Harlem World niggas / Everybody I'm running with is the highest paid in what we do/That's why this shit is Pay Per View . . ." Later, he raps: "A.I., Betha in Miami/G's in our pockets/Pullin' out on these bitches like Tubbs and Crockett . . ."

As the night wore on, Mase grew more and more outspoken about his own hoops game vis-à-vis Iverson's. Around two in the morning, Iverson had had enough of Mase's trash-talking. "Man, you keep running your mouth, I'll play you one-on-one for ten grand," he said, issuing his standard offer, a challenge so outlandish its mere mention served as an act of intimidation. "We'll play to twenty, I'll give you nineteen and the ball five times in a row. Then I'm gonna score twenty unanswered."

They went to Run and Shoot, an all-night inner-city gym. As promised, Iverson stopped Mase five times in a row. Then, with a crowd forming, he hit 19 in a row, even though Mase was trying to foul him on every shot. With the score tied at 19, Mase started to fret. Iverson missed a jumper; Mase, knowing the momentum was clearly against him, got the rebound and—without taking the ball back—put it back up for a layup. Then he started jumping around, hands in the air, as though he'd won. "Hell if I was about to pay him," Iverson would later recall.

Still, it didn't stop Mase from spending the rest of the night boasting about how he'd beaten the Answer. From Run and Shoot, they went to Atlanta's The Gold Club, a spot that would later make headlines for providing ballplayers (including Patrick Ewing and Iverson's future teammate Dikembe Mutombo) with sexual favors. There they were ushered into a private part of the club. Women were sent in. The bouncers at the door assured them that they wouldn't have to worry about anybody coming in and that they could do whatever they wanted. Royster didn't like the vibe. " 'Chuck, something's wrong here," he said. "I don't like the way they're force-feeding us. There could be cameras in here or something."

Iverson didn't necessarily share Royster's suspicions, but he didn't like the executive-type feel of the place. "Let's just go to one of our down-and-dirty spots," Royster suggested.

"That's what I'm talking 'bout," Mase agreed.

Once they got to a more downscale club, Mase regaled the crowd with chatter about his hardcourt "conquest." When Iverson took a sip of his Texas Tea, Mase boasted, "That's right—drown your sorrows!" When Iverson got a lap dance, Mase yelled to the girl to "ask him who beat his ass!"

"Yeah," Mase called out while Iverson laughed at his friend's playing the fool. "I just come from shutting Allen Iverson's lights out."

Then it was back to laying down tracks. Later, Iverson would speak about how much he learned from Mase in the studio. But he also realized something else. Rapping was fun, but basketball was his life. He yearned to get back on the court.

The lockout ended on January 7, 1999, leaving roughly three weeks for abbreviated training camps before the commencement of a fifty-game regular season in early February. The union agreed to a limit on the earnings of individual players. As a result, the new collective-bargaining agreement would cost Iverson more than $30 million. There was no doubt that as a franchise player he would get the maximum salary for a player beginning his third year. David Falk called the Sixers' Billy King and consummated the deal in about ten minutes, King would later tell Iverson. It was for six years and $71 million.

"I'm not greedy," Iverson said, when questioned about the effect the new agreement had on him. "I don't have to make twenty million dollars a year to play basketball, to do something I really love."

Unlike almost all other sports superstars dotting the public landscape, Iverson singled out his team owner as one of the main reasons he wanted to sign the deal and stay in Philly long-term. One day, shortly after the season opened, he sat in front of his locker wearing baggy jeans, Timberlands, and an Enyce sweatsuit, and he made it clear where his loyalties lay. From day one, he said, Pat Croce had kept it real with him. "He didn't shoot me no curves," Iverson said. "He didn't come in and kiss my ass or try and show me that he wasn't going to kiss my ass. He just ain't phony. Coach Brown is my coach, and I respect him for what he's taught me. But for whatever reason, Pat knows how to handle himself."

In the off-season, the Sixers had become Iverson's team. The other big names were gone. Coleman's contract, in keeping with Croce's wishes, had been bought out. Joe Smith was similarly jettisoned. Instead, the team signed shot blocker Theo Ratliff to a long-term deal and brought in free-agent center Matt Geiger, who had been a serviceable backup in Charlotte. Geiger was seven-one, with a reputation for toughness and soft shooting skills. With his shaved head, goatee, "Carpe Diem" tattoo, and avant-garde fashion sense, he added color to Brown's suddenly egoless locker room. Geiger, Ratliff, Tim Thomas, and Carolina alum George Lynch held down the frontcourt spots, and Eric Snow, Aaron McKie, and first-round draft choice Larry Hughes—the national freshman of the year at the University of St. Louis—complemented Iverson in the backcourt.

This is the team that got off to a 4–1 start, despite Iverson's early-season shooting woes. In one early-season win, Iverson hit on only 4 of his 17 shots. Afterward, McKie, who had become closer to him than anyone else on the team, noticed how upset Iverson was by his subpar shooting. "Would you rather have forty points and a loss or fifteen points and a win?" McKie asked him. "You choose. That'll show what type of player you are."

Beginning with Stackhouse, Brown had cleaned house of big-name offensive talents in favor of those willing to do defensive-oriented grunt work. Since his arrival in Philly, he had relentlessly preached defense; now his sermons finally began to pay off. Even when his team followed up its 4–1 start with four straight losses, he remained upbeat. "This is the proudest I've been in a long, long time," he said after a 76–69 loss to Atlanta. "It was as good a defensive period as we've played."

It was just one example of Brown's penchant for seemingly counterintuitive coaching. There was value, he'd learned, in being tough and critical when your charges were riding high, and in being soothing and understanding when times were tough. During a horrendous losing spell while coaching the University of Kansas in 1988, Brown had entered his team's locker room and was met by a squad expecting a Bobby Knight–type tirade. Instead, he told them he'd "never been prouder" of them, that he felt things were on the upswing thanks to their effort and unselfishness. It became a self-fulfilling prophecy, as Kansas went on to win the national title.

Brown's comments, combined with his early-season decision to move Iverson to shooting guard and play Eric Snow at the point for over thirty minutes a game, were panning out. Freed of the responsibility of running the team on every play, Iverson found new ways to distribute and create. Thanks to the intricate screens Brown devised, he often found himself with the ball in his hands only after all of his teammates had touched it. He was named the NBA Player of the Month for February, averaging 28.5 points, 6 assists, 5.8 rebounds, and 2.31 steals.

On March 11, the Sixers' record stood at 11–8, their best start since the 1990–91 season. But Brown—ever counterintuitive—was suddenly not happy. He pulled Iverson from an 85–70 win over Charlotte after Iverson launched a series of ill-advised shots while there was still plenty of time on the twenty-four-second clock. Iverson, for his part, never had much use for twenty-four-second clocks. He played on feel, not by design—a tendency that, given his preternatural self-confidence, led him to disregard such matters as the shot clock or his teammates' "touches." Brown, with his constant scribbling of intricate plays, didn't coach feel; despite his own emotional nature, he was the ultimate rationalist as a coach.

As Brown and Iverson struggled over issues like shot selection, the stakes were raised on the morning of March 12, when Royster called in Iverson's absence from practice. Tawanna, now living with Allen (along with their two kids), had recently suffered a miscarriage. The message was that she was sick and Allen had to stay at home and help with Deuce (Allen II), two, and Tiaura, five.

Brown was livid and complained publicly that he hadn't heard from Iverson himself—only "his guy," Royster—and stated that Iverson's unexcused absence was "not the first time." When Brown addressed the local media horde after the missed practice, there was no doubt whom he was speaking of, even though he didn't mention Iverson by name. "You've got to be a team in every sense of the word," he said. "That means you respect your teammates. You show them respect by how you act, how you practice, how you play . . . We have a lot of people who have good character and care, but that's not enough. You need all your people to do that."

Iverson wasn't happy about Brown's public airing, and he was even more upset by the comments of unnamed teammates in the *Philadelphia Inquirer,* one of whom said, "We simply can't have that. If he doesn't have a legitimate excuse, he's got to pay the price. Any one of us would have to. The same should apply to him."

Of course, as Jordan had proved in Chicago, rules tended to be different for superstars. Such was the case even before Jordan. In Philadelphia some thirty years before, after Wilt Chamberlain missed a game-day shoot-around, he told his complaining coach: "I'm coming to the arena once. You can have your choice: I'll come to shoot-around or the game." Come game time, he was in the lineup.

Iverson, in addition to feeling betrayed by his coach and teammates, was puzzled over just what the rules were. In the past, he'd had Royster phone in his absences and no one had said anything. As Croce had long feared, Brown's reluctance to confront his players face-to-face was now reaping consequences.

The truth was that few in the Sixers organization believed Iverson's excuse. They knew that Mase had been in town the night before and that the two had gone out clubbing till the wee hours. Their night started at Friday's, where they hung until closing. Then it was on to Club Risqué, where Iverson kept knocking down Texas Teas. Then they ended up at the after-hours Palmer Social Club. Mase had been trying to turn in early all night; he was in the process of being saved and would soon give up his lucrative recording career to become a preacher. It was Iverson who kept dragging his friend to the next spot. "C'mon, you're in my town now," he'd say. (Many in hip-hop were skeptical of Mase's later conversion; Iverson, however, believed it. It had to be real, he said, because Mase wouldn't "go to no titty bars no more.")

Of course, both things could be true: Iverson could have been out all night *and* Tawanna could have been under the weather. That's basically what Iverson said when confronted by the media over whether he'd been out on the town with Mase. If ever there was a moment that best symbolized his anti-Jordan status, this was it, as Iverson stood before the TV cameras and defended his right to party all night with a rap star. "I guess people felt one of my friends was in town, I was hanging out all night," he said. "Well, I hang out all night anyway, if I want to. But I still come in here and give these people the same thing I always give them."

During the controversy, Iverson scoured both the *Daily News* and the *Inquirer* for critical public comments from Croce. He found none. "He kept it in the family," Iverson said. "He'll rip me man-to-man, but he won't go to the paper and try to tear me down, because he already knows they're not for me, they're against me. That's okay. People been against me my whole life. So it would shock me for Pat to talk about me like that."

Meantime, the Sixers traded Tim Thomas to Milwaukee for power forward Tyrone Hill, who would become a critical player for the team. The next night, the New Jersey Nets came to town, having just completed a blockbuster trade to acquire Stephon Marbury from Minnesota. Marbury didn't play on this night because he hadn't taken the mandatory posttrade physical yet. Nonetheless, when Iverson came out for the pregame warm-up, he was surprised to see David Falk sitting courtside with Nets owner Lewis Katz. Falk had recently taken on Marbury as a client and was said to have been the driving force behind the trade. Iverson said hello to Falk before the game, but he had not been pleased when he heard that his agent would also be representing his rival, nor was he happy that on this night, Falk was sitting with the opposing team's owner in *his* house.

Some had thought Brown would suspend Iverson for missing the practice. Instead, Iverson not only played, he started and scored 28 points—again flourishing at the center of a storm. Ratliff was dominant, with 23 points, 11 rebounds, and 7 blocks. The Sixers fought back from 13 down to win in overtime. As always, a win seemed to bury the controversy.

But Falk's appearance at the game—seemingly to support someone else—was the final straw for Iverson. Saying he "felt like the prey," Iverson severed ties with the agent some were calling the most powerful man in sports. The issues had been building up. Despite the fact that his new contract took all of ten minutes to hammer out, Falk charged Iverson his standard 4 percent. From Iverson's standpoint, since it was such an easy deal, he should have charged an hourly rate, as Ray Allen's lawyer had done. Moreover, there had been a recent news story about Iverson defaulting on his car payments to Mercedes-Benz. In his view, Falk's office was responsible for that. Then there was Ann, who said Falk's office had made travel plans for her; when she got to the airport, there were no tickets awaiting her.

Finally, the jettisoning of Falk signified far more than an agent-client dispute. Falk was a paradigmatic figure, a man who had taken a simple surname, "Jordan," and turned it into a cultural touchstone. Thanks to Falk, the Jordan name not only meant something to America (many things, actually), it *provoked* an emotional response. Jordan was—particularly to his white crossover audience—a soothing figure. He was a beautiful and beautifully athletic black man who, unlike so many other beautiful and beautifully athletic black men, was not "angry."

The Jordan crossover, as engineered by Falk, succeeded because white Americans got to participate fully in what was "Jordan" without ever having their race guilt triggered. Jordan's white fans didn't think of him as black the way Ali's white fans thought of *him* as black; Jordan didn't construct his public persona out of his blackness. As a result, the world's most dangerous man on the hardwood was utterly unthreatening as a symbol; he "transcended" race, which is to say that in his planed, smiling face, white Americans (unconsciously) sought and found permission to *forget* about race—both his and theirs. Thus the Jordan appeal, while giving the impression of having "overcome" race—of having "solved" the race problem—merely sidestepped the issue altogether. For creating this phenomenon, Falk was, unquestionably, a genius.

Unfortunately, he was also a one-trick pony. Which meant, almost by definition, that a Falk-Iverson relationship could only come to a sorry end. Was there ever a man more ill-suited than Iverson to become a soothing crossover figure—someone who could willfully and skillfully obviate his race by giving white America permission to forget it? There was not. Nevertheless, Falk tried to do with Iverson what he'd done with Jordan, to subject Iverson to the old crossover model of marketing. He constantly counseled Iverson against the tattoos and cornrows and baggy jeans, arguing that such style choices didn't attract corporate interest. That's why Falk had been able to get Iverson only one major endorsement deal, Reebok for $50 million. But as Que Gaskins was always pointing out, there was an emerging youth culture Iverson could tap into. Gaskins noted that DMX had the number one CD in the country—and those were suburban white boys buying those raps. And there was Lauryn Hill, braids and all, on the cover of *Time* magazine.

Falk was the ultimate handler, and Iverson wouldn't be handled. As he'd later say, he fired Falk in part because "I wanted to be in charge of my own shit." Iverson was aware that, in music, the crossover era had given us artists who were the product but who had little or no control. Stevie Wonder and Al Green didn't own their own master recordings, for example. It was hip-hoppers like Puff Daddy, Dr. Dre, and Master P who made themselves the product *and* the entrepreneurs behind it.

It was a distinction pressed upon Iverson by Earvin "Magic" Johnson, whose counsel he sought before getting rid of Falk. Johnson was managing Mase's career, and he spoke to Iverson while Mase was with him during a taping of the NBA TV show *Inside Stuff.* Iverson saw that Jordan, under Falk's tutelage, had made his money the old-fashioned way: by selling himself as a pitchman. Johnson, however, was building an empire by growing businesses in minority communities, employing people where they live. There were his string of Magic Johnson movie theaters and his groundbreaking partnerships with Starbucks and TGI Friday's, Iverson's favorite hangout. When Iverson sought Johnson's advice, the basketball legend didn't mention Falk but didn't hide his disdain for agents, either. "Too many guys forget the agents work for us, not the other way around," Johnson said. "The problem young athletes have is they let their agents and managers speak for them."

It was rumored that Johnson was getting into the agent game, though as a part owner of the Lakers, he was prohibited from doing so in any explicit way. But Johnnie Cochran had made public his plans to become a sports agent, and Iverson had already talked to Puff Daddy about his interest in steering Iverson's career. And Master P's No Limit Sports was signing up athletes as well.

But Iverson took Johnson's message to heart and decided it would be unwise to have anyone other than his lawyers, Shuttleworth and Woodward, look out for him. Aligning himself with Magic, Johnnie Cochran, Puffy, or Master P might make for a cool story, but at the end of the day, he didn't trust that putting his career in the hands of someone who was arguably a bigger star than himself would work to his benefit. Besides, though he wanted to learn about this business stuff and become a businessman like Magic, he didn't want to be distracted from ball. His team was finally winning, and as he observed to Gaskins one day, all this business stuff takes care of itself if you're winning.

"Winning means everything," he said.

Y'all got any new questions for me?" Iverson said, surrounded by the daily journalistic pack on the court at St. Joseph's University, just after Sixers practice. The questions, as he knew full well, weren't new. But they were fired at him anyway, and he answered, as usual, in a deep monotone behind droopy eyelids.

It made for a telling scene, one that played out in professional-sports-team locker rooms across the country. A young black athlete accosted by a sweating, jostling pack of overwhelmingly white, middle-aged sportswriters and broadcasters. The clichéd questions would come, the athlete would answer in like-minded clichés, and the whole interaction would smack of the impersonal. Both sides seemed unaware of their roles in a generational, racial, and cultural divide. The men—and they were mostly men—who presented Iverson to the world were alienated from him in at least two significant ways: they couldn't relate to his upbringing—eight friends killed in one summer!—nor could they grasp the riches in which he now basked.

Add to that schism Iverson's history with the media, how, at the tender age of seventeen, he felt turned on by the press of his hometown, *judged* by them, and his current bored, disinterested media mask became understandable. That history even explains the markings on his skin. It wasn't until his rookie year, when he didn't recognize himself in all the breathless coverage of him as a "thug" with a "posse," that he decided to use his body as though it were his own personal billboard. He would advertise who he was on his very own skin, because if he couldn't control how he was portrayed or perceived, he knew he could control his own body. It's the one thing he'd always been able to control, the one thing that had gotten him where he was today. And so he started going down to South Street in Philly, to a place called Body Graphics; he liked to say he got addicted to the needle, but he really got hooked on expressing himself, on the notion that he could carve into his own skin announcements of who he was. You want to know who I am, he'd say, "Just read my body."

Yet few in the media did. So used to judging athletes based on how athletes treat media, the writers and pundits and talking heads instead focused on the dour outward demeanor, and invariably contrasted it to the ingratiating gregariousness of Jordan. Ironically, it was their portrayal of Iverson that so captivated a wide audience of young people; seeming disinterest, combined with stunning achievement, has always been the province of cool. But those who knew Iverson say the somber postpractice demeanor was more a defense mechanism. They saw the chattering class clown, the cutup who, when Sixers traveling secretary Allen Lumpkin teased him one afternoon, scribbled out an uproarious caricature of Lumpkin on the locker-room chalkboard, complete with an exaggerated big belly.

That's what Croce saw one night after another home win. The Sixers owner and his wife, Diane, stopped by the family room, where the players' wives, girlfriends, and children were waiting. When five-year-old Tiaura Iverson saw Croce, she burst into a wide smile. "Uncle Pat Croce!" she yelled. But her attention was soon diverted when her father appeared, looking not much more than a kid himself, loping down the hallway, the personification of cool. Tiaura ran to him and the tough-guy pose melted; Iverson scooped her up and there he was, laughing and tickling his daughter under her chin. "How can that be a bad guy?" Croce said to his wife. "You can't be a thug with that smile!"

It was a smile that Iverson displayed on the court, but rarely showed the press. On this day, however, after the dispersal of the media pack with their predictable questions ("What do you have to do in tomorrow night's game?" "What were you thinking when you hit that shot?"), Iverson's eyes widened as though he'd just seen a sliver of an opening in the lane. His mouth expanded into the grin that so captivated Croce. He was asked about his kids.

"Deuce had a stomach flu," he said, explaining a recent *excused* practice. Iverson stayed home to help Tawanna nurse him back to health. "Now, Tiaura, all she wants to do is go to Chuck E. Cheese all the damn time. There be a whole lotta noise in my house. All these kids do is run around and tear up the house. Man, Tiaura, I don't even have to say nothing to her, I just give her a look and she knows: 'I better calm my ass down.'"

After games, Iverson seemed to take refuge from the press pack in his kids. Indeed, as more and more scrutiny rained down upon him, he had

Twirling daughter Tiaura in the air in July 2002.

turned increasingly to children, his and others. Kids don't heckle or boo or judge, after all, and his face would light up—as Croce noted—any time he'd wade into a crowd of them. Onetime boy-wonder soprano Bejun Mehta wrote in his essay *A Process of Prodigy* that his "childhood relationship" to his own voice had been "taken over by the opinions and expectations of the adult world"; like Mehta, Iverson was learning that the purity of his gift had been compromised by the chattering negativism of adults. But then he'd step onto the court and all the blather from the pundits and reporters and nervous coaches would fade away. He'd hear the kids. And he'd perform for them.

Even during the heyday of the rivalry, it was never like this. Back in the day, when Magic and Kareem would lead the Lakers into the old Spectrum, where Doc and Moses and Andrew Toney lay in wait, there had never been twenty-thousand-plus maniacal fans drowning out the PA announcer. Especially for a regular-season game.

Shaq and Kobe and all-star Glen Rice led the Lakers into Philly in late March to face the league's leading scorer, Iverson. Two days earlier, Sixers newcomer Tyrone Hill was surprised to hear Iverson on the team plane bemoaning an ensuing off day. "I wish we could play the Lakers right now," he'd said.

"Relax," the veteran Hill had said. "The game will come soon enough."

Come game time, there was a play-off-like buzz in the air. It was a triumphant return home for Bryant, whose parents were in the stands. He'd become a star in his own right, despite ongoing chemistry problems with Shaq, who dubbed Bryant "Showboat" and who felt the young star cared more about stardom than winning.

The Lakers had championship aspirations under coach Kurt Rambis. But the team was in some disarray: Dennis Rodman, whom they'd picked up as a free agent to bolster their rebounding, had bolted for an unspecified leave of absence. Something about trouble in his marriage to actress Carmen Electra. Still, with Shaq, Bryant, and the deadly outside eye of Rice, the Lakers were considered to be among the league's elite.

The game began as a showdown between Bryant and Iverson. Iverson missed 6 of his first 10 shots, while Bryant hit 4 of his first 7. But their one-on-one game within the game didn't bode well for the Lakers. His teammates stood around while Bryant time and again dribbled twenty feet away from the basket, before pulling up for jumpshots. At the other end, Iverson ran Bryant through screen after screen off the ball and was getting his shots in the flow of the Sixers' offense; Geiger or newcomer Hill would pop out to the top of the foul line and find Iverson open behind a double or triple screen. In the second quarter, he started to hit the open shots. And once Iverson's outside game was cooking, there was no stopping him. Bryant had to fight through the screens to get on him before another jumper could be launched; that meant Iverson could use the decoy of his sizzling outside shot to blow by Bryant and get to the hoop, where he'd draw Shaq to him and either loft a high, feathery scoop shot over the behemoth or lay the ball off to either Geiger (who would finish with 8 points, 8 rebounds) or Hill (11 and 10).

When McKie stripped Rice at midcourt and slammed home a fast-break dunk with 2:33 left and the Sixers ahead by double figures, Rambis called a time-out and the arena erupted in deafening cheers. Iverson chest-thumped McKie and skipped to the baseline adjacent to his team's bench, cupping his left hand to his left ear and looking pleadingly at the crowd, *his* crowd. The roar dutifully grew louder.

It was becoming something of a habit at key moments, this singular interplay between Iverson and the crowd. Other players at similar junctures during a game mugged for the TV cameras on the baseline; their celebration was about *them*. Iverson always peered over the cameras and appealed to the fans, suggesting, in effect, that every die-hard sports fan's fantasy is true, that he or she *is* integral to the game. Unlike Bryant, a cool craftsman who had brought former Sixers strength-and-conditioning coach Joe Carbone out to Los Angeles to work him out *after* grueling practices, Iverson's game was all inspiration. And his playing to the crowd was a tacit acknowledgment of a symbiosis between him and his fans.

Coming out of the final time-out, Iverson snuck a peek at the scoreboard and saw that he had 41 points. Uh-oh, he thought. I hope this isn't going to backfire on me. Ever since his rookie season, when he'd scored 40 or more points in five straight losing games, he'd been aware of his team's record when he scored 40 or more points. It now stood at 0–7. When the final buzzer sounded, and he'd led his team to a 15-point win with 41 points, 10 assists, 5 rebounds—one more than Shaq—and 2 steals, Iverson shouted heavenward, "Get that monkey off my back!"

The Sixers soon went to Miami, where they stunned Pat Riley's Heat,

88–84, behind Iverson and Geiger, who had become the team's second-leading scorer at 13 points per game. But, this being Larry and Allen's Sixers, the good times couldn't last too long. In the Lakers game, Iverson had suffered a bruised right quadriceps on a drive to the basket that ended up as a collision between his thigh and the solid steel of Shaq. When the Cleveland Cavaliers came to visit the Sixers, Iverson felt he was at 75 percent. He could play, but long periods of inactivity caused his body to stiffen up.

Against the Cavaliers, the Sixers came out sluggish. When Iverson missed badly on a three-pointer to close out the first quarter, Brown pulled him. Iverson mumbled his displeasure, but took a seat on the bench. With nine minutes, fifty-seven seconds remaining in the half, Brown called for Iverson to reenter the game. Iverson got up and, walking past his coach, was heard to say, "About fuckin' time."

Brown immediately called him back to the bench, where he sat, grim-faced. During time-outs, he only joined the team's huddle at the urging of teammates Geiger and Rick Mahorn, whom Brown had added to the roster to be a stabilizing force on Iverson. Iverson talked of getting dressed and going home, but his teammates persuaded him to stay.

He never reentered the game. Afterward, he told his coaches he wouldn't play again until he was 100 percent; some wondered if his sudden switch—before the game, he'd said he'd never take himself out of the lineup because "my team needs me"—was really motivated by a petulant urge to stick it to Brown. For his part, Brown kicked Royster out of the locker room after the game and exhibited uncommon testiness when questioned by Comcast SportsNet's Michael Barkann during Brown's postgame press conference.

"I'm not going to comment," Brown said tersely. "He said he was hurt, so he didn't play."

Barkann tried to follow up. "There's no need to follow up," Brown snapped. "I made the answer, all right?"

Barkann tried again. "Hey, hey, I'm the coach, all right?" Brown fumed. "I have the right to play a guy and not play a guy, all right . . . Hold it! Hold it! I ask a guy to go into the game, they go in the game. I ask them to go out, they go out. That's the way I coach."

Clearly, the rift between Brown and Iverson was wider than ever. Rather than seeing Iverson's disrespect for him as an utterance in the heat of battle, born of his star's desire to play, Brown saw it as a challenge to his authority. And given that it wasn't the first time that Iverson—among the league leaders in minutes played—had cursed at his coach about playing time in front of the team, who could blame him?

The coach and player would emerge from a twenty-minute meeting within the coming days, and they'd make nice for the cameras. "If y'all think that Larry Brown and myself are not going to have any altercations, I mean, that's just crazy," Iverson said.

In the aftermath of the controversy, none other than Charles Barkley weighed in with some incendiary comments about Iverson in *Sports Illustrated.* "I can't stand that guy," Barkley said. "He has a responsibility to cut the crap and not have some drama with the coach every week. He's showing no respect to anyone, least of all the game."

In true hip-hop form—you dis me, I dis you—Iverson responded by going nuclear. "He's nobody, man," he fulminated. "Why am I on his mind so much? Why is he thinking about me? What has he done to criticize somebody like that? He hasn't done anything but throw [somebody] through windows, spit on little kids. You can't say that about me. You can talk about my game all you want, but I've never spit on a kid. I can't understand why he tries to dog me out like that. I can't stand him, either. How many times has he been to the Finals? One time. Tell him to think about that. Think about that before you start criticizing."

Despite all the media attention and controversy—or, maybe, given both Iverson's and Brown's lifetime embrace of tumult, because of it—the Sixers were in the thick of the play-off hunt. The regular season ended with a thrilling home win over Detroit. The Pistons led, 93–89, with twenty seconds left when the Pistons' Stackhouse blew a kiss good-bye to the sellout Philly crowd that had heckled him all night. Snow, who had come into his own by now as a point guard, scored on a drive to the hoop. Then McKie stripped Stackhouse at midcourt—much to the fans' delight—and Iverson found himself with the ball on the baseline, some fifteen feet from the basket, as the clock wound down. Running at him was six-foot eleven-inch Christian Laettner. A seldom-talked-about facet of Iverson's game, overshadowed by his leaping and quickness, is his sense of spatial dimensions; when he challenges giants, he has a knack for knowing just how much of a looping arc to use in the shot. So it was here, with Laettner rushing him, arms outstretched. The jumper seemed to go straight up, a rainbow. It fell through the net, forcing overtime and a deafening chant of "MVP! MVP! MVP!" from the crowd.

When the five-minute overtime period ended with a win, the Sixers were the play-offs' sixth seed with a 28–22 record. A jubilant Iverson spontaneously grabbed the courtside microphone from the hands of the arena's public-address announcer.

"We need the kind of enthusiasm you guys showed now all through the play-offs," he barked. "We're gonna play hard because we owe this to you!"

Philadelphia was starved for a winner, but not just any kind of winner. Some winners of the city's past, though celebrated, failed to capture the imagination of the gritty, working-class town. Much had been made of the Philadelphia fans over the years, how they'd booed Santa Claus and came down hard—harder than any other city would—on superstars ranging from Dick Allen and Wilt Chamberlain to Mike Schmidt and Randall Cunningham.

It was all true. Traumatized by years of disappointment, the Philadelphia fans were well schooled in self-protection, wary of falling in love again. But once they fell, they fell hard. The dawning of the 1999 NBA play-offs marked the beginning of a tempestuous love affair.

It made sense that the fans would be smitten by this team, for like the town itself, it embodied grit and hustle. Philadelphia had long been a sucker for hustle, for guys like Pete Rose, Larry Bowa, and hockey's Bobby Clarke—lesser talents who overcame odds by virtue of work ethic and competitive fire. More than any other recent superstar in Philadelphia history, Iverson was beloved because, like the overachievers, he didn't come with any glitz. He excelled through heart, hustle, *and* talent.

Similarly, this Sixers team, having allowed opponents just 87.6 points per game, won thanks to a scrambling, frenetic defense and a marked selflessness. Gone were the days when Iverson's teammates would complain about his league-leading number of shots and minutes played, or the fact that, at 41 percent, he had the lowest shooting percentage of any NBA-leading scorer (26.8 points per game) since 1958. It was part of Brown's master plan to surround Iverson with players who, as he put it, "allow Allen to be Allen." Now that the team was winning, Brown was not only tolerant, but encouraging, of Allen being Allen.

The play-offs opened with the Sixers splitting the first two games in Orlando against Chuck Daly's Magic. In preparation for the series return to Philly, Pat Croce stoked the fires of the local faithful by shaving his head—and offering to shave fans' domes before game three. At game time, a sea of bald heads led the roar when the *Rocky* theme blared out and, on the arena-vision, an animated Rocky decked a reeling Mickey Mouse time and again with a left hook.

Sitting courtside was Philadelphia native Will Smith, the actor and rapper. "This is almost like a concert," he told the *Daily News*. "Allen Iverson is basketball's rock star."

And the star didn't disappoint. He scored 33 points and set a play-off record with 10 steals. As impressive as the points were, the steals spoke to the hustle he and the Sixers had come to embody. The only time the ear-numbing cheers for Iverson were surpassed was when, after a call, Daly grabbed the ball while complaining to the ref; ready to inbound, Geiger reached over and ripped the ball from the Magic coach. The Magic were done. The Sixers romped in game four to move on to the next round. Julius Erving, now a vice president with the Magic, was quoted criticizing Iverson—calling him, ironically, "playground"—but not even Erving's old-school lamentations could dull the moment for Iverson.

Next up for the Sixers was Brown's old team, the Pacers, led by Reggie Miller. The Pacers' experience showed against the Sixers, who fell in four straight. As game four ended, along with his season, Iverson took solace in the affectionate applause from the home crowd. His third NBA season was complete. And he was finally a winner.

chapter | 10

THE PANTHER

this used to be a grim reaper holding a basketball, but i
had it changed to a panther after my friends teased me and
told me it looked like a damned flying monkey.

The secret was out. Allen Iverson had been a novelty act during the Sixers' eight-game play-off run the previous spring. After all, until the play-offs, the Sixers hadn't played a single nationally televised game on NBC all season long. Most basketball fans across the country had long been exposed to the *idea* of Iverson before seeing his game; they'd either first heard of him when he was a playground legend in jail, or when he was running amok in John Thompson's once tightly controlled system, or when, these last few years, he was presented as a corn-rowed, bejeweled, tattooed threat to all that was Jordan. But all that would soon change. As the 1999–2000 season loomed, it was announced that his team would play eleven times on NBC. Moreover, just before training camp, he would make his national television-interview debut.

"I can curse, right, this is cable?" he asked upon first sitting down with Chris Rock, taping a segment for the comedian's HBO show before a live studio audience.

The eight-minute conversation could have served as a snapshot of the new NBA. Rock's audience ate up Iverson's laid-back candor, his mix of shyness and bravado. Rock joked about Iverson's friends—"I seen them in the green room, and *I* was scared," Rock said—before asking if Iverson hung with any white people. The guest paused, then smiled sheepishly. "Yeah. I mean, my lawyers."

The crowd roared. Rock then proceeded to list the hoops stars who were branching out into movies and rap CDs, before turning to his guest. "So, how you gonna embarrass yourself?" he asked.

Iverson laughed. "I don't look at it like that, man," he said. "I look at it like, the sky's the limit."

Walking off, Iverson was met with thunderous applause. For him, it was confirmation of all that Gaskins, among others, had been saying all along: that while he might be seen as a threat in the retro, corporate world of the NBA, there was a sizable audience out there who would identify with and embrace him for who he really was and what he represented.

Inside the world of the NBA, meanwhile, he continued to encounter difficulty. The Sixers got off to a desultory 0–3 start, all road games, with Allen shooting a paltry 33 percent from the floor. In the home opener, however, he busted out by scoring 37 points in a win over Seattle. In the next game, Iverson scorched the Magic for 46 en route to a 110–105 victory.

Afterward, Iverson found himself once again in the headlines for issues that had nothing to do with his game. Brown, it turns out, had consulted with McKie, Snow, and George Lynch and instituted a team dress policy. Brown was known throughout the league for his impeccably tailored suits. Now his players would have to wear suits or sport coats on road trips. Iverson wasn't having it. "If they take my money, so be it," he said nonchalantly. "I'm going to wear what I want to wear."

The season had just started and already Brown and Iverson were talking past each other. Brown, for his part, had come to appreciate fine clothes years before. Though he had grown up wearing his cousin's hand-me-downs, the cousin happened to be a stylish dresser, so Brown always had neatly fitted blazers and suits. At the University of North Carolina, he played his freshman year for legendary coach Frank McGuire, one of the sport's most debonair of dressers. "Coach McGuire could walk into a room with a thousand people and he'd be the only one you'd notice," Brown recalls today. McGuire used to tell Brown, "It's unfortunate, but people get a feeling for who you are by the way you present yourself."

When Dean Smith took over, there was no drop-off in the emphasis on style. After graduation, Brown was an assistant coach. "We had to wear a tie and jacket every day," he says. "There might be a prospect who showed up that day with his family and Coach Smith wanted them to understand what we were about."

For Brown, the fact that his team would be on national TV so much this season *meant* something. It was time to make an impression. For Iverson, all this talk about wearing suits meant that people—white, middle-aged people—were trying to change him. It wasn't that how he dressed was unimportant to him; on the contrary, his style choices had always been very consciously thought out. The image he projected was how he expressed himself; for someone to dictate how he dressed was, to him, tantamount to being denied the right to speak. To Iverson, the low-hanging jeans, the Timberlands, and the billowy, untucked designer shirts spoke of, and to, the generation that spawned him. He'd seen the photos of Larry Brown back in his ABA days, with the hilariously wide bell-bottoms and paisley shirts. Brown had once been of his time, too.

Ultimately, the dress code was never enforced, especially after Brown said he didn't care what his players wore "as long as they're neat and clean." That settled it; Iverson always dressed "neat and clean," even if he dressed differently from Brown. But the episode left Iverson feeling sour. Why couldn't people let him be himself?

Even the NBA seemed determined to change him. When the holiday issue of the league's *Hoop* magazine came out with him on its cover, Iverson was aghast to see that league officials had airbrushed off his tattoos and diamond earring. He was outraged. "It's like a slap in the face," he said. "Don't put me on your damned magazine if you don't want me as I am. Those tattoos are part of me, they mean something to me. What gives them the right to change me?"

The NBA apologized. Croce, who sports a couple of tattoos himself, thought that, once again, Iverson had prodded the system into having an open mind. "Maybe now people will realize that tattoos are not a threat to the game or the world as we know it," he said.

In December, Iverson broke his shooting hand's thumb against the San Antonio Spurs and was sidelined for three weeks. (The injury happened early in the game; he not only played with the break, he finished with 35 points.) Meantime, trade rumors circulated around Larry Hughes. Hughes was talented, but Brown was having a hard time finding him minutes now that Iverson was playing almost exclusively at the shooting-guard position—Hughes's natural spot. Plus, Hughes was moping about his diminished playing time—a no-no in Brown's universe. Concern over one's own minutes meant that individual issues were being placed before the team.

While Iverson was sidelined, the Houston Rockets came to town for Barkley's final visit to Philadelphia. He'd announced that this would be his last year in the NBA, even though he remained a good—though not great—player. Still fuming over Barkley's public criticisms of him the last few years, Iverson called in sick, saying he had the flu. That, in and of itself, wouldn't have merited headlines. But when he was spotted eating at TGI Friday's during the game, his no-show was taken as a huge dis of the onetime Sixer great.

Iverson soon returned to play. In his absence, the team had gone 6–4. After his return, they went 2–2, with Iverson connecting on just 38.8 percent of his shots. But then, as Christmas approached, he lit up Toronto for 37, and it looked like the rest of the season would be clear sailing. But this was the Larry and Allen psychodrama. All would cease to be harmonious on one Saturday night in Detroit.

At 11 P.M. on the Saturday before Christmas, Pat Croce's phone rang. It was his brother, John, the Sixers strength-and-conditioning coach. The team had just lost at Detroit and there was something about John's voice that prompted in Croce a sudden, sinking feeling.

"I'm on the bus with the team, Pat," John said. "Coach told me to call you. He wants Allen traded, Pat—now. He wants him traded now."

In the first half, the starters were sluggish and uninspired. They fell behind Detroit by 23 points. At halftime, Brown told the team, "If we don't start off showing some emotion, I'm going to play the second group." After four minutes of the second half, Brown pulled his starters: Iverson, Snow, Hill, Lynch, and Ratliff. Snow, Ratliff, and Iverson, who had 19 points at the time, did not return. The reserves whittled the Pistons' lead down to 7 before the Sixers lost, 104–91.

After the game, with Brown standing maybe ten feet away, Iverson waited until the media surrounded him—and then he vented, demanding a trade. "For some reason, my style doesn't fit this team anymore," he fulminated. "Something needs to happen. Something's got to give. If I'm hurting this team, I need to get out of here. I don't like what is going on. When I get back to Philly, I'll let that be known. I've never been done like that ever in my career."

The next day, Croce tracked down both coach and player. Neither had calmed down. During the afternoon, Iverson was at Dave & Buster's, a family restaurant and arcade, for Tiaura's birthday party. He went into the men's room to talk to Croce on his cell phone. "How can I be so disrespected?" Iverson shouted. "I'm a starter. I'm the only fucking all-star in the league who has to put up with this shit. I done everything for this fucking team and this is what I get?"

When Croce got Brown on the phone, the volume was turned down, but the hurt was palpable. "I'm not coaching him ever again," Brown said. "Get rid of him."

Croce told Brown what he'd told Iverson. "I hear you, it's not right for both of you," he said. "So, okay, we'll make it right. We'll have a meeting tomorrow morning."

Iverson agreed. Brown, however, refused. "I'm not coming," he said. "I'm not coaching him again."

For the first and only time as president of the Philadelphia 76ers,

Croce pulled rank on his highly sensitive coach. "I'm the boss," he said. "And you *will* be at that meeting."

Croce went to bed that night thinking that his franchise was blowing up. He needed both men; one without the other did him no good. After a fitful night, he decided to go for broke. If he got both men in the same room—and there was no guarantee Brown would show—he would mediate by instigation. He would pick at every grudge both men had zealously guarded and nurtured the past three years. He would orchestrate one of two endings: a catharsis or a mushroom cloud.

The next day, the Sixers were to host the Pistons in the second of a home-and-away series. Croce arrived early to the game-day shoot-around at the practice facility. Croce, Brown, Billy King, and assistant coach Randy Ayers were chatting in the conference room, just off the basketball floor. The door flew open and Iverson came storming in, the veins in his neck bulging. "I am fucking fed up with this shit!" he yelled, pacing.

"How about if we talk about this after shoot-around?" Croce said.

Iverson stopped and looked at him as if Croce had just been dropped onto the planet. "I ain't practicing, man."

They'd talk about it now, then. Brown and Iverson sat down across from each other, both leaning back with their arms folded over their chests. Croce had hoped to set the meeting's agenda, but Iverson wasn't done venting. He started ranting about all the past slights Brown had inflicted upon him, about how he was the only star in the league never to be consulted on personnel moves, about how Brown talks about family and then runs his mouth off in the media about family business. As Iverson ranted, he grew more and more incensed and stood up over Brown, shouting down at him, his fingers jabbing at the air. Finally, he paused.

"Are you through?" Brown asked calmly.

"Do I ask you if you're through when you're talking to me?" Iverson shot back, taking his seat.

Croce began as he'd planned to do earlier, by stating the crux of the problem: "Each of you perceives the other one as disrespecting you," he said. "Coach, I don't know if you realize it, but Allen's never been pulled from a game. To him, pulling him like that was an act of public disrespect. But, Allen, Larry feels you disrespect him when you come off the court and you 'motherfuck' him all the time. You say it right to his face in front of the fans and the team. When he's just trying to win the game."

There was a pause. Croce wasn't about to let silence fill the air—because who knows what crazy thoughts either man could bring to the surface? "You know, you both might as well just stand up and look in the mirror— both of you!" he said. "Because the reason we're in this situation right now is because you're both so similar. Not dissimilar. Similar. Headstrong and sensitive and talented and set in your ways. Take a good look at each other."

Another pause.

"There's a communication gap here," Croce continued. "Coach, Allen has told me this. He thinks you treat him like those white guards did when he was in prison—'sit over there, nigger, and don't move.'"

Brown had no visible reaction, but inside, he was stunned. Neither Croce nor Iverson knew it, but Brown had grown up idolizing Jackie Robinson, and not just for his athletic ability. Robinson stood for the triumph of merit, fairness, and racial parity. Brown had grown up a true liberal, someone who basked in his own color blindness. He often spoke movingly about how "our league" provides opportunity to young black men like his own Billy King, whom he had long mentored. Brown never imagined that anyone might interpret the way he communicated as somehow racially insensitive. But then he thought about it, how so many kids just like Allen had had little or no experience with a white authority figure. "Why *would* they have any trust?" Brown would later say, giving voice to the thoughts he entertained that day. "Because a lot of times in their life, no white person has ever shown them any respect at all."

Croce stuck to his plan: every time a sore seemed ready to heal, he'd rip the scab right off. "And, Allen," he said, "I don't think Coach likes you."

Now Brown had to speak.

"It's not about liking," he said. "It's about being a part of a team." Brown went on to reiterate his team-first philosophy, how, in his view, the minute one individual gets preferential treatment, a team becomes a loose collection of individuals. It wasn't about Allen and Larry, in his view; it was about Allen and a team. Brown came from a certain tradition, he explained; from coaches like Henry Iba, Frank McGuire, and Dean Smith he learned that if you were part of a team, you respected your teammates by showing up and being on time.

Nothing between him and Allen, Brown said, had ever been personal. And then he spoke from the heart, about his personal relationship with Allen. He talked about how, no matter the issues separating them, any-

May 2001: The MVP and his coach, Larry Brown.

time Allen walked out of the locker room and saw Brown's wife and kids, he'd always, in Brown's words, "treat them positively." Not everybody does that, the coach noted. He'd had players whose wives, if their husbands weren't playing, would have nothing to do with him or his family. On a personal level, Brown said, he knew what Allen was about—because he'd seen the player interact with his kids. Maybe Croce was right, maybe what divided them was their similarities, not their differences.

"Allen is a lot like me," Brown would later reflect. "Sometimes things happen right away and you react and don't have time to think about it. And when we do have time to think about it, we realize things could have been handled a different way."

Now it was Iverson's turn to unburden himself. By now, both men were leaning forward, engaging each other—calmly. Just as Croce's comment about race had touched Brown somewhere deep, so was Iverson moved to let his defenses down after hearing Brown.

"There are times when I'm listening to you and I can tell you're looking at me, thinking I ain't listening," Iverson said. "That's just the look on my face. My face is just my face. But I'm hearing you. You think I'm like, 'Man, get outta my face,' but I'm really right there with you." And then Iverson said the thing that would cement his relationship with his coach for a long time to come. "All I've wanted," he said, "is to have a relationship with my coach like Magic had with Pat Riley and Michael had with Phil Jackson. That's all I've ever wanted."

Croce erupted. "That is an arrow into the heart—dipped in honey!" he exclaimed, and—for the first time on a very tense morning—laughter filled the air.

More talk ensued. Billy King spoke of his relationship with his college coach, Mike Krzyzewski, about how, now, he looked back on things his coach said and did and realized that the coach only got on him so much because he cared so much. If a coach isn't pushing you, King said, it means he doesn't care about you.

Finally, Croce said, "Let's shake hands and get back to winning games." Iverson got up and walked around the table to shake his coach's hand.

Afterward, Iverson would say the meeting began as an "alley fight" and became "the most real talk we've ever had." Brown felt good as well, save for the fact that he had to be in the room in the first place. That afternoon, Croce received a call from his coach at home. "How dare you take sides." Brown said.

"Coach, it was a great meeting," Croce said. "I didn't take sides. I mediated." He apologized to Brown if Brown felt he'd been unfair. "No one ever teaches you how to handle these situations," he said.

As they had done so many times before, Brown and Iverson followed up on their turmoil with a pressure-packed on-court triumph. It was as though each man, on some level, created their soap operas in order to script a dramatic ending.

On this night against the Pistons, Iverson was everywhere. He scored 32 points to take the game into overtime. With time in the extra session ticking down, the Pistons held a 121–120 lead. Iverson drew the defense to him and found Snow wide open on the right baseline. Snow's jumper left his hand as the buzzer sounded; it swished through the net, the fans went wild, and Iverson leaped into Snow's arms while Brown ran from the sideline to embrace both of them. In the ultimate homage to Brown, Iverson had played a consummate team game, trusting an open teammate with the game's outcome on the line. Returning the respect, a smiling Larry Brown entered his postgame conference and said, "After all the junk, I would have liked to see Allen make the last shot."

It wasn't official yet, but it was in the air. Iverson knew it. Despite his being the league's scoring champ, the leading vote getter among Eastern guards for the all-star game and a first-team all-NBA player the year before, rumor had it he would not be named to the U.S. Men's Olympic Basketball team for the games in Sydney, Australia.

If the rumor was true, odds were that the Bucks' Ray Allen would fill the last available roster spot. Unfortunately for Ray, his team's schedule brought him to Philadelphia to face Iverson and the Sixers on the eve of the announcement that he'd beaten Iverson out for the spot.

It is said that, after he was cut from his high-school basketball team, Michael Jordan became expert at turning perceived slights into motivation. It was as though, from then on, every opponent, in Jordan's mind, wore the face of that high-school coach who so misjudged him. He always needed someone to stick it to. So it was with Iverson. Often, that foil would be Brown; he'd take to the court determined to show his nagging, doubting coach what a warrior he was. But just as often, it could be anything, something seemingly innocuous that Iverson seized on and used as fuel. It was a personality trait common among kids from ghetto upbringings who managed to succeed, who come from a hardscrabble world where nothing good ever just "happens," but must instead be fought for. Seen this way, to Iverson, excellence could only be achieved by way of conflict, by proving someone wrong. The subtext, of course, was race; in "showing them," a ghetto-born overachiever not only shows up whoever conveyed today's real or imagined insult, but everyone who ever doubted him.

Few close to Iverson doubt that when he lit up Ray Allen's Bucks for 45 points in early January, he wanted to show the Olympic committee—which included the 76ers' newly appointed general manager, Billy King—what a mistake they'd made. It wasn't just that Iverson scored at will. He also scored big baskets, late in a close game, to win it.

In the days that followed, the official Olympic announcement was made and the media crowded around Iverson's locker, asking why he thought he hadn't made the team. And why someone like Ray Allen—who had been chosen to do public-service announcements for the Thurgood Marshall Fund—did make it. "I knew I wasn't going to be on that team," Iverson said. "With the question you're asking, you want me to tell you the reason you already know, and I'm not going to do that. Everybody knows. It's no big deal."

Someone asked, would it bother him if his past were held against him? "People are going to do that," he said. "It's not right, but it's something I kind of understand, that people would kind of be scared. After the things I've been through, I can't blame people if they say, 'Maybe he's not the right guy,' but when they talk about basketball, I'm the right guy. Simple as that."

Not surprisingly, Iverson went on a tear after the snub. He scored a career-high 50 points on 40 shots in a win over the Sacramento Kings and their exciting point guard, Jason Williams. (The hype surrounding Williams, a white player with streetball flair, was indicative of just how thirsty the NBA was for a Great White Hope; the fact was, Williams, especially compared with the likes of Iverson, wasn't quite the genuine article—clichéd comparisons to "Pistol" Pete Maravich notwithstanding.)

At the all-star break, the Sixers were 27–23, and Iverson made his all-star debut in San Francisco. That weekend, he gave Arnie Steele $80,000 to throw an all-star bash in his name. Then he went out and totaled 26 points and 9 assists, and would have been named the game's MVP had the East prevailed.

In February, the Sixers finally dealt Larry Hughes, getting Toni Kukoc from the Bulls in return. Finally, it appeared Iverson would be paired with another legitimate scoring threat, someone defenses would have to double-team. At the press conference to announce Kukoc's arrival, Iverson showed up, all smiles.

But with twenty-two games left in the season, all smiles dissipated. With a record of 34–26, the Sixers were to play at division-leading Miami, whom they trailed in the standings by two and a half games. Croce, who has a vacation home in Florida, came to the game with his bags packed. He'd fly back with the team. When he entered the locker room, he was met by a pale, irritated Brown.

"Go talk to your kid," Brown said, motioning toward the trainer's room.

"What's the matter?" Croce asked.

"Just go talk to him."

Croce looked to King for help. "Allen missed shoot-around this morning," King said.

Here we go again, Croce thought. Iverson had been out late in the Miami clubs the night before. He had a headache in the morning and called Sixers trainer Len Currier to say he'd be staying in his room. By now, Croce was realizing that one of Brown's coaching tenets was to keep his distance from negative confrontations. So he confronted Iverson. "Bubba, you can't do this," Croce said to him. "I'm going to discipline you." Iverson was suspended for the game; Croce hurriedly got Ann on the phone so she'd hear the news first from him. "Ann, what can I say?" he said. "Bubba fucked up."

Just as back in high school, when Mike Bailey made sure to get Ann on board when he punished Allen, Ann was fully supportive. "I know you care about my baby, Pat," she said.

Of course, Iverson was unrepentant. "You think I'm going to come to Miami and not go out? I go out if I want to," he told reporters that night. "But don't question my heart. Don't question my health. I don't think this was fair at all."

Late in the season, Brown's contract was extended. He would now be the coach for the next five years, at roughly $6 million per year. Iverson, ever brittle but always resilient, played the last weeks of the season with a broken big toe on his left foot, but it didn't stop him from scoring 28.4

points per game, second in the league. The Sixers won fifteen of their final twenty-two games to finish 49–33. They'd face Charlotte—and Derrick Coleman—in the first round of the play-offs.

I t was a locker room full of dropped jaws.

"I can't even begin to figure out where it comes from," said Aaron McKie, shaking his head slowly.

Dressing in front of a nearby locker, Matt Geiger offered his own theory. "It comes from God, that's where," he said.

They were talking about the performance just turned in by their superstar teammate in game one of the play-off series at Charlotte. The Hornets had come into the game as the hottest team in the league, winners of fourteen of their last sixteen games. But then they ran into Iverson. On this night, he scored 40 of his team's 92 points, hitting 13 of 25 shots. The basket, he would claim, "looked like an ocean" all night long.

The evening could be summed up in one stunning sequence. In the third quarter, Iverson stole the ball and raced up the court. It's a cardinal rule in basketball that you don't leave your feet with the ball without knowing precisely what you're going to do. It's a rule Iverson routinely ignores. For that is precisely when his creative inspirations hit, when he commits to a course of action while all is still possibility. On this play, he darted full speed into the lane with Charlotte's David Wesley squarely in front of him, and elevated while looking back, over his left shoulder, for a trailing teammate to pass to; Wesley, reading Iverson's eyes, lurched that way. But there was no one there; seeing no one, Iverson seemed to lengthen his stay in the air while completely turning, a floating, soaring, 360-degree spin, followed by an eight-foot bank shot on his way down, the ball released just before his feet regained contact with the floor. Those in the arena were confused; it happened so quickly—that couldn't have been legal, right? Instant replays showed that, indeed, it was. It was a move that couldn't be planned, let alone explained.

"It comes from within him," Tyrone Hill opined after the game.

For his part, Iverson had no answers for his zone-like performance, although in front of his locker after the game, he may have inadvertently provided one. While his teammates were jubilant, he was venting about comments Billy King had made in that morning's Charlotte newspaper. King had been asked if the marriage between Iverson and the Sixers could last, and he responded, "I want to think it can. But I think a lot of soul-searching has to take place by everyone."

Iverson had read the comments earlier and had been stewing all day. "If I can hear my general manager say that he doesn't know if the marriage is going to work in the paper to some reporter, it's time to stop feeling that way," he said. "I don't feel like they treat me like a franchise player. I'm treated nowhere near like a franchise player. I'm treated like the twelfth guy on the bench."

What had so wounded Iverson? On the face of it, King's comments were hardly incendiary. (King would nonetheless apologize.) Some saw Iverson's reaction as yet more evidence of a hair-trigger oversensitivity; others claimed he was astutely reading between the lines, sensing that the brass of his team—despite all the lovey-dovey bromides coming out of the December dustup—just might give up on him this off-season. Both views were onto something. Iverson, so skittish by now about trusting male authority figures, may have had reason to suspect Brown's motives where he was concerned, but he most certainly was also inventing a slight, which related to a third possibility. Was it possible that he was looking to invent hard feelings on the morning of the game in order to do what he did on the court?

As the series unfolded, Coleman played solidly, but didn't haunt his old team. In fact, Philadelphia sports-radio personality Angelo Cataldi riled up Philly fans before game three by having hundreds of doughnuts delivered to the hotel room of the power forward, whose weight had long fluctuated. The Sixers would go on to eliminate the Hornets in four games, despite the fact that Snow and Iverson were both nursing ankle injuries. With Snow out and Iverson hobbled by a chipped bone in his left ankle, McKie and Geiger stepped up, though Iverson admonished the hometown fans for having turned on the oft-injured Geiger recently by booing him. "That doesn't help a guy's confidence," he'd said.

Next up for the Sixers was a rematch with the Indiana Pacers. Though the Pacers were the higher seed, they were virtually the same team that had eliminated Philadelphia the year before. This year, the Sixers' youth would be buttressed by the experience gained from last year's play-offs. Besides, the Sixers were out for revenge.

Nonetheless, the Pacers won the first two in Indiana and then stunned Philly with a 97–89 win on the Sixers' home court. The Pacers' Jalen Rose, who had butted heads with Brown when he was in Indiana, was unstoppable. No team had ever come back from a three-games-to-none play-off deficit before.

After game three, the Pacers had written AND NOW . . . THEY SLEEP, R.I.P. on the chalkboard inside the visiting team's locker room. Iverson vowed that the series wasn't over, and the Sixers won games four and five, setting up a pivotal game six in Philly.

The day before the game, local sports-talk radio personality Rhea Hughes checked her usual bevy of E-mail messages from the Philadelphia less-than-faithful. One was from a retired math teacher who called himself a "Philadelphia sports hater for years." She was about to hit the delete button when the writer began questioning Iverson's intelligence, and just how he had gotten into Georgetown. Something about the E-mail's harsh tone made Hughes keep reading. Then the writer named Iverson's daughter. Then, in the most chilling language Hughes says she's ever read, he threatened to take Tiaura from Iverson, chop her up, and return her to the star in a box.

Hughes forwarded the E-mail to Sixers vice president Dave Coskey, who immediately contacted the police and the FBI. (An arrest would later be made.) Iverson was used to stalkers, even to threats. There was, for instance, the woman who had moved to Philadelphia from Los Angeles because she thought she had become his girlfriend after he'd politely said hello to her in a restaurant. But this was something different. Earlier in the season, discussing his "Fear No One" tattoo, Iverson had said that the only thing he feared was "something happening to my family, to my kids." So it was no surprise when he showed up late for game six, wearing green fatigues. He was in the bunker, embattled.

Iverson and his team played their hearts out, but lost game six, 106–90. Late in the game, he came to the bench, draped a towel over his head, and broke down, crying. His mother raced to the bench and embraced him from behind. When the final buzzer sounded, Ann accompanied her baby into the trainer's room. It had been a draining, emotional season, yet much of the melodrama would have been worth it had he led his team past Indiana. Now it had been topped off with the threats against his daughter. And his team had lost. Again. It all just spilled out. Iverson sat on a training table, his face nestled in the crook of his mother's neck, and he sobbed while Ann held him and soothingly rubbed his back. Her comforting presence might have suggested things would get better. And they would.

But first they'd get worse.

Only The

Strong

chapter 11

THE ANSWER

This was my first tattoo, when I was nineteen. I went straight to the tattoo parlor from the park to get THE ANSWER the day the guys gave me the nickname.

Almost as soon as the season ended, Larry Brown went on the offensive. Iverson had gone back to Virginia, taking a room at the Radisson Hotel in Hampton when he wasn't crashing at Uncle Stevie's house or pulling all-nighters in a recording studio with Cru Thik, where he was putting the finishing touches on a hard-core rap CD to be distributed by Universal Records.

Meantime, Brown surprised many by drafting tiny point guard Craig "Speedy" Claxton in the first round of the NBA draft, saying, "Maybe Allen's got to learn to share some time with other people." The comment was aired nationally, as were a series of other thinly veiled threats. Fed up with being asked about his relationship with Iverson—and still smarting over Croce's insistence that he sit down, face-to-face, with a player over whom he was supposed to wield authority—Brown said, "I don't know what any of you would do if you had an employee who didn't come to work or who always showed up late for work."

The groundwork for a trade was being laid. Throughout the league, rumors abounded. One had Iverson going to Detroit for Grant Hill. Another had him shipped off to the Los Angeles Clippers for Lamar Odom. Neither was a real possibility, but Iverson didn't know that. Knowing that the Clippers had long been a doormat organization, he dreaded a return to the losing days of his first two seasons.

"If they trade me, they'll be sorry," he vowed to Ann's boyfriend Jack. "I'm gonna average fifty points a game against them. I'm gonna average thirty-five points against everybody."

As the trade talk swirled, Iverson hosted his third annual Summer Celebrity Classic in Hampton. This time, it was a star-studded weekend, capped by a Saturday-night softball game before a throng of over five thousand fans. Croce attended, even while his coach was blasting his star player in the press. The day before the weekend, an even bigger story brewed. Dean Smith had called Croce, asking for permission to talk to his protégé, Brown, about the head-coaching position at the University of North Carolina. Croce granted the request. "If his heart isn't into staying here," he told Billy King, "I don't want him." Suddenly it looked like Brown was readying to pull another nomadic move and the Allen and Larry saga would meet an anticlimactic end.

Croce couldn't reach Brown by phone for days while Smith was talk-

ing to him. Meantime, Croce started running names past Billy King and
Sonny Hill as possible replacements. He wanted to know if Isiah Thomas
or Julius Erving might be interested—and how good they'd be as head
coaches.

Privately, Iverson hoped Brown would take the college job and that
John Thompson would become his pro coach. (Croce had also floated
Thompson's name, but after his experience with Johnny Davis, he was
reluctant to hire anyone who hadn't coached in the pros.) But when
Croce arrived for the charity weekend, there was no talk of Brown's
coaching status. Instead, Croce hung out in Iverson's suite as a stylist
braided Iverson's hair. Then the owner and player made their way to the
softball field, where they met up with Magic Johnson, whom Iverson had
again called for career advice during the NBA Finals. The three men met
for an hour in the trailer that would serve as a locker room for the evening's softball game.

Those around Iverson had long maintained that their man's close relationship with Croce ensured that Iverson would last longer than Brown
in Philadelphia. "This is your team, not Larry Brown's," Iverson's friends
would tell him. Now that Brown had a new, long-term deal, however (ini-
tiated by Croce's senior partner, Ed Snider, who was becoming more
active in Sixers business now that the team was winning), the balance of
power had shifted. The organization was committed to Brown—that is, if
he stayed in the organization. (Within a matter of days, Brown rebuffed
his alma mater, in part because his wife and their two young children were
happy in suburban Philadelphia and uninterested in another move.)

Croce didn't want to trade Iverson, but his management style was to
defer basketball decisions to those he'd empowered in that area. So, as he
did with the jettisoning of Coleman, he'd told Brown, King, and director
of player personnel Tony DiLeo his preference—"I'd like to take another
shot, one more year with this group"—but gave them the freedom to
make a deal, provided they were unanimous in their belief that they'd be
getting equal value for Iverson.

"I can't defend you when you're tardy and you don't do what the
coach says," Croce said now, in front of Johnson, explaining that he
would be unable to veto a trade if one were made. "We go back, Bubba.
We came in together as rookies. And I've told Billy and Larry what I'm
telling you, that I don't want you traded. But I can't stand in the way of a

trade because you're not doing what you're supposed to do, like coming to practices and doing off-season training." Iverson sat there, looking down. By now, Croce knew that, even when he wasn't making eye contact, Iverson was listening. But Johnson leaned in closer.

"You see this man here?" Johnson said, pointing to Croce. "It means something that he's here. Not too many guys have relationships with their owners like I've had with Jerry Buss. But you can have that, Allen, 'cause this guy's here. But you've got to make it work.

"People love you, Allen," Johnson continued. "Wait till you see the crowd tonight. My son is eighteen, and he's in love with you. He's all Mr. Tough now, see, and he's got that 'A.I.' attitude. He can come to Lakers games with me and sit courtside, but if you're on the dish, he's staying home to watch A.I. You've got the younger generation sewed up, and you don't even realize it. You just gotta stop making things hard for yourself. The kids are going to love you regardless, but the dads like me might have to say, 'You can't follow Allen because of the choices he makes.' I always loved practice, man. I came early and was the last to leave. If you're the best player, that's the job. It's not enough to just be the best player. You've got to set the example, too."

Johnson was simply reiterating messages from countless authority figures—from Brown to Cheeks to Rick Mahorn to Croce—but Croce sensed this was different. Since it was coming from Johnson, with all those championship rings, Iverson might take the advice as information—and not as a threat. Now Johnson burst into the wide smile that had made him millions in endorsements. "I know what a pain in the ass coaches can be," he said. "Don't forget, I played for Pat Riley. He was much tougher than Larry Brown. But I loved it. And I loved him, because that's how he cared about me."

Iverson looked up. "I don't hate Larry Brown," he said. "People think I hate him. I don't hate him. He didn't do anything to my kids or my mom. People think I'm gonna go back to Philly and be spiteful, but I'm not about that. I'm going to go back there and this is all gonna be about business."

If he got back to Philly, that is. Shortly after his weekend in Virginia, Croce learned that a trade had indeed been made. It was a blockbuster deal between the Sixers, Lakers, Pistons, and Hornets. Iverson and Geiger would go to Detroit and the Sixers would get all-star guard Eddie Jones from Charlotte, Glen Rice from Los Angeles, and Iverson's collegiate teammate Jerome Williams from Detroit. From Brown's perspective, Jones was a defensive upgrade, and the combination of Jones and Rice would compensate for Iverson's scoring.

As a lifelong Philadelphian, Croce knew the trade made no sense from a business perspective. He knew that Iverson was more popular than Wilt Chamberlain, Julius Erving, or Charles Barkley had ever been. Moreover, in the last year, he'd watched Phil Jackson lead the Lakers to an NBA title in his first season in L.A. He saw Jackson earn his salary—roughly in line with what Croce was paying Brown—by using his communication skills to bridge the chemistry gaps between Shaq and Kobe Bryant. Jackson was paid to solve a problem, not to throw up his hands and start fresh. "But I don't know if Larry's capable of solving this problem," Croce wondered to friends.

Faced with no other choice, he called Iverson. "It breaks my heart," he said, "but it looks like you're about to be traded, Bubba." He expected to hear either resignation or anger in Iverson's voice. Instead, he got breathless passion as Iverson pleaded for one more chance. "I just turned twenty-five, Pat," Iverson said. "If you're going to fuckin' trade me, trade me for someone who's better and who will help the team. But if you're trading me because of little things like coming late, missing a shootaround, I can change all that. I want to come back and be a captain, I'm gonna get married, I'm gonna start doing the right things." Croce loved what he was hearing, but he feared it was too little, too late.

And then Matt Geiger, with, ironically, an assist from David Falk, saved Iverson and, ultimately, the Philadelphia franchise. When Geiger signed as a free agent with Philadelphia, his agent, Falk, had negotiated for a 15 percent "kicker" to be paid by any team acquiring Geiger in a trade. Now Detroit would only go through with the deal if Geiger waived their obligation to pay him the onetime fee. Geiger refused. The trade was scuttled.

Still, it was unclear whether Iverson could really start anew. In late August, Magic Johnson appeared on *The Tonight Show with Jay Leno* to promote *his* upcoming charity basketball game, which, he announced, would feature Allen Iverson. Come game time, however, there was no sign of Iverson.

Johnson knew firsthand what the no-show was about: Iverson's posse. He knew his mentoring of Iverson was seen as a threat by those already in

With teammate Matt Geiger, who, upon first seeing Iverson's "What Would Jesus Do?" bracelet, quipped, "You should add, 'Not This.'"

the young star's ear. "Those guys around him should have made him come to my game, but it was the other way, for sure," Johnson said. "I've told Allen, you can't reach a certain level if you have guys who haven't been there. None of those guys have ever been to this level. I get guys asking me all the time how to get to this level. Allen has asked. And I've told him, number one, I don't deal with the posse. When you come meet with me, *you come meet with me.* When we do something, it's gotta be you and I and somebody who's going to execute this thing, but not all these other guys. See, I had to pass a test. Businessmen I've done deals with couldn't believe I was on time to meetings, that I didn't bring a hundred guys with me, that I wasn't wearing all the jewelry. I was in a suit and tie, I was up early, and I knew my numbers."

Shortly after Iverson's no-show, Johnson bumped into Iverson at a Mary J. Blige concert. "Man, don't stop calling me," Iverson said sheepishly. "Don't be mad at me."

"Look," Johnson said. "You got a get-out-of-jail-free card from me now. But the next time, that's gonna be it for me."

Meantime, perhaps the makeover Iverson promised Croce had begun. In September, he purchased a $2.4 million mansion on the Main Line, just minutes from where Croce, Snider, and Brown all lived. It came with five bedrooms, six baths, three fireplaces, and $25,000 in yearly taxes. He rented his previous home—and ultimately sold it—to Geiger, for $834,000. He and Tawanna began planning a wedding. He met with Brown and asked to be a team captain, a request Brown granted. And he finished up the rap CD. It was, he felt, like taking a page out of Magic's playbook; rather than constantly handing out money to his friends, he'd empower them with record deals, as they'd long fantasized. When a promotional single from the CD was released on the eve of training camp, though, it hardly appeared that Allen Iverson was changing anything.

We're about to shock the world," Ra said, smiling. He was dressed in a wifebeater top and baggy jeans, standing by the recording studio's pool table, chatting with Dan DeLuca, music writer from the *Philadelphia Inquirer.* In the other room, Iverson was putting the finishing touches on a cut entitled "Virginia Ain't for Lovers."

DeLuca's ears perked up at the lyrics. "Bitch niggas take cover/Virginia ain't for lovers," and "This ain't for kids with action figures/This is for the hardcore niggas." Great line, DeLuca thought. Over the next five hours in the studio, he grew convinced that Iverson's rapping would be much better than Shaq's goofy rhymes or Kobe's lame attempt. (*Vibe* magazine would later give Iverson's CD a respectable three stars.) Throughout the evening, Ra and "E" and others took turns with Iverson on the mike. As Coronas were drained and pizzas devoured, Iverson and his boys kept coming back to Ra's point: This was *their* time. This was what they'd been waiting for all their lives. The world might see them as nothing more than a bunch of hangers-on and sycophants, but the CD would show them to be equals in this artistic endeavor.

Days later, DeLuca received a copy of "40 Bars," the CD's promotional single, from the record company. Only it was the uncensored version. He heard Iverson rap, "Man enough to pull a gun, be man enough to use it" and "Come to me with faggot tendencies, you be sleeping where the maggots be" and "Get money, kill and fuck bitches/I'm hitting' anything and planning on using my riches."

DeLuca called Croce and read him the lyrics over the phone. "That doesn't sound too positive to me," Pat Croce was quoted as saying in DeLuca's story. "This is going to be a problem."

Training camp was about to start, and now this. The Philadelphia chapter of the Gay and Lesbian Task Force denounced Iverson's lyrics, as did civil-rights activist C. Dolores Tucker, who, along with Bill Bennett, had taken on Time Warner over the gangsta raps of Suge Knight's Death Row label.

When training camp at Penn State University opened, there Iverson stood, cornered by a press pack bewildered by the rhymes he had written. Iverson stood among them, defiant and defensive, refusing to discuss his CD, saying that, with the exception of the rap-specific press, no one in the media "understands hip-hop because y'all don't want to understand hip-hop."

For one of the few times in their relationship, Iverson felt Croce had spoken out of turn. Together they found a conference room away from the media throng and Iverson made his displeasure known. "If you got something to say to me, you can just talk to me," he said. "I gotta read in the paper that you think I'm doing something that isn't positive?"

"You're right," Croce said. "I apologize. I shouldn't have talked to the press before I spoke to you."

Iverson, naively, was taken aback by the controversy. When he heard that gay groups were outraged by his use of the word "faggot"—which he and many hip-hoppers used as a synonym for "weak" without regard to sexuality—he was upset to think he'd offended people. "I have a gay cousin," he said. "I'd never want to insult him." He couldn't understand what all the fuss was about. "I'm just talking smack, rapping," he said. "It's an art form. Bruce Willis don't do the things he do in a movie, right? It's just a movie."

Among those who didn't quite get the distinction was league commissioner David Stern, who summoned Iverson to New York. Theo Ratliff, the team's player rep, accompanied his teammate, and later regaled the Sixers with his version of the meeting's highlight. Stern, known for a ferocious temper, at one point yelled, "If you go through with this, I'm going to kill you!"

"See, I don't think you *really* gonna kill me," Iverson coolly replied. "You just talking smack, like I did on wax."

Once again, Iverson found himself a combatant in a cultural and generational clash. On one side were his overwhelmingly white and middle-class interlocutors, who reacted to his rhymes literally, at face value. On the other side of the divide were a generation of young hip-hoppers with their own set of mores.

Iverson issued a written apology and met with the offended groups. After all her public posturing, Tucker was a no-show; Jerry Mondesire, head of the Philadelphia NAACP, not only attended, but praised Iverson for squarely facing the issue—and then asked for his autograph. Meantime, Iverson's old friend Spike Lee was in Philadelphia, promoting his new film, *Bamboozled.* On local TV news, Iverson saw Lee criticize him; Lee went so far as to call Iverson's type of hard-core rapping "the new minstrelsy." Iverson vowed never to speak to Lee again, not because Lee had criticized him, but because he had done so publicly. In Iverson's view, Lee had aided and abetted a media eager to bring him down.

From Iverson's perspective, his naysayers simply didn't understand his art form. Chuck D, pioneer rapper of the group Public Enemy, once said that hip-hop was the "CNN of the ghetto"; it used literary technique to tell gritty, sometimes offensive stories that were, above all else, a real depiction of inner-city street life. That's what Iverson thought he was doing, as evidenced by his CD's original title, *Non-Fiction.* (It was later changed to *Misunderstood;* still later, he decided against releasing the CD, because the controversy took all the fun out of it for him.)

As Iverson well knew, nearly 70 percent of rap records are bought by suburban white kids, in large part because hip-hop offers a safe and authentic travelogue to another culture. Those consumers were aware of the multiple fictions rappers used to tell stories. They knew, for instance, that Eminem was an artist who had created the character Slim Shady, a rap protagonist who mouthed offensive lyrics for dramatic effect, like countless characters in popular movies. Similarly, there was Iverson's alter ego, Jewelz, who presented a snapshot of street life that brought down this torrent of judgment upon the basketball star.

Iverson saw himself as an entertainer; The Answer was his basketball character. Jewelz was his rap alter ego, who chronicled underworld violence—which is not necessarily the same thing as endorsing it. (In fact, the CD's cover read: "Allen Iverson *as* Jewelz.") When Iverson reacted defensively to the media horde, it was because he felt they were there to judge him, and that the controversy was being fueled by a deep-seated animus toward young black men who wear the hip-hop "uniform." After all, he pointed out to Gaskins and others, where was the outrage when the Lakers' Rick Fox played a murderer on the violent HBO series *Oz?*

Plenty of pundits weighed in, arguing that this latest controversy proved that Iverson's pledge to rededicate himself to the game was nothing but lip service, words he'd had to utter to avoid being traded. But Larry Brown sensed something else. While the national news crews descended upon training camp, Iverson not only avoided the media swarm—he took solace in the cocoon of his team. He got to every practice early, he practiced hard, and he hung with his teammates at night.

One day during training camp, Iverson's high-school coach Mike Bailey visited. He was now coaching nearby, in Williamsport, Pennsylvania. That night, Iverson agreed to follow Mike and Janet Bailey to Mike's sister's house, twelve miles outside State College. Allen and Gary Moore, plus Tawanna and the kids, drove behind the Baileys, deep into the woods. "I want a house like this," Iverson said, getting out of the car and taking his first glimpse of Bailey's sister's secluded farmhouse. "You got to be lost in order to get here."

They stayed and visited for two hours. Moore, who had spent a good part of the previous four seasons shuttling between Virginia and Philly, was now committed to spending the season by Iverson's side, as his personal manager. Some around Iverson were suspicious of Moore's motives when it came to Iverson. At times, even Iverson pointedly joked about Moore's stewardship of the Crossover Foundation charity: "You better give some of that money to the kids, Mo," he'd say. But Gary Moore had been there for him in Newport News, had clothed him and fed him when no one else could. Now that Moore, who was in his forties, had committed to being by Iverson's side, the Baileys were convinced he would be a steadying influence.

As the evening wore on, Iverson, as always, gravitated toward the children in the room, sitting cross-legged on the floor and playing with his kids and Bailey's young nieces and nephews. At one point, Iverson reminisced over old high-school exploits, even telling Bailey he was still mad that Bailey hadn't intervened when Coach Koz tried to punish him one time by making him do a hundred push-ups in front of the crowd during a timeout of a JV basketball game.

As Iverson and Moore were about to leave, Iverson turned serious. "How long have y'all been married?" he asked the Baileys.

"All our lives," joked Janet Bailey.

He looked at his former coach. "You think I can make the long haul?" he asked.

"You mean the championship?"

"Nah, man. You think I can get married and stay married?"

The Baileys smiled while Tawanna shyly blushed. "I have no doubt," the coach said.

The 76ers team that opened the 2000–2001 season was Larry Brown's kind of team. Up front, Ratliff was a shot-blocking intimidator, and Hill and Lynch egolessly did the little things that account for winning: setting screens, rebounding, defending. In the backcourt, Snow was a steadying floor general, intent on feeding the ball to Iverson. On the bench, McKie was fast becoming a clutch outside shooter and defensive stalwart. Geiger—though oft-injured now and the focus of the boobirds—was a big body able to defend legitimate centers. Kukoc was still a question mark; he seemed uninspired defensively and tended to defer to Iverson on offense, rarely asserting himself.

On the eve of the regular season, Brown signed veteran shooting guard Vernon Maxwell. "Mad Max," as he was known, had a troubled NBA past, but there was no doubt he could play. He had been a starter on Houston's championship teams in the midnineties and none other than Jordan had once described him as among the league's toughest defenders. At thirty-four, his career was winding down, but Brown thought he could add depth to the bench. Iverson was ecstatic to see Maxwell in a Sixers uniform. "Don't tell me they brought this crazy nigga in here!" he shouted, upon seeing Maxwell at practice for the first time.

The year before, Seattle's Gary Payton had lobbied his team to sign Maxwell, saying, "We need some ghetto in here"; the two, both combustible personalities, ended up feuding, however (Maxwell threw an iron plate at Payton in the locker room, striking and injuring their teammate Horace Grant), and Maxwell was traded. Now Iverson quickly struck up a friendship with this most unlikely of role models.

Once the regular season opened, the Sixers followed up their focused and disciplined training camp by storming out to a league-best 10–0 start. Even though Iverson once again started off shooting poorly from the field, the team was winning Brown's way—by playing hard-nosed, scrambling defense. In fact, Iverson, perhaps seeing how much Maxwell liked to practice, seemed newly dedicated. On defense, especially, he was making great strides. Brown couldn't stop praising his best player.

"He's all about playing the right way," the coach said of Iverson. "His defense is one hundred percent better, his turnovers are down, he's getting rid of the ball sooner and enjoying it more. I hear a couple of jerks in the stands yelling for him to shoot. But the one thing I had always hoped, once he won the scoring title and made the all-star game, was that he'd start to realize all of that is great, but the bottom line is about winning. You can't convince a player until he buys into the program. His overall game is the best since I've been here."

When Eric Snow went down for nearly three months in early December with a stress fracture to his ankle, the love fest didn't miss a beat. McKie stepped into the starting lineup and put up better numbers than Snow had. The Sixers remained one of the hottest teams in the league. Because the team was so workmanlike, it captured a wide fan base.

Inevitably, the first bump in the road hit, and it was much more than a pothole. It was a crater, and it jarred everybody aboard.

With a first-place record of 17–5, the Sixers lost to the Dallas Mavericks at home, 112–94. Dallas forward Dirk Nowitzki was unstoppable, scoring 37 points. In the locker room afterward, Brown, in keeping with his counterintuitive instinct to be tougher on a team when it's doing well, was harshly critical. Iverson spoke up for the team, criticizing Brown for not adjusting during the game to provide George Lynch with some defensive help in trying to contain Nowitzki.

The next morning, in a team breakfast meeting in Chicago, the rhetoric escalated. Iverson, apparently with the green light from his teammates, told the coach in front of the squad that his constant carping was wearing thin. "We got the best record in the league and you treat us like we're in last place," he said. Moreover, guys were afraid to speak up about it, for fear that Brown would cut their minutes. Iverson told Brown that he was "whining all the time like a little bitch."

Brown was horrified. He coached that night in a stupor, barely communicating with his team during a win over the lowly Bulls. The next day, the Sunday before Christmas, Pat Croce awoke and commented to his wife, Diane, "Can you believe it was a year ago today that everything blew up between Allen and Larry in Detroit? Now we're in first place. What a difference a year makes."

Not exactly. When Croce returned from church early that afternoon, Diane had a message for him. "Billy King called," she said. "It's urgent."

What could be so urgent—we're 18–6, Croce thought. Then he got King on the phone. "Pat, there was a blowup before the Chicago game," King said. "Coach is offended and taking time off to reflect and he's thinking of quitting."

"No!" Croce exclaimed.

"I think he just needs some time off," King said.

Croce called Brown at home. Shelly Brown answered and told Croce her husband couldn't come to the phone: "He's too upset." The next day, she called in her husband's absence from practice, saying he was still "too emotional."

It was unheard of in professional sports: an AWOL coach. When the players showed up for practice on Monday, Croce addressed them. "Coach is at home, reflecting on his relationship with you," he said. "He just doesn't want to have a negative relationship with you, like he had with Reggie Miller and the Pacers at the end. He doesn't want to let you down."

There was silence. Then, according to one player who was there, Iverson spoke up, angrily. "This punk is quitting on us, then," he spat out. "Well, fuck him."

"Allen, it's not just you, it's his relationship with the team," Croce said. " He's emotional right now. The best way you can show support for him is to practice hard."

When Iverson had spoken up against Brown in Chicago, it marked the first time that it was Iverson *and* the team versus Brown. In previous controversies, Brown had always allied with the likes of Snow and McKie in trying to bring Iverson around to their shared vision of what constituted a team. But now this. It was all too similar to what had gone down in Indiana. During Brown's fourth and last season there, he'd lost that team. This was now his fourth year with the Sixers.

"Larry's a great builder, but not a finisher," said one NBA head coach of Brown's strange sabbatical. "He builds teams up, and then when they're ready to kill his ass, he leaves."

That's what had happened in Indiana. "Those were guys who were really important in my life," Brown recalls about his last year with the Pacers. "I didn't treat them the way I should have. The word was out: I was too demanding, I never let up on them." His riding of the Pacers was so bad, in fact, that when Brown first returned to Indiana as head coach of the 76ers, even some of his mild-mannered former players, like Rik Smits, took snarling, trash-talking delight in beating their old coach.

It's a fine line, Brown maintained. He had always felt an obligation to teach, even if his teachings might grate. Then, too, he was aware of his less-than-tolerant nature. "I can't coach assholes," he says. "I know that about myself."

When coaching Kansas in the 1980s, Brown had been the subject of an academic study that gauged his positive-to-negative reinforcement ratio. He was pleased to find he was an overwhelmingly positive coach. "The problem is that players don't hear when you're positive," he says. "They have selective hearing."

In Indiana, one of those refusing to listen was a young, prodigiously talented hip-hop player. After Brown left, that player, Jalen Rose, became a star, blossoming under Brown's replacement, the laid-back Larry Bird. Brown knew how much Rose loved to play and he wished that more players cared so deeply for the game. But the six-eight Rose wanted to be a point guard, seeing himself as the next Magic Johnson, and Brown saw him as a small forward. Brown held firm, and Rose retreated into himself. "I'm still disappointed I couldn't reach Jalen," Brown says even now. Once Rose was lost, the rest of the team followed and Brown became convinced Indiana needed a new coach.

Could it all be happening again? Was Larry Brown about to flame out in his fourth year in Philadelphia? Doug Moe, one of Brown's closest friends in the coaching fraternity, once quipped that Brown "is only happy when he's unhappy." Brown took exception to the remark—"Doug's the one with the ulcer, not me"—but if he bolted now, with a first-place team, his coaching epitaph would be forever sealed: *Great basketball mind, victim of his own tortured genius.* For the story of Brown's life was a story of abruptly severed relationships. There was the succession of jobs, the father who died when Larry was seven, the three marriages, the long and mysterious estrangement from his brother Herb—a recently repaired split that had developed because both coaches (Larry then with Denver, Herb with Detroit) coveted Marques Johnson in the 1977 NBA draft. (Neither got him.)

After missing two practices, Brown finally spoke to Croce. "Coach, you can't quit now," Croce said. "You finally have the players you want. We're in first place!" Then came calls from McKie, Lynch, and Snow, urging his return. The Brown who came back, these and other players would later attest, was a kinder and gentler one. Larry Brown had obsessed over the way his tenure had ended in Indiana and he was determined to do one thing when he returned. "I didn't want what happened in Indiana to happen again," he said.

By early January, it had become clear that the change in Brown involved a subtle alteration in tone; he hadn't compromised on matters of coaching principle. His team would still play like a well-schooled college squad. At a time when most NBA offenses lacked imagination— how often did they dump the ball into a big man down low, wait for the double-team, then kick it out for a three-point bomb?—Brown's team led the league in classic backdoor cuts and give-and-go's.

Nor did he deviate from his usual practice regimen. During one practice, he whistled a play dead to reprimand Kukoc for the way he was setting a pick, one of the game's most fundamental acts. "It's not that complicated," Brown chided. "Set the screen *even* to the ball, and then roll." Kukoc had been setting the screen perhaps fifteen inches from where Brown wanted. "Those fifteen inches," McKie would later explain, "could be the difference between an open shot and a blocked shot."

But according to players like Geiger, with whom Brown had a long heart-to-heart once the coach returned, Brown seemed more aware of the effects his words could have. On January 9, the Sixers visited New Jersey to face the Nets and Marbury, Iverson's longtime rival. During pregame warm-ups, a fan let Iverson have it, calling him a "gunner" who cared only about himself and his scoring average. Iverson turned on the fan and bellowed: "Man, I already won a scoring title. I'm going for that ring now!"

Just a few feet away, Brown almost let himself smile. He had more reason to smile during the game, when Iverson took only 14 shots but played a flawless floor game en route to another win. The next day, Brown called his star into his office at the practice facility. "There are a lot of things I've been proud of you for, things that you've done, what you've become," he said. "But that might have been one of the most satisfying games I've ever coached last night, because I know that playing against Marbury is big for you, and you just played to win."

As the all-star game approached, it became commonplace to hear Brown laud Iverson not just for his guts and hustle and talent, but also for how he kept his teammates involved—giving them touches—and how he was finding his scoring chances out of the natural flow of the offense. Similarly, Iverson could be heard praising his coach. "He's got a tough job," he said. "He's always drawing up and calling the right plays. He's got to make tough substitutions, 'cause we got twelve guys who want to play. And he's got to keep me happy."

For his part, Croce had given up trying to figure out both men. "They're both geniuses," he said. "And genius is something I can't relate to."

Brown smiled when he heard what Croce had said. "I don't know about being geniuses," he said. "But Allen and I both have loose wires."

The good feelings showed on the court, where the Sixers were 13–3 in January. Iverson averaged 34.6 points, 4.6 assists, and 2.67 steals a game and was named NBA Player of the Month. The only downer came in the last game before the all-star break, when Ratliff, who was to join Iverson as an all-star starter, suffered a stress fracture to his right wrist. He'd be out at least six weeks and maybe much longer.

Brown coached Iverson in the all-star game, for which Iverson won

Forcing teammate Dikembe Mutombo to double over in laughter on the bench.

MVP honors. He scored 25 points, including 10 of his team's final 16, and elicited a string of oohs and aahs from the Washington, D.C., packed house every time he crossed someone over or skied for an alley-oop. Manning the middle for Iverson's squad was Atlanta's Dikembe Mutombo. Against the best players in the world, Mutombo grabbed a game-high 21 rebounds. Because of Mutombo's dominating presence, Brown was able to "go small"—play shorter, quicker guys like Marbury and Iverson together. The East won; afterward, when David Stern presented Iverson with the NBA trophy, the star searched the crowd. "Where my coach at? Where my coach at?" he called. "I couldn't have done this without Coach Brown."

The Sixers won five straight after the all-star break, giving them an NBA-best record of 41–14. On the morning of the league's trading deadline, Brown did something he'd never done before, something few coaches would ever do. Before practice, he pulled aside his three team leaders: Iverson, McKie, and Snow. "This is just between us," he began, "but I want to tell you what we're thinking of doing, and I want your input."

Brown proceeded to spell out the details of a possible trade that would send Ratliff and Kukoc to Atlanta for Mutombo. With the best record in the league, some could argue Brown was aiming to fix what wasn't broken. But with Ratliff injured and his future unknown, and Geiger often out of the lineup with chronic knee problems, the center position looked like a gaping hole. Besides, if his team did make it to the NBA Finals, Mutombo would give them a presence in the middle to at least match up against Shaq and the Lakers or the twin towers of Tim Duncan and David Robinson in San Antonio. As Brown outlined the deal to his players, he withheld one key fact. He didn't tell them he was giving them veto power. If just one of them strenuously objected to the deal, he planned to nix the trade.

McKie was the first to respond. "Coach," he said, "you know I'm going to be loyal to the guys who got us in this position. But that's personal, that's not about basketball."

"I wouldn't expect anything else but loyalty from any of you," Brown said. He looked at Iverson, mindful of Iverson's longtime complaint that he was seldom consulted on personnel moves.

"Coach, I love Theo," Iverson said. "But if you think this is going to make us better, I guess you gotta go for it."

"Well, you never know, Allen," Brown replied. "But I keep coming back to the fact that we don't have Theo now, and who knows when we get him back and how he'll be when we do?"

Snow, Ratliff's best friend on the team, looked up. Brown knew that his reaction would be key. "If we don't have Theo, Coach, and we don't know when we're getting him back," Snow said, sighing, "I can't stand in the way of this."

That night, the deal for Mutombo was made. Iverson was ecstatic to play with a legitimate all-star center for the first time in his pro career—a fellow Georgetown product, no less. Sitting in front of his locker before Mutombo's debut, McKie thought back to Brown's pretrade consultation with the players. "It meant a lot that Coach came to us, that he involved us in the decision," he said. "In the past, it was more like Coach might just as well have gone up to a club box seat and yelled down orders *at* us."

It was a bold move on Brown's part. Seldom does a league-leading team make a blockbuster deal. But Mutombo was a seven-foot one-inch, 280-pound shot blocker who was a three-time NBA Defensive Player of the Year and who was currently leading the league in rebounding at 14 per game.

But the adjustment to Mutombo's plodding style didn't come easily. At the time of the trade, there were only twenty-eight games left in the season. Iverson wouldn't play in nine of those because of the injuries to his hip, tailbone, and elbow that had been plaguing him all season. The Sixers would close out the season with a mere 15–13 record after acquiring Mutombo. Still, the Sixers ended the season with the best record in the East, 56–26, and Iverson had had his best season as a pro. He scored 31.1 points per game, good enough for his second scoring title and making him the first player since Jordan to average over 30 points per game for a season. He was favored to win the MVP award. In fact, shortly after the close of the regular season, the Sixers swept the postseason awards, when McKie was named Sixth Man of the Year, Mutombo Defensive Player of the Year, and Brown Coach of the Year.

Now all that remained was a lengthy play-off run. And the first team that stood in their way was—who else?—the Indiana Pacers.

Under first-year head coach Isiah Thomas, the Pacers were rebuilding after having advanced to the NBA Finals the year before. They had barely qualified for the eighth and final play-off spot. Still, Brown knew that any team with Reggie Miller and Jalen Rose presented challenges.

The play-offs are different, and the Pacers veterans had been there before. Iverson had had his way against the Pacers during the regular season, but Thomas designed a defense to frustrate the all-star guard for game one.

Before a boisterous, packed crowd in Philadelphia, the Sixers built an 18-point third-quarter lead. But Iverson was stymied by Thomas's swarming, double-teaming defense. Every time he touched the ball, guard Travis Best would be joined by either forward/center Jermaine O'Neal or Miller or Rose, and they'd play Iverson two on one. Iverson couldn't get a rhythm going. He'd either force the issue or find the open man—who would, more often than not, miss. In the second half, the Sixers' other starters shot a paltry 3 for 14, with the usually deadeye McKie hitting just 3 of 10.

Iverson scored a mere 16 points. With 2.9 seconds to go, Miller—who had connected on only 4 of 20 shots—eluded Iverson behind a screen and George Lynch failed to leave his man and switch out on one of the great clutch shooters in NBA history. Miller drained a game-winning three, stunning the crowd into silence. "Our asses got tight," Iverson succinctly said after the game.

The Sixers had worked all season long for home-court advantage, and they'd given it back on the first night of the play-offs. The next morning, Iverson was the first to arrive at the Sixers' practice facility. Before practice, he and Brown went over the tape of game one. Thomas had said after the game that the purpose of the aggressive double team was to turn Iverson from an instinctive player into a thinking player. Brown countered by drawing up a series of offensive sets designed to get Iverson free off the ball. He'd be tougher to double-team if he was running off screens without the ball. When he did have it, Brown told him to trust his teammates.

In game two, the Pacers again threw swarming double teams Iverson's way, but the outcome this time was strikingly different. Iverson didn't waste time dribbling, as he often did, to set up his man. He came off screens and made moves the moment the ball touched his hands. In the third quarter alone, he scored 19 points, using a vast repertoire of moves to keep the defense honest. On one play, he jolted Miller with a crossover and sensed forward Austin Croshere coming over to help; in midair he faked a pass to Croshere's man, freezing the defender. At the last possible instant, he arced a floater over O'Neal and through the hoop. He also hit from outside, which enabled him to start driving to the basket. He made 15 of his 27 shots, scored 45 points, and trusted his teammates, as evidenced by his 9 assists. The Sixers won, 116–98.

Afterward, Iverson couldn't stop talking about his coach. "I learned a lot more about Larry Brown as a coach," he said. "It's unbelievable how he prepared us for this game. Coach put in so many things to help me, so many different plays where they couldn't double-team me like they wanted to."

The Sixers won game three behind Iverson's 32 points and 6 assists, while McKie added 22. In game four, Iverson went for 33 points and the Sixers closed out the series, three games to one. As they were walking off, Miller embraced Iverson. "You've got to make your team believe they can win," the veteran told Iverson. "We've put you through enough wars. This is your first step." Iverson was jubilant, recalling how, just a year earlier, the Pacers' dismissal of his team had caused him to break down, sobbing.

Next up came Vince Carter's Toronto Raptors, a series that would pit two of the game's rising stars against each other. NBC billed it as "The Answer versus Vinsanity." Once again, the Sixers made things hard for themselves, dropping game one at home. Iverson and Carter canceled each other out, with Iverson scoring 36 and Carter 35. The difference was Toronto's outside shooting specialist Dell Curry, who totaled 20 points.

The pressure was on for game two. It was a seesaw battle; the longer the game stayed close, the more pressure it put on the Sixers. Yet it seemed as though, on this night, Iverson would not let his teammates' asses get tight again. In the fourth quarter, he was unstoppable, seeming to will high, arcing shots into the basket while opposing players frantically clutched at him. He made an astounding 21 of 39 shots, for a franchise play-off record 54 points. Amazingly, he scored all of his team's last 19 points—in a 97–92 win. Afterward, when asked where such a clutch performance came from, Iverson provided a telling two-word response: "Poverty. Life." After the press conference, with his kids tugging at his legs, he walked to his car in the center of a large entourage that included Ann and Jack. "If you lose this game, the series is basically over," someone said to him. "Surely you felt that pressure?"

Iverson stopped and look puzzled. "Pressure?" he said. "After all the shit I've seen in my life, you think I'm gonna feel pressure from a muthafuckin' *basketball* game?"

The series against the Raptors was epic. Carter scored 50 points to lead Toronto to victory in game three, before Iverson's 30 helped the Sixers eke out a game-four win on the road. With the series tied at two games apiece, Iverson was named the league's MVP the day before game five in Philadelphia.

During the ceremony, Croce had a beaming Iverson sit on his coach's lap for a photo op that appeared in papers across the country. In his off-the-cuff speech, Iverson, in addition to paying homage to his boys in the back of the room, singled out his teammate Aaron McKie as an influence. "I told Blue [McKie] that it was going to be important for me to become a professional, like he is day in and day out," he said.

When Brown spoke, the Larry and Allen narrative had come full circle. "I'm so proud of what Allen has done," he said. "Maybe I didn't give it enough thought or time to understand what this kid is about, and that's the neatest thing about my improved relationship with him. He doesn't always do it the way I would expect or sometimes like. But I know where his heart is. This kid has great character."

Before game five, Iverson was presented with his MVP trophy. And then he decimated the Raptors with 50 points for another Sixers win. When Toronto held serve at home, a pivotal game seven loomed in Philly.

The morning of the game, Carter was in North Carolina, taking part in his college graduation ceremony. He took a private jet back to Philly by game time; the media had a field day with "should he" or "shouldn't he" debates. Meantime, Iverson was ailing. The long season, and the brutal beatings he'd been taking, were adding up. Early in game seven, Iverson collided with Toronto enforcer Charles Oakley, further aggravating his chronically bruised tailbone. He was hobbled; his outside shot was front-rimming, a sign that the usual lift wasn't coming from his legs. So he did the next best thing: he reined in his offensive impulses and concentrated instead on setting up his teammates. It was like he was a point guard again, only wiser and more careful with the ball. McKie led the team with 22 points, but Iverson, who scored 21, tallied a career-high 16 assists. When Carter missed a long jumper at the buzzer, the Sixers had won, 88–87. Iverson went running, arms raised, to the opposite baseline, where he flung himself into his mother's arms while fans stormed the court.

Things didn't get any easier, though. Ray Allen's Milwaukee Bucks came to town next. In game one, Iverson torched George Karl's team for

Iverson's Tarzan yell after scoring 54 points, including his team's final 19, in a 2001 play-off win over Toronto.

34 points and the Sixers finally won an opener at home. In game two, however, the Bucks evened the series behind Ray Allen's 38.

Iverson, still hobbled by the tailbone, opted to sit out game three. He and Gary Moore watched the undermanned Sixers take on the Bucks from Iverson's hotel room at the Pfister Hotel while Iverson tried to rest. The Sixers fought valiantly, but lost by six. When they got back to the hotel, Iverson was in the lobby, grinning proudly, applauding his teammates as they got off their bus.

Game four found Iverson not only playing but seeming to gain strength in the second half. At one point, Ray Allen elbowed him in the mouth. Iverson played on, knowing that if the refs saw that he was bleeding, he'd have to leave the game. So he kept letting his mouth fill with blood before swallowing—this while scoring 11 of his team's final 13 points in a 89–83 victory.

Snow, playing with a stress fracture in each ankle, scored 18 points, including the game winner in game five. The Sixers dropped game six to the Bucks in Milwaukee, despite a furious comeback attempt led by Iverson, in which he scored 26 of his 46 points in the fourth quarter.

Once again, it was win or go home as the Sixers hosted the Bucks in game seven of the Eastern Conference Finals. Before the game, Iverson limped slowly around the Sixers' locker room, looking brittle and sore. When asked how he was feeling, he shrugged. "Like shit," he said. "But I won't feel a thing once I'm out there."

Forty-four points, 7 assists, 6 rebounds, and 2 steals later, Iverson was hugging Brown and Croce at midcourt while he and his teammates donned "Eastern Conference Champion" T-shirts and caps. There was Mutombo, who had totaled 23 points, 19 rebounds, and 7 blocks in game seven, bending down to embrace Iverson. And there was Ann, as always, right near her baby, looking on with pride while confetti littered the court. Her son was going to Los Angeles to kick Goliath's ass.

The Los Angeles Lakers had not lost a basketball game in sixty-seven days, ever since, appropriately enough, April Fools' Day. Since then, Shaq, Kobe, and Phil Jackson had decimated the best teams in the Western Conference. They swept Scottie Pippen and the Portland Trailblazers, Chris Webber and the upstart Sacramento Kings, and—most stunningly—they rolled right through Tim Duncan and the San Antonio Spurs. Eleven games, eleven wins. They didn't just beat these teams; they demoralized them. As

Bryant was fond of saying, they "ripped the hearts" out of their opponents.

There wasn't a pundit alive picking the Sixers to win the series. Most weren't picking Philly even to win a game.

Though he rarely played the media game, Iverson liked to read virtually everything written about him. Now he was national story number one, given that the various story-line permutations of Shaq, Kobe, and Phil had all been exhausted long ago. Iverson was new and different. He was showing up to press conferences wearing a 'do rag covered in dollar-sign insignias, dressed in trendy hip-hop clothes, with Deuce bouncing or, depending on the time, asleep on one knee.

But Iverson didn't like all of what he was reading. Other sports stars might have bought into the cliché-ridden sportswriter hype about how, suddenly, he'd "grown up" this season. To Iverson, it was much too simplistic a take. Yes, he'd matured—the same way any young man grows between the time he's twenty and twenty-six, which he'd turn the day after game one. In the press conference the day before the big game, a questioner, anticipating a wholesome, feel-good response, prompted him: "It must be nice, the way the public has seemed to embrace you?"

Iverson licked his lips. "I don't care," he said, without a trace of rancor in his voice. "All I care about is what my family feels about me, my friends, my teammates . . . [There is] nothing easy about being Allen Iverson where everybody is looking at your every move, criticizing you for just saying a curse word when you get mad. Making you feel like you're some type of villain, the smallest man on the court but the biggest villain in life."

The Lakers should have been taking note: Iverson was fine-tuning his "me against the world" outlook. In fact, Tupac Shakur's song by that very name was one Iverson could often be heard humming to himself. Come game time, he played as though the world were indeed aligned against him. When he saw fans in the stands holding brooms, meant to signify "sweep," he took note. He'd use that. When the crowd booed him, he smiled. He'd use that. When the refs blew a call, he clapped his hands together and looked skyward. Just another obstacle. He'd use that.

In the game's first twenty-nine minutes, Iverson scored 38 points. He hit jumpers, he hit fastbreak layups, he challenged O'Neal, despite being more than a foot shorter and half the giant's weight. The Sixers forced overtime, where Iverson rose to the occasion again. Trailed doggedly by speedy Laker sub Tyronn Lue, Iverson hit a three from deep in the corner with 1:19 left; Lue, having lunged at him, lay at Iverson's feet while the ball sailed through the air. Once it dropped through the twine, Iverson made an emphatic show of stomping over the prone, disbelieving form of Lue—as if to say, *There. Take that.*

Then came a jumper from the corner, for a 4-point lead with forty-eight seconds left. Then came a runner by Snow to seal the overtime win.

On the way to the locker room, Iverson shouted, "Put the brooms away!" He told his team, "We didn't do nothing yet. We got a long way to go." The Sixers announced that McKie had suffered a chip fracture in his right ankle. But he'd continue to play, as Snow had been playing through twin ankle fractures, as Iverson had been playing with his deep tailbone bruise and an elbow in desperate need of surgery. "We've got heart," Iverson said after his 18-for-41, 48-point performance. "We're going to play with that first, play with the talent second."

Jackson, who had coached Jordan for so long, couldn't quite believe what he'd just seen. "Here's a young guy that's as slight or small as almost anybody we've had in this league, and he's not only able to get off shots but lead the league in scoring," he said. "How he does it, I'm still in a quandary about."

The next day was Iverson's twenty-sixth birthday. He wanted to hang in the hotel room with his friends, but there was business to be done. *GQ* magazine had set up a photo shoot for its October cover. Reebok was scrambling to produce a national TV commercial to capitalize on Iverson's stunning national popularity—and to counter Kobe Bryant's marketing blitz for Adidas.

It seemed like a Bryant ad was airing during every time-out on NBC. Yet it was the unpackaged Iverson who was capturing the attention of America. His sneakers were outselling all others; in the week ending June 3, retailers took in roughly $1 million in Iverson jersey sales alone, far outdistancing all other athletes. Sales of Sixers-related team merchandise dwarfed that of the Lakers and Knicks. How critical was Iverson to Reebok's bottom line? Just three years prior, the multinational corporation announced massive layoffs and didn't renew O'Neal's $3-million-per-year endorsement deal. Now Reebok announced that Iverson had boosted their sales by 20 percent during the first half of the year. Thanks to Iverson, said Reebok CEO Paul Fireman, his company posted second-quarter earnings of $14 million, or twenty-four cents a share, up from $10 million and nineteen cents a year earlier.

Part of Iverson's appeal seemed to be that he didn't give a shit about any of the aforementioned facts. Across the country—these Finals would be the highest rated since Jordan had retired—fans were taken by Iverson's single-minded passion for the game. So it should have come as no surprise to *GQ* or Reebok that, on his birthday, he just didn't feel like doing anything. No prior commitments. Just wanted to hang. "Man, I give Reebok a commercial every time I step out on the muthafuckin' court," Iverson said.

Needless to say, this made for a stark contrast to Bryant, who very consciously signed on to the Jordan crossover marketing model. Bryant's name seemed to be attached to every product with an advertising budget: Adidas, McDonald's, Spalding, Coke. Bryant's father, Joe, had played for the 76ers in the seventies, and then professionally in Italy, where Kobe lived until he was fourteen. While there, Kobe's grandparents would send him videotapes of *The Cosby Show* and of Michael Jordan's games and press conferences. He'd study Jordan's moves with his father, using the VCR's freeze-frame to analyze and break down his idol's game. From Jordan's public statements, Bryant learned how to conduct himself in a non-threatening, if seemingly prepackaged, way.

They were a study in contrasts, Iverson and Bryant. Bryant was classically trained; Iverson was a freestyling rapper. Bryant took 1,500 jumpshots a day; his teammates had once resented the competitive zeal with which he attacked practice. Iverson's game was less about the repetitive training of his muscle memory than it was about being open to spontaneous bursts of creativity. And practice? Much to Brown's chagrin, Iverson would duck out of it to gulp down a handful of Taco Bell burritos, or he'd lie on his belly and exaggeratedly grunt while his teammates—suckers!—did push-ups all around him.

But they had many things in common, these two stars: their indomitable spirits once a game got under way, their utter fearlessness, their shared addiction to competition that, as with Jordan, could seem borderline unhealthy. All of these qualities were on display at the close of game two, after the Sixers had nearly opened up a commanding two-games-to-none lead. The Sixers were down just three with two minutes to go when Jackson had to call a time-out to settle down his team. "One shot is not going to bury them," he told the Lakers, who shakily held on for the win. Just before the final buzzer, there was Iverson, excitedly clapping his hands and smiling, jawing at Bryant, who gave it right back. Neither man would comment on the exchange, but one Sixer overheard Iverson chirping, "Y'all better respect us now! We heading to our house now!"

And a rocking house it was. Philadelphia had caught Sixers fever, in a way that felt unparalleled in the city's history. They'd had winning teams before, but none so beloved. Partly, the chord struck between this team and its city had much to do with the scrappy style of these wounded Sixers—a much-talked-about *Daily News* cover photo even had McKie, Snow, and Iverson doctored up in Revolutionary War garb under the headline THE SPIRIT OF THE 76ERS. And then there was Croce, a local working-class hero, who saw to it, somehow, that practically every car within the city's limits sported a Sixers pennant and who climbed to the top of the 374-foot Walt Whitman Bridge to hang a banner reading GO SIXERS, BEAT L.A. (He wanted to rappel into the water from the top of the bridge, but was told he needed permission from the police.)

But mostly the bond between city and team had to do with Iverson. Had there ever been a player more aptly placed? Philadelphia, after all, was a city of resentments, nestled as it was in the shadows of New York and Washington, D.C., a city that made a folk hero of pitcher Tug McGraw because, in a packed stadium during the city's 1980 World Series parade, he'd inexplicably told New York to "stick it"—even though his team had just beaten Kansas City, not one of the Big Apple's franchises. Who better, then, to carry McGraw's legacy than Iverson, someone who not only resented, but turned resentment into triumph, time and again? He was a cornrowed, tattooed, real-life Rocky; when an L.A. journalist asked before game three, a bit hopeful, if Iverson was "feeling fatigue yet," he snorted. "Fatigue is army clothes," he said.

Game three was another nail-biter, with Iverson pumping in 35 points and grabbing 10 rebounds. In the last thirty seconds, he cut the Lakers lead to one with three free throws, but the Sixers were ultimately no match for O'Neal. The Lakers took command of the series with a 96–91 win. As the clock wound down, Brown took Iverson out. The fans rose en masse and serenaded their team with an ovation normally reserved for winners; Iverson clapped back, applauding the fans and his teammates.

Then he stood next to Geiger and gently put his head on his teammate's chest. "It got away," Iverson said after the game. "We had our chances."

Los Angeles went on to close out the series, four games to one. O'Neal was named the play-off MVP, but Iverson had left an indelible mark. He scored more than 35 points a game on 40 percent shooting, but measuring his game by his statistics was akin to judging Martin Luther King Jr. on his administrative skill. Iverson had played with a passion and a defiance seldom seen on the public stage. He'd spent the long play-off run battered and bruised but not beaten, spent it talking about "heart"— his and his team's—in a way that only boxers, alone among athletes, commonly did. Because that's what he was, Iverson would tell you: a basketball player with a pugilist's spirit.

When it was all over, he came into the interview room with Tawanna and the kids. Shaq was at the podium. Unbeknownst to Iverson, Bryant was on the other side of the room, awaiting his turn to face the press. When Shaq got up and left, both Iverson and Bryant started for the microphone—with Bryant getting there first. Iverson about-faced, suddenly pissed, muttering to Tawanna, "Let's get the fuck out of here." Exiting the room, someone called to him, "A.I., what about the interviews?"

"Fuck that, man," he said. And then he was off for the summer.

As always, the now abbreviated off-season would be action-packed for the Sixers. First, Croce announced he was resigning as team president. In a series of highly publicized negotiations with his senior partner, Ed Snider, he had sought assurances that he'd be Snider's heir apparent as chairman of Comcast-Spectacor. When nothing could be worked out, he stepped down in an awkward press conference, claiming that "the keys to the kingdom" had been "dangled" before him; Snider claimed Croce had misunderstood him. (Though, three years earlier, Snider had publicly fantasized about Croce eventually taking over for him; that was before their relationship soured. As time went on, Croce felt Snider treated him more like an employee than a partner. For his part, as the Sixers' fortunes turned around, Snider seemed irked that Croce was often referred to as "the owner" of the Sixers.)

Once Croce announced his resignation, Brown felt compelled to come back and coach again. He'd been 90 percent certain he was going to retire. But once Croce left, he didn't feel he could leave Ed Snider in the lurch.

August 4, 2001: Iverson and longtime girlfriend Tawanna Turner tie the knot.

One of Brown's first acts in preparation for the next season was the trading of Tyrone Hill—who had disappointed in the play-offs—to Cleveland for six-foot seven-inch Matt Harpring.

Over the summer, Iverson was named *Time* magazine's Athlete of the Year. But his attention was far from the basketball court. He was busy preparing for the social event of Philadelphia's season: his own wedding, set for early August. He and Tawanna registered at Bloomingdale's ($4,200 in china and stemware) and Williams-Sonoma, where, among their desired items, was a $26 mini-muffin pan and $649 chrome bowl mixer.

Three days before the big day, however, Gary Moore started making calls: the wedding was off. Later, word came again: false alarm. It was just another example of a tumultuous but loving relationship that had lasted close to ten years and produced two children. But before the big night, Iverson had a score to settle. He was waiting in the hotel lobby for Michael Jackson to arrive. Jackson was now getting a Ph.D. in education administration from Ohio State, but to Iverson, he was still that twelve-year-old "Thrilla" who had beaten him in a sprint.

"Let's race now! Let's race now!" Iverson said after the two men embraced. They went out into the parking lot while a lobbyful of guests looked on. Iverson, in Timberlands and droopy jeans, won.

Two days later, on Saturday, August 4, the bad boy of the NBA wore a black tuxedo jacket, white vest, and a broad smile in front of 210 guests in a ceremony those in attendance described as "touching" and "spiritual."

It was held at the Mansion in Voorhees, New Jersey, an upscale banquet hall, although the location, despite intense media scrutiny, was kept a secret—even among invited guests, who were shuttled from area hotels. Ann arrived late, so the ceremony started well past its scheduled time of 7 P.M. The wedding program read: "This day, I marry my friend, the one I laugh with, live for, dream with, love . . ."

When Allen saw Tawanna stride down the aisle in her ivory strapless gown, a tear came to his eye. Three-year-old Deuce, seeing his father tear up, started to cry himself. Smiling, Iverson's groomsmen, among them Gaskins, Ra, and uncles Gregory and Stevie, patted the man of the hour on the back. The best men were Gary Moore, Michael Freeman, and Arnie Steele. Iverson, as on the court, was fully in the present, nodding his head solemnly when Reverend Barber from back home intoned, "When times are hard, don't call on others to make things right. Call on

God." The couple kissed and marched off to "Ease on Down the Road" from *The Wiz*.

Afterward, during the elegant affair's cocktail hour, Iverson sought out Sue Lambiotte. She'd never met Tawanna. "This is what I've always wanted to see," Allen said as the two women—who had long heard about each other—hugged. Later, there was a two-foot-high wedding cake and a seafood buffet. In attendance, seated at tables identified not by numbers but by names such as "Hope," "Faith," and "Commitment" were Allen's teammates and their wives, Larry and Shelly Brown, Pat and Diane Croce, and Billy King.

At 2:40 in the morning, the newlyweds emerged outside onto the street, with Allen holding a bottle of champagne. Several days later, Allen and Tawanna escaped to a tropical locale for their honeymoon—but not alone. Que and Cindy Gaskins and Ra and his fiancée, Sherri, all joined them, at Allen's urging; the only way he could make sure he'd stay on the trip for a whole week was if he broke up how he spent his time, he explained. This way, during the day, he, Que, and Ra could ride jet skis while the girls got manicures and pedicures. At night, the couples could go do their couple things.

In two months, and for many thereafter, Allen Iverson would be unable to stop picturing his friend Ra's smiling face on his honeymoon.

chapter | 12

HOLD MY OWN

I was at the tattoo place and I said to myself, "who can look out for me better than me?" so I came up with "hold my own" 'cause so much of life is up to me.

It was, Allen Iverson would later recall, a real bad feeling. A sinking, short-of-breath, empty feeling, like when he used to get hit on the football field and the air would be crushed from his body. That was the feeling of September 11, when Tawanna came upstairs and turned on the TV, waking him up by softly saying, "I cannot believe what just happened."

A lot of people he knew watched the TV all day. They saw the buildings fall, they saw city streets morph into war zones. After an hour, Iverson clicked it off. He'd seen more than his share of bad shit; he knew early on when something sure as hell wasn't about to end well. "All those innocent people who woke up that morning just like me and went to work like any other day, for them to just die like that?" Iverson would later say. "If that can happen, that tells you that anything can happen. I didn't know anybody in there, but it hurt so bad thinking about those people's families."

Four weeks later, the feeling was back, though this time it didn't just remind Iverson of having the wind knocked from him. This time, when the news came, it was worse than any hit he'd ever taken. It was worse than when Tony Clark was killed, because at least that was back in the day when corpses and chalk outlines were everyday sights. Word came that Ra, the most affable Cru Thik member, had been murdered back in Virginia, shot outside a bar, left leaking in the street.

On the night of October 13, Ra had been with friends at the MVP Sports Bar in downtown Newport News. So had somebody named Gregory Fox. Iverson was hearing that Fiend was there, too, a guy known to both Iverson and Ra. Fiend knew Fox, too—and now Fiend was nowhere to be found. Inside the bar, Ra may have teased Fox about having a lazy eye. There was speculation that after the two groups had left the bar, Ra and Fox argued over which one was the better rapper. Then there were eight gunshots. And Ra was no more.

Ra, the court jester of Cru Thik. The one who'd tease the others unmercifully, who'd say, "Oh, so I'm the scapegoat tonight, everybody gonna crack on ol' Ra," when the barbs were shot right back at him. Ra, the best father of the bunch; some of the other guys, you'd meet their kids on the sly. Ra was always with his three kids. He'd tell Allen he was heading back to Virginia to see his kids and Allen would instead send for them, just to keep Ra around. Because Ra always made things better. "I went to bed with two kids and woke up with five," Iverson told Royster when he called him with the news of Ra's murder. "Now I gotta take care of these kids and let them know what a great father they had."

At the funeral, just two months after he officiated at the Iverson wedding, Reverend Barber eulogized Ra and again put things in perspective for a grieving Allen. "Look at your life as a book," the reverend counseled. "And stop wasting pages complaining, worrying, and gossiping."

Iverson's mourning was made all the more painful because he didn't have his customary refuge available to him. He couldn't escape his pain on the basketball court because he'd delayed undergoing arthroscopic surgery on his elbow all summer. In the past, his body had always healed itself. In fact, this very elbow, which had been a problem at least since Georgetown, had always come back on its own after a summer of rest. That's what he was banking on all summer, even while the doctors were telling him he'd need surgery. Easy for them to tell a guy to go get himself cut. Friends would later say that on a certain level, Iverson's reluctance to go under the knife had something to do with a cultural predisposition, a reaction to the often exclusionary nature of the medical establishment in general—an establishment with a storied history of treating black people poorly or not at all (or even maliciously, as with the infamous Tuskeegee experiments).

He reluctantly went under the knife just before training camp. (As did his teammate McKie; the last act of Croce's presidency of the team had been to call McKie in July to congratulate him on his new, lucrative contract and to urge him to get the surgery he needed. Given Croce's penchant for attending to details, many connected to the Sixers doubted that the surgeries for Iverson and McKie would have taken place so late had Croce still been with the team.) An arduous rehab process followed, one that Iverson wasn't always diligent about.

Already, the new season differed significantly from a year before. Then, Iverson had come to training camp with something to prove and, when the rap CD imbroglio hit, was more deeply committed to his team than ever. Now his prevailing mood was grief, not determination, and, as he was unable to play, the court was suddenly no longer his sanctuary.

There were other differences as well. This year, because of injuries, McKie and Snow missed training camp along with Iverson. (Snow would begin the season on the disabled list with an injured thumb.) In addition, unlike a year earlier, when Geiger's refusal to waive his trade-kicker had certified that the off-season roster changes would be minimal, Brown made sweeping moves. Gone were Tyrone Hill, Jumaine Jones, and backup center Todd MacCulloch.

With Croce gone, the setting was ripe for Derrick Coleman's return. In Charlotte, Coleman was coming off his worst season as a professional. His relationship with his coach and onetime mentor, Paul Silas, had deteriorated. Charlotte would have been happy to give him away. But Brown traded starter George Lynch for him because Lynch felt underpaid by the Sixers and Brown knew Charlotte had the money to take care of him. For those who feared that Coleman's lackluster practice habits might rub off on Iverson, Brown said, "When Derrick was here before, he didn't have to practice all the time. This time, I've made it clear what will be expected of him."

Suddenly Iverson was on a vastly different team. Instead of the egoless, defensive-minded Lynch and Hill up front, there would be Harpring, a hustling player with an inconsistent outside shot, and Coleman, with his proficient offensive game and slow-footed defense. The combination of Mutombo and Coleman up front helped turn the Sixers from a young, athletic team into an older, plodding one.

The league was different as well, having finally legalized zone defenses. (In a zone, defensive players play an area of the floor rather than a man.) Now opposing teams could dedicate themselves to stopping Iverson with impunity. They could double-team him all over the court, whether he had the ball or not. Other coaches, like Flip Saunders in Minnesota and John Lucas in Cleveland, would adopt zone defenses early in the season with some success. Brown not only stuck with his tried-and-true defensive principles, he also refrained from adding an offensive "zone buster" to the team, someone who could score over packed-in defenses.

Without Iverson, the Sixers started the season 0–5. With his elbow still hurting, Iverson made his season debut at Dallas; before the game, Gary Moore gave him a black armband with the name Rasaan inscribed on it. Moore had been like a father to Ra; neither man said a word to the other as Iverson somberly placed the armband on his left elbow. (The right elbow was already encased in a black protective sleeve, as it would be all season.) Iverson vowed that before every free throw for the rest of the season, he'd tap the armband in a symbolic show of love for Ra.

On the court, Iverson scored 18 points on 7-for-28 shooting with nine assists in forty-four minutes. "Allen makes us a totally different team," Brown said afterward. "To play as many minutes as he did without that much practice time is incredible."

With Iverson back in the lineup, the Sixers ran off seven straight wins, a streak promptly followed by losses in seven of their next eight games. Iverson appeared to be playing with as much passion as ever. But off the court, the trauma of his friend's murder lingered. At Miami, Iverson missed practice the day before the game, telling the Sixers that Royster's mother had passed away and that he had to be with his now former bodyguard, who was from the Miami area.

Late the previous season, Royster had intervened when Iverson couldn't find about $300,000 worth of jewelry. Through police contacts, he traced the jewels to a pawnshop back in Virginia; a couple of Iverson's friends had apparently stolen and pawned the goods. As prominent a member of society as he had become, Iverson had never shed his belief, instilled by the social chaos in which he was reared, that the police were simply not to be trusted under any circumstances and that matters of justice were always to be handled "in-house"—within the community. (Iverson's outrage over Brown's public airing of their spats had similar roots; "family business," he maintained, ought to be handled internally.) When Royster used his police contacts to find out what had happened to the jewelry, it was as though he were *informing* on Cru Thik—a more grievous betrayal, at least in Iverson's eyes, than that of the friends who had stolen from him. After all, no human connection in this world, save that with his mother, was more essential to Iverson than the one he shared with Cru Thik. After Royster solved the mystery of the missing baubles, he was told his services would no longer be needed.

While it was true, now, that Royster's mother had passed away, it wasn't the case that the bodyguard was in Miami. He was in North Carolina, where Iverson reached him to express his condolences. Iverson, according to Royster, was "torn up" about Royster's loss, and spent a long time talking about how to deal with such tragic losses.

The next day, some two hours before game time, Iverson sat in the trainer's room, getting treatment on his elbow. His shooting percentage—never great—was way down, thanks in part to his continuing inability to fully extend the elbow on his shot. The malady would haunt his game all year and underscore in Iverson a distrust of those who had urged him to have the surgery.

But on this night, as on so many others of late, whether the subject was his elbow or his team's chances, the conversation always circled back to his dead friend. "It's always on my mind, except when I'm on the court," Iverson said; in a couple of hours, he'd score 25 points and lead the Sixers to a road win, but now he sounded morose and sapped of energy, as if to compensate in advance for his later expenditure. "I think about the good times we had, the things we went through. Most of all, I keep telling myself that he did his job with helping somebody—me. He helped me so much just by being a real friend and always telling me when he thought I was wrong. And I needed that in a friend, instead of a bunch of people telling me everything I want to hear. I feel good about the friendship I had with Ra. He saw things he might never have seen, he been to places and he experienced things. I know he had fun, because he was a happy-go-lucky guy. I just miss laughing with him. I even miss arguing with him, and me and him used to argue damn near every day."

Gary Moore came in. "You okay?" he asked.

"I'm cool, cat-daddy," Iverson said. In about fifteen minutes, he'd morph into what he'd always been, a chirping, class clown of a teammate. Turns out, Iverson's rookie teammate Samuel Dalembert had spray-painted a pair of his own sneakers, and after this therapy session, Iverson relentlessly rode the rookie: "This the NBA, man! You can call up a shoe company, say you in the NBA, and they'll send you boxes of the shit—in all colors!"

But first, after a moment of silence, his thoughts returned to Ra. "I know I'll see him again, and we'll have fun just like we always had," he said. "That's why, you watch me on the court, and you tell me if that guy is good or bad. I think you can tell who I am. I think you can tell I'm trying to get better as a person. Believe that. Because I want to go to heaven. When I die, I want to go see Ra, man. I know he's in heaven, and before I die I want to know that's where I'm going. I don't want to have to guess."

In November 2001, Reebok tore up Iverson's existing endorsement deal and announced it was signing him to a lifetime contract. No details were reported, but one industry source placed the amount at $121 million. It was just in time, too, because Iverson was feeling a cash crunch, thanks to all the houses and cars and living expenses he was having Woody's office dole out to some thirty-odd people (many of whom had kids to support). From Reebok's perspective, the new deal tied up their top endorser forever and gave the company final say over all his marketing plans. From now on, all of Iverson's business interests would dovetail with the image the company was promoting.

As November gave way to December, the Sixers' woes continued. Eric Snow was still sidelined with a thumb injury. Geiger's knees were worse, but the Philadelphia fans were unsympathetic. Their booing of him, he said, "at times broke my spirit"; he retired and swiftly moved back to Florida, leaving the Sixers without a backup center. McKie missed multiple games with an irregular heartbeat and back problems, Coleman sat out after hyperextending his knee, and Iverson missed games with a sprained left thumb.

But it wasn't just injuries plaguing the Sixers. The team suddenly seemed much older; Mutombo, in particular, seemed to have aged considerably since the play-off run last spring. Chemistry was also an issue. Coleman's physical problems were limiting him from practicing, and Iverson began to sense a double standard. Coleman was always talking basketball with Coach, sometimes dissecting tapes of games on the team plane with Brown and his assistants. Iverson saw that Coleman was able to go half speed, if need be, during practice, or take practices off when his knees swelled, and he began to complain within the confines of the team that Coleman was being afforded "franchise player" status.

The coaches felt it was a ridiculous argument, that Iverson was equating being a "franchise player" with getting away with special privileges. It never occurred to them that, in his own unique, and typically macho way, Iverson might have actually been jealous of Coleman's favored status in Brown's eyes. Maybe Iverson wanted to be the player Brown continually praised to the media as someone "who will make a great coach someday," as he often said of Coleman.

Meantime, Brown felt Iverson was reverting to his old habits. On December 17, Royster, seeking a security gig with the team, met with

Brown before practice and heard his complaints. "I've been in this business thirty-one years and I've never gone through something like this," Brown said. "I can't take it. He comes to the team plane late. He came to practice yesterday reeking of alcohol. I took one look at him and said, 'He's not going to make it through practice.'"

Three days later, the issues between the two men became public. The Sixers had lost the night before to Charlotte at home, dropping their record to 10–15. Iverson, bothered by the pain in his right elbow, left while practice was in midsession. "We had everybody here but Allen, which is typical," Brown said to the media afterward. He also returned to a pet peeve when it came to Iverson's game: "Everybody tells me we need a shooter," he said. "But we don't have anybody that will pass it to a shooter."

Iverson's response? He missed the next day's shoot-around before a win over Atlanta. At the end of December, the team left on a seven-game, thirteen-day West Coast roadtrip. While the team was on the road, rumors started swirling that Brown was about to resign. In Denver, he was asked if he'd be interested in coaching the Nuggets, who had named Mike Evans interim head coach after Dan Issel resigned the day after Christmas. Brown was circumspect and didn't rule out returning to coach in Denver someday. His coy response, plus his longtime friendship with Denver general manager Kiki Vandeweghe, helped give the rumor legs.

On the morning of the game against the Nuggets, Brown pulled Iverson aside for a lengthy, and overdue, heart-to-heart. "We've got to do this together," he said. "If we don't, with Pat gone, everybody's going to blame the two of us."

It was a productive clearing of the air, but it was undermined come game time when Iverson learned that Brown wouldn't be on the bench. Brown reportedly had taken a muscle relaxant for back and neck pain before the game; he was in no shape to coach. He stayed and rested in the training room instead. After a heartbreaking loss (Coleman, who had otherwise played well, failed to block out power forward Raef LaFrentz on a critical offensive rebound put-back late in the game), Iverson was despondent. His team had lost, and from his perspective, a father figure had once again reached out to him—only to disappoint. "If he's not coaching tomorrow night," Iverson grumbled on his way to the team bus, "he better just quit." It was no secret that Brown had wanted to retire after last season; Iverson believed that his coach's heart wasn't in the current season. "If he doesn't want to be here, he shouldn't have come back," he said.

On January 10, 2002, after the Orlando Magic came to Philly and manhandled the Sixers, 102–91, dropping the Sixers' record to 15–20, Iverson's team was eight games behind first-place New Jersey in the Atlantic Division. He spoke out after the game. "A lot of stuff that goes on on the court didn't go on last year, and nothing's being done about it," he said. "I don't know what the plan is, night in and night out, as far as the offensive end. At the defensive end, it should be obvious. We need to get stops and hustle, scramble like we always did. But we don't have that team no more." Later in the same media session, Iverson said, "Sometimes, if it ain't broke, don't fix it." Brown was reportedly angered by the comment, interpreting it as a reference to all the off-season moves that had changed the team.

Two days later, Iverson was a couple of minutes late to shoot-around. Brown told him to leave. That night, the mighty San Antonio Spurs were in town. Of course, they didn't stand a chance, not with Iverson having been kicked out of the shoot-around, not with the coach and player feuding once again. Iverson scored 37 points to go with 6 assists and 4 steals in forty-three dominant minutes. The Sixers won, 101–84. Mutombo, who had yet to see this once commonplace type of rift between his coach and teammate, observed that this spat "was like a father and a son."

By the end of January, the Sixers climbed back to the .500 mark after a 106–90 win at Boston, thanks to Iverson, who had 47 points. Though a Sixers insider described the relationship between Brown and Iverson as "beyond repair," the coach heaped affectionate praise upon his star player. "The little kid was sensational," he said, referring to Iverson by a moniker that some close to the team felt infantalized the player. "He took it to another level."

Iverson was leading the league in scoring again and his team might have been on a modest upswing, finally. The all-star game loomed, but it wouldn't be just any all-star game. It would be in Philly, and Allen Iverson was real serious about being a proper host.

He was everywhere. The Cru Thik guys threw two massive parties in his name at The Gallery, an inner-city Philadelphia shopping mall. Iverson was there the first night, in a VIP area, looking out over the crowd that had gathered to catch a glimpse of him. Then it was on to the jazz club Zanzibar Blue, where, along with hip-hop impresario Russell Simmons and comedian Chris Tucker, Iverson was one of the hosts for a bash benefiting Inner-City Games, Arnold Schwarzenegger's charity.

Simmons, Tucker, and Run-D.M.C. may have been in the house, but it was Iverson the crowd had come to see. Though he normally shied away from crowds—"People look at you like you ain't even human, like you need to be caged up or something," he said—Iverson found himself standing against a wall with Gaskins and Moore while a packed room of fans and media turned his way, watching his every move, camera lights glaring into his eyes. There he stayed for much of the evening; fans would approach with kind words, and he'd respond with shy thanks. Unlike, say, Charles Barkley or Magic Johnson, both of whom would work a room like this with the smooth skills of practiced politicians, Iverson stood, back against the wall, eyes downcast, forcing himself to adopt a public persona. After a few hours at Zanzibar, it was on to the center-city lounge Gaskins had rented for an all-night, laid-back after-hours party.

Meantime, the Philadelphia media seemed unimpressed that Iverson was spending time among the fans during all-star weekend. On talk radio, he was criticized for putting in brief appearances at parties thrown in his name; in fact, that was part of the plan. Iverson tried to hit as many parties as he could, to be with as many fans as he could, instead of spending all his time at just one venue.

The big story was that he'd blown off Friday's mandatory media session, as had Michael Jordan, whose stirring comeback at age thirty-nine had become a major story. Both were fined $10,000. When the two did meet with the press together, Jordan praised his younger rival. "I see traits of me in him in terms of just a competitive nature," Jordan said, while Iverson beamed sitting next to his childhood idol on the podium. "[He has] overcome any negative outlook from anybody. And he's taken it as a challenge to prove people wrong. And those are things you just can't teach."

Game day began with Iverson as a guest on Tim Russert's *Meet the Press.* Asked about September 11, Iverson paid homage to the New York City police without pointing out that he'd once been, in his view, unfairly prosecuted by police. The game itself was proof of just how integral the

NBA product had become in terms of showcasing African-American culture. Stars lined the court. Angie Stone and Alicia Keys movingly performed the African-American national anthem. Even if the game was anticlimactic, it had become a pop-culture happening.

Come game time, Iverson seemed listless, prompting more criticism from the talk-show snipers, who complained that his partying interfered with his play. Kobe Bryant dominated the game and was named MVP. Much to Iverson's chagrin, Bryant was booed mercilessly throughout the game, especially when he was awarded the MVP trophy.

Of course, the lack of hospitality afforded Bryant in his hometown made national news. Defenders of the Philadelphia fan noted that the Sixers got only a few thousand tickets for local fans; most of the crowd was made up of NBA heavy hitters from out of town. But this was Philly, after all, where a few thousand irate leather-lungs could sound like an arenaful.

After the game, Bryant said he was "upset" and "hurt" by the fans' reaction. Iverson rose to his defense. "I think [the booing] was wrong and I feel bad for him," he said. "I think a lot of people should take the time and think, what if that was their kid up there? But that's the way this profession is. You want to bring up a reason for it, but for something like that, you just can't find a reason."

Of course, the reasons were there. Just seven months before, Kobe had marched into Philly, his self-proclaimed assassin's game-face on, saying he'd come to "cut [the Sixers'] hearts out." And then he had. But something else was very likely afoot, too. Iverson had long since supplanted Bryant in the collective heart of the City of Brotherly Love—a nickname that, originally, at least, was not meant to be taken ironically. In the Age of Iverson, Bryant had become the unreal. Iverson was the player who kept it real, who showed up with a kid on each knee at the same indoor press conferences for which Kobe donned expensive sunglasses.

Maybe the fans booed Kobe because, on some level, they suspected Bryant had "gone Hollywood." To Iverson, such a view overlooked what Bryant's game said about him. He knew that Bryant worked his ass off. He knew that when Bryant's rookie season ended with a procession of play-off airballs, Kobe awoke the next morning, procured the key to the Pacific Palisades High School gym, and spent the afternoon and evening there, taking the same shots he'd blown the night before over and over again, willing himself into a clutch player.

Iverson knew that he and Bryant differed in approach and style. But when it came to the substance of his game, the man deserved respect. He tried to cheer up his rival. "I've played in Philly for six years," Iverson said, "and they boo us in the first quarter if things aren't going right."

In the second half of the season, injuries continued to decimate the Sixers. They hovered around .500 for much of the season's remainder, while Brown and Iverson maintained a steady truce. There were flare-ups, of course.

After a late February loss to Portland, Iverson spoke publicly about "some players not knowing the plays at the end of the game." He didn't name him, but he was talking about Mutombo, whose level of performance was waning as the season wore on. From Iverson's perspective, he was exhibiting leadership. He'd never single out a teammate for criticism by name, as Jordan had been known to do. (Jordan, who'd refer to his teammates as his "supporting cast," used to shout at Phil Jackson the names of the players he wanted to go back in for when he was on the bench.)

Mutombo was offended, however, as were many in the media. Mutombo was on the local news, saying Iverson had "pointed fingers." Before the next game, against Miami, Iverson confronted his teammate in the training room.

"You say shit about pointing fingers, that's a fuckin' slap in my face!" he shouted.

Mutombo was stunned. "Shut up! Shut up!" he yelled, in a hoarse baritone.

Days later, Iverson showed up a couple of minutes late for shoot-around. That night, with the first-place New Jersey Nets coming to town, Brown did not start Iverson. After five minutes and fourteen seconds of play, he entered the game to stirring applause and drained his first two jumpers. He scored 43 points and the Sixers raised their record to 29–28. After the game, Iverson was philosophical.

"I broke a team rule," he said. "You break a rule, so you've got to pay for it. But I wonder, what do you do when a player that doesn't start comes late? What's his punishment? I guess that rule was made for me."

The press pack laughed. But Iverson was still having a tough time. Though he played with undeniable zeal, he privately talked about how, all season, he'd been having trouble "finding the love." Unlike in past years, he was having difficulty putting a lot of off-court stuff aside.

"It's been hard, man," Iverson said one late-season day, stretched out in front of his locker, his elbow encased in a bulky ice pack. "I still can't straighten my arm out. But I ain't gonna use that as an excuse. It's just been hard, man."

Off the court, it had been a season that began with surgery and his best friend's murder. Another friend from back home, Jamil Blackmon, had filed a lawsuit against Iverson seeking a quarter of all proceeds Reebok derived from the nickname "The Answer," which Blackmon had given to Iverson. With Ra gone and Blackmon now turned against him, Iverson was face-to-face with the downside of the posse phenomenon. Having a crew might have been a necessary survival mechanism on the streets, but it lost its traction and very tenability once Iverson began moving in the "real" world. In Newport News, Cru Thik held its center because there *were* real threats, real enemies who needed to be kept at bay. But once Iverson moved on and up, those threats were no more; could it be that the psychic energy the posse had once directed toward outsiders was now, inevitably, turning inward?

Lately, one friend of the Iversons had even speculated that their marriage had hit a rough spot, owing to Tawanna's efforts to get her husband to cut at least some of his friends from the payroll. (Some of those friends were actually closer to Arnie Steele than to Iverson.)

Add to the mix a season of tough losses and problems with Brown that Iverson had thought they'd gotten behind them a year ago. "A lot of shit has gone down within the organization that's been tough," he said.

As the Sixers made a late-season run, there were moments, though. In a game at Toronto, Iverson scored 42 points and emitted an open-mouthed, openhearted warrior roar after sealing the game with back-to-back steals and driving layups.

"Maybe I'm getting the love back," he said shortly after the Toronto game, before again showing that heartache still haunted him. "I know that Ra is with me and that he wouldn't accept anything but me loving it out there, like I always have. I mean, it's a feeling you get. And you can't force it. Maybe it's coming back. I mean, the play-offs are coming. You know what Ra would say, right? He'd say, 'It's the play-offs? Well, let's get this party jumping, man.'"

But just when it looked like Iverson was getting into his groove, his regular season ended prematurely. In the first half of a game against Boston, Tony Battie chopped down on Iverson's left hand, fracturing the second metacarpal. On the bench, Iverson told Snow his hand was broken. Yet he played until he could undergo X rays at halftime—scoring 20 points *after* the injury.

The doctors said he could have surgery or try to let the injury heal on its own. Successful surgery might get him back a week sooner. This time, there was no hesitancy. The talk-show mavens could blather on all they wanted. Nobody was about to cut on him again. His regular season over early, Iverson won his second scoring title (31.1 points per game) on a career-low 39 percent shooting. He'd be back for the play-offs, which the Sixers qualified for as the number six seed, with a 43–39 record. A first-round, best-of-five matchup against the up-and-coming Celtics awaited them.

When the Sixers practiced at Harvard University the day before game one of the play-offs, it marked the first time all year that Brown had every one of his players available to him in the most injury-plagued season he'd ever coached. With the benefit of just one practice, Iverson pronounced himself ready. "I feel great," he said.

The matchup between the Sixers and Celtics marked a renewal of basketball's most-storied play-off rivalry. In the past, Wilt did battle with Bill Russell, Dr. J with Larry Bird. This series promised to be a war between Iverson and Paul Pierce, the sharpshooting small forward Brown had passed on in the 1999 draft in favor of Larry Hughes.

Five seconds into game one, Iverson buried his first shot, a jumper. In fact, he made four of his first five attempts, but as the game went on, his shooting touch went south. He missed his last 10 shots, finishing 4 for 15 for 20 points. The Sixers lost, 92–82. With their expert outside shooting, the Celtics spread the floor and pulled Mutombo out from beneath the basket. On the perimeter, he was rendered ineffective. Late in the game, they sent cutters behind him for backdoor baskets.

Iverson was unable to take over the game, conceding afterward that he'd been "kind of hesitant." Players often speak of "letting the game come to them," but that had never been Iverson's style. He had always stubbornly stamped his imprint on the game, always been an instigator of action.

The day before game two, according to the Sixers' public-relations staff, Iverson didn't practice. He vociferously denied the report. Brown said he "ran up and down the court a few times" but had mostly sat out with a "sinus infection." In any case, Iverson was thinking ahead to game two. "I'm all about bouncing back," he said.

In that game, with Iverson resting on the bench, the Sixers went on a 14–2 fourth-quarter run to go ahead 75–71, behind 10 straight points from McKie. But with seven minutes left, Iverson checked back in and McKie came out. With the Sixers up four, Iverson missed two jumpers; the Celtics went ahead to stay and won, 93–85.

Iverson had hit 11 of 30 shots for 29 points, but he missed five of his last seven shots, including the two with the Sixers ahead by four. After the game, Iverson reacted angrily when a reporter asked if, in retrospect, the decision to take those two shots was a "smart" one. "That stuff happens in the flow of the game," he said, annoyed at the second-guessing and, perhaps, the racially charged insinuation about intelligence. "I don't care about that. They were shots that were missed."

Meantime, in his postgame comments, Brown set off a couple of days' worth of controversy. "I think their star players are thinking about winning the game and not dominating the game," he said.

By now, Iverson had grown accustomed to his coach's none-too-subtle public digs. There was that time early in the season, after a loss to Toronto, when Brown observed that "[Toronto's] superstar is unselfish." Iverson had held his tongue, but he felt it was Brown's way of name-calling and finger-pointing.

At practice the day after the Celtics loss, Iverson responded. "I don't know why he would want to think that I don't want to win," he said. "I want to be dominant and I want to win. You should've asked him, did he feel like I want to win? Because he'll tell you I want to do both."

Brown offered a strange pseudo-rebuttal: "I think I'd rather have him say he wants to win and then dominate," he said.

The back-and-forth—carried out through the indirect agency of reporters—typically glossed over some critical points. Iverson believed that the odds of his team winning were *enhanced* if he dominated—no matter what order you put the terms in. Otherwise, the Sixers' record in games without him this season wouldn't have been 7–15. (For his career, his team is 22–34 when he wasn't in the lineup.) More important, from Iverson's perspective, the "is he more interested in dominating than winning" question was further proof of a lack of respect accorded him—a disrespect no other player of his stature seemed to receive. It led Iverson to declare, somewhat mysteriously, that he is not "a franchise player."

Over the next couple of days, many in the Philadelphia media interpreted the remark as a sign that Iverson was shrinking from his responsibility as the team's go-to man. Instead, Iverson meant to say he wasn't being *treated* as a franchise player by management. All season long he'd voiced this complaint, whether it was in observing that Coleman got away with missing practices he'd have been disciplined for skipping or in pointing out that when his shots didn't fall at the end of games, his coach got on him—something few "franchise" players had to tolerate.

Iverson even entertained the notion that he could be traded. Since jettisoning Falk, he hadn't had—or needed—an agent. But that would change if he were suddenly on the trading block. His lawyers weren't known in NBA circles. So he hired Leon Rose, McKie's agent, to start representing him on basketball matters, and now, on the eve of game three, he raised the issue of a trade.

"I mean, after going to the Finals last year, you see how many changes we made, so anything can happen," he said. "I could be gone this summer. I know it's a business. And I know once things start going bad, the first thing you think about is making changes instead of just trying to get better . . . I've always said from day one, I want to be a Sixer. I want to remain a Sixer for the rest of my career. And I'm not going to let anyone drive me out of here. But if people think me leaving is the best for the team, then make that decision."

In the first two games of the series, Iverson shot a paltry 15 for 45, while his backcourt mate Snow was a chilly 4 for 25. And now, thanks to Iverson and Brown's latest Kabuki dance, the pressure was palpable. *Philadelphia Inquirer* columnist Stephen A. Smith went so far as to suggest that if Iverson didn't single-handedly stave off the Sixers' elimination by playing like a superstar, he ought to get ready to pack his bags—because he'd be as good as traded. "Iverson has had many challenges in his basketball career," Smith wrote, "but maybe none as tough as this one."

Perhaps predictably, Iverson not only responded to Smith's challenge—he proved that, when he dominates, the Sixers win. The final score was 108–103, and he had 42 points, connected on 19 of 20 free throws, and made 5 steals. In a close fourth quarter, he scored 13 points. Snow helped keep the defense honest by nailing 9 of 14 shots. "Pressure is in tires," Iverson quipped after the game. "Basketball is what I love to do. It's not supposed to be any type of pressure. It's supposed to be fun."

For his part, Brown was contrite about the controversy leading up to game three. "Our stars the last two games are trying to do it the right way," he said. "I've got to be real careful the way I word things. This is typical of what goes on with us when things go bad, and I think people equate 'things go bad' with when you lose a couple games."

Game four had a different feel. The teams were tied with less than two minutes remaining; Iverson had spent much of the game missing shots, hitting only 5 of 21. Miraculously, he scored eight points in the final seventy-seven seconds. First, he snared an offensive rebound off a McKie missed foul shot and drove the lane, lofting a high, soft shot that bounced around the rim and finally through it. After a McKie steal, Iverson knifed through the lane for a driving layup. When Boston's Rodney Rogers tied the game at 79, Iverson raised up and hit a twenty-foot jumper while falling to his right. That proved to be the game winner. When his two free throws iced the game with seconds left, the crowd chanted "MVP! MVP!" while Iverson, childlike, skipped off the court.

"I've been around stars," McKie said after the game. "But he's in a league by himself."

The deciding game five in Boston, however, was a disaster. Paul Pierce riddled the Sixers' defense for 46 points, including 8 of 10 three-pointers, in a 120–87 Boston blowout. Defensively, the Sixers—particularly Mutombo and Coleman—were unable to cover Boston's perimeter shooters. On offense, Mutombo was again a nonfactor and Snow hit only 2 of 12 shots, making him 18 of 56 (32 percent) for the series. Alone among the Sixers, Iverson, who liked to boast that he "plays every game like it's my last," played with urgency. He hit 11 of 24 shots for 31 points. But it was Celtics point guard Kenny Anderson who summed up the Sixers' season best after the game: "They are nothing like the team I saw last year," he said. "They have Allen Iverson. Everything else was so different."

Their season was over, but—this being Brown, Iverson, and the 76ers—the drama was just starting.

The day after the end of his team's season, Larry Brown met individually with all but one of his players. When Iverson was a no-show, Brown would later say, he was "crushed." And so he told members of the press what Iverson might otherwise have heard in private.

"My problems with Allen have been the same for five years," Brown said. "I love him, I love his competitiveness. The issues I have are all the things he has control over. He'll have a problem if that doesn't change. I'm looking at a kid that tells me he wants to win. I've heard him say it to the media, he doesn't have a selfish bone in his body, that he's going to be the first guy to practice and last to leave. He said that publicly. Now let's do it."

Brown's comments filled a gaping sports-news hole in Philadelphia. The Sixers' and Flyers' seasons had both just ended, it was two months until football's training camp, and the Phillies were already mired in last place. The big story became: Was Allen Iverson about to be traded? WIP, the all-sports talker, debated the issue around the clock and the newspapers were filled with speculation. On Tuesday, May 7, 2002, Iverson finally had a meeting with Brown. Sixers sources said it went swimmingly; afterward, Iverson held a press conference at the arena that would be carried live on TV in Philadelphia. When the fireworks started, ESPN2 would jump to the story live as well.

Iverson began the session talking about the meeting he'd just had with Brown. "I just let him know I'm that pit bull in his yard, and if anybody tries to intrude, I'm going to be the one that's going to bite and protect his home," he said. But he was also upset by Brown's public comments. "No question," he said. "[We're] not as tight as I thought we was by this shit happening right now . . . If you're going to get rid of Allen Iverson, then get rid of Allen Iverson. Do a trade. But you don't have to assassinate his character."

The words started coming faster now, tinged with fury. He couldn't believe he was here, facing the judgment of a roomful of journalists—when his teammates were long gone. "I know I do all I can for this city, for this team, for my teammates. I know don't nobody in the world plays harder than me. And for me to go through this is just tough, man. Everybody in Philadelphia know, all y'all know I want to be here. That ain't no secret. Everybody knows I want to be a Sixer for the rest of my career, but I'm tired. I'm hurt, too."

Someone asked about missing practices. For a brief moment, he was silent, staring at his questioners. "If I can't practice, I can't practice," he said. "If I'm hurt, I'm hurt . . . I know I'm supposed to be there. I know I'm supposed to lead by example. I know that. I know it's important, I honestly do. But we're talking about practice."

And then he was off on what would commonly be referred to in the press as a "rant" about practice. He would use the word seventeen times, prompting Brown to joke that Iverson *said* "practice" more than he came to it. "I'm supposed to be the franchise player, and we're in here talking about practice," he said. "Not a game. We're talking about practice. How silly is that? . . . I don't feel like the franchise player because—look at this press conference, look at what we're talking about . . . Practice. Franchise players don't go through this. Franchise players' daughters don't have to go to school and hear, 'Is your daddy coming back? What's going on with your daddy and Coach Brown?' She's seven years old and that's what she's got to deal with. It hurt."

Iverson scoffed at the notion that he could make his teammates better by practicing. "How the hell can I make my teammates better by practicing?" he shot back. "So my game is going to deteriorate if I don't practice with those guys? Is my game going to get worse?"

He sat on the edge of his seat, ready to do battle. Off in the wings, Sixers general manager Billy King reached for his cell phone with a worried look. Meantime, Iverson turned the tables on his questioners. When Comcast SportsNet's Michael Barkann suggested that such criticism comes with the territory of being paid $11 million to play a game, Iverson waved away the Sixers public-relations official who tried to intervene and shot back: "Don't you get paid to do what you do? I don't go around saying I don't like the way you mispronounced this or that word, man." When Phil Jasner, longtime beat writer for the *Philadelphia Daily News*, posited that, if Iverson worked out with weights, maybe he could increase the strength in his legs and, thus, his shooting percentage by a couple of points, Iverson said: "You ever play basketball?"

"Yes," Jasner muttered.

"Well, I don't know Phil Jasner as no basketball player," Iverson said, smiling slightly. "I know Phil Jasner as a columnist." (The next day, the *Daily News* would run a photo of Jasner playing pickup basketball.)

Later, members of the media marveled at Iverson's aggressive defensiveness. From his point of view, however, his work ethic and character were on trial—and he was particularly sensitive to being on trial. Moreover, on a practical level, Iverson believed his low shooting percentage wasn't a function of weak legs; he'd always known his body, always had preternatural energy and stamina and strength. No, he shot a low percentage because he took low-percentage shots, which had been part of Brown's system for five years now. Without another scorer capable of drawing a double team, paired in a backcourt with a guard who couldn't consistently hit open jumpshots, Iverson had long been relegated to leading the league in scoring, yes, but also in degree-of-difficulty shots.

But he said none of this—why should he have to? He railed on and on, about practice—"we talkin' 'bout *practice*, man,"—but beneath the lashing out was a tension born of his own dawning, but not yet fully conscious, knowledge. He'd improved every year of his basketball career—until this one; perhaps he was advancing to the point in his career where talent alone was no longer sufficient to cut it. Could Iverson's anger have had something to do with a nascent realization that, to continue being a brilliant grasshopper, he'd have to change his ways and become a worker ant, too?

But the pundits saw Iverson's performance as a defiant announcement that he'd never change. There you have it, they said: he's as much as told us he'll never consistently come to practice. In fact, he'd explicitly said the opposite, beginning by saying, "I know I'm supposed to lead by example" and by acknowledging his missteps: "I got some shit that I need to get better in." No, as Iverson kept upbraiding the press pack for its focus on "practice," it was clear, in his own unique way, he was serving up a media critique. They'd taken his coach's bait and scapegoated him, he seemed to suggest, after a series in which—though he'd never name his teammates—Eric Snow couldn't hit an open twelve-foot jumpshot and Dikembe Mutombo couldn't catch a simple entry pass into the post. "We talking 'bout *practice*" was nothing short of Iverson's way of stating the obvious: "I'm not the problem with this team."

The media didn't get it. There were comparisons to Mike Tyson; the press conference was more than once referred to as a "meltdown." One columnist called for Iverson to be immediately traded, describing the event as the "truly bizarre ramblings of a scolded, wounded and obviously confused Iverson." But the public reaction, in interviews and anecdotal evidence, seemed much less reactionary. Fans had seen the series, they'd seen game five, when only Iverson seemed to be hustling in the fourth quarter. They heard him respond to being dissed by his coach by proclaiming his love for the man and reiterating his desire to stay a Sixer throughout his career.

Most of all, after all the deadening postgame clichés served up by athletes over the past couple of decades, they'd been treated to a raw, heartfelt exhibition. You wouldn't find Kobe Bryant holding such a press conference. The next day, Brown held a press conference of his own. He said that, in his meeting with Iverson before the player's press conference, he'd told him, "You can tell your daughter not to worry about it: Daddy is going to be living in Philadelphia and we're going to see him at training camp at Penn State and move on and try to figure out a way we can get better."

"The way you saw him act is maybe why he does so many special things on the court," Brown continued. "Maybe why every time I take him out of a game he dresses me down publicly . . . It's my responsibility to teach him the right way without inhibiting him. I have to let him grow; I've got to grow myself."

Watching Iverson's news conference, Brown suggested, was like watching "a young kid reaching out for help." In that sense, maybe it was all a fitting end to a turbulent, wrenching season. At one point during his press conference, Iverson had lowered his volume and taken a step back. "You want to know why I'm upset? I just didn't want to have to be here, that's all," he said. "My best friend died, my team lost, and this is what I've got to go through for the rest of the summer until the season starts over again. This is what I've got to go through. This is my life, in a nutshell."

Just before the curtain closed—only temporarily—on the drama that is Allen Iverson, he stood up and said, "Y'all have a happy life," and then he was gone, scaling a fence outside the arena en route to one of his three Cadillac Escalades, pausing only to hug Comcast SportsNet's Barkann, with whom he'd just tussled, when Barkann called to him, "A.I., have a great summer." Looking back at the tailing media over his shoulder, he called, "It's going to be a happy ending," a note of reassurance in his voice, as though he were suddenly comforting his chroniclers. Then he slapped hands with the black parking-lot attendant before peeling out of the lot. Finally, summer.

Event#:   181174087
PID#: 948473
Name: IVERSON
        ALLEN
Arrest Date: 07 / 16 / 02
Age at Arrest: 27
Height: 6'00"
Weight: 165
Hair Color: BLACK
Eye Color: BROWN
Phila. PD ARREST

epilogue

these are tough times, man. everybody's taking the chance to throw their darts at me.

In Tom Wolfe's *The Bonfire of the Vanities*, the protagonist, an uppity yuppie named Sherman McCoy, is unaware that he is surrounded by people itching for his comeuppance. He finds himself in an altercation. At first, it doesn't seem like a big deal. The fallout, however, is anything but minor. McCoy's life spirals into an absurd nightmare peopled with self-interested politicians, Kafkaesque denizens of the criminal "justice" system, and tabloid hacks out to make a quick buck. It is more than a novel; it is a deconstruction of a singularly modern development: the all-consuming media feeding frenzy.

Allen Iverson never read Wolfe's book, but as Iverson's life blew up in the summer of 2002 and made headlines the world over, it was as though Wolfe were workshopping a sequel. Within a matter of weeks, Iverson found himself at the center of a narrative that featured a stranger-than-fiction cast of characters.

There were the cops, with their pronouncements straight out of *Dirty Harry*. There was the tabloid paper, running Iverson's image on the cover for seven straight days—and seeing an average increase in sales of five thousand papers per day. There was Iverson's flamboyant accuser, who wore revealing, high-cut "poom-poom pants." There was a city's black mayor, whose spokesman publicly tried to rein in the police. There was a rabid radio talk-show host, unleashing incendiary charges of "cover-up" early on. There was the pricey, hotshot lawyer Iverson would turn to. There were the TV stations camped outside Iverson's mansion around the clock. There were the gay-rights groups who wanted to know just why the accuser's sexuality—not to mention the type of pants he wore—was relevant.

In Wolfe's novel, a fictional character stood at the center of the storm. Now it was Iverson's turn.

Over the July Fourth weekend, the cops started to leak the news. They were looking into a complaint regarding Allen Iverson and a home invasion. Something about Allen and Tawanna having a fight, and Allen searching for his wife late at night in a West Philly apartment.

It had been a slow news summer in Philadelphia; the specter of an Iverson scandal instantly energized the fourth estate in the nation's fourth largest media market.

The apartment in question belonged to Iverson's first cousin Shaun Bowman, Aunt Jessie's twenty-one-year-old son. Tawanna often turned to Shaun when she and Allen argued. After a quarrel, Tawanna stormed out and headed over to Shaun's. Later, Iverson, accompanied by his uncle Greg, went to find his wife. Only Tawanna and Shaun weren't there. Charles Jones, Shaun's roommate, was in the apartment with seventeen-year-old Hakim Carey, an upstairs neighbor.

Iverson would later tell friends that shortly after he entered the apartment, Jones, who is gay, gave him some finger-snapping, head-bobbing attitude. Iverson, ever the mimic, would even crack up friends with his impression: "Listen here, Mr. Allen Iverson," he'd screech. "Don't be coming in here like you're all that!"

No doubt, words were exchanged. Jones and Carey alleged that Iverson locked the apartment door behind him, forced them to call Bowman, and picked up his shirt so they could see a gun tucked into his waistband. "Either I'm going to die or I'm going to jail, and I guarantee that I am not going to die," Jones and Carey claimed Iverson said. They alleged that he wiped his fingerprints off of the phone and made more threats before leaving.

By midweek, WIP sports talk-show host Howard Eskin was raising the stakes, turning a routine criminal complaint into a political football. He claimed the mayor's office was trying to orchestrate a cover-up, and none too subtly implied a racial cabal, referring to both Mayor John Street and Iverson as "brothers."

Eskin was a longtime Philadelphia broadcaster known for a bombastic style and short fuse. He also had a reputation as a reporter; he didn't just opine, he dug around a story. Ironically, Eskin had long championed past controversial Philly sports stars such as Charles Barkley and Mike Schmidt, cultivating friendships with both men. But for some time, he'd been a fierce critic of Iverson's. (Schmidt, in fact, once explained Eskin's methods: "If you're his buddy, he'll never rip you," said the Hall of Famer. "Like Barkley—for the most part, he'll support everything that Barkley does, because Barkley's his buddy. Same with me.") In the aftermath of the CD controversy in the fall of 2000, Iverson, offended by something Eskin had said about him, ceased to speak to the broadcaster. Once, when Eskin tried to say hello in the locker room, Iverson snapped, "Kiss my ass," and brushed by him.

Ann defending her son in July 2002 as she is driven up to Iverson's estate. "I'm not frontin' no games," she said.

THE
ALLEN IVERSON
CELEBRITY SUMMER
CLASSIC
ALL ACCESS

At his 2002 Celebrity Summer Classic, Iverson listens to Pat Croce.

Now Eskin filled the airwaves with invective, calling Iverson a "thug" with "a drinking problem." When African-Americans called in, he'd tease them by breaking into Ebonics—"wassup, dawg?"—or an impression of Iverson's "we talkin' 'bout practice" screed. The problem, Eskin said, was Iverson's friends—though he glossed over the fact that, in this case, Iverson's friends weren't alleged to have been involved. In any case, Eskin argued, Iverson was receiving preferential treatment. If it were anyone else, he argued, the suspect would already be in jail.

Shortly thereafter, mayoral spokesman Frank Keel called into the same station's morning show and rebutted Eskin. "I can tell you that it's going in the opposite direction," Keel said. "There are some detectives within the rank and file of the police department who may actually be a bit overzealous about nailing Allen Iverson in this thing."

Now, with the mayor's office publicly chastising the police, the case—like any cause célèbre—took on a life of its own. Time and again, innuendo and hearsay were repeated as fact; the *Inquirer* printed the transcript of Jones's 911 call, which took place some eleven hours after Iverson had been in the apartment. In the call, Jones told the dispatcher that earlier in the night, Iverson had thrown his wife "out the house naked." Within days, national news outlets were repeating the allegation as though it had been independently reported: "According to published reports, Iverson threw his wife out of the house naked."

The police—challenged now by the mayor's office—leaked to the press that blood had been found in one of the Iversons' cars. Later, it turned out to be jelly from one of the kids' sandwiches. Nothing could stop the media circus. *Nine* detectives were sent to the Iverson mansion to execute a search warrant in search of a gun while news choppers hovered above. The ABC affiliate broadcast Iverson's address. The CBS affiliate led off one newscast with "exclusive" still photos of Iverson stepping onto his patio to rescue his dog, whose head had gotten caught in the porch's wrought-iron gate.

The police couldn't find a gun, but publicly announced they had probable cause for an arrest. The district attorney asked for further investigation. "This isn't over yet," lead detective Lieutenant Mike Chitwood said into the cameras. "Stay tuned." It was a telling choice of language, for the case had quickly morphed from legal issue into *show*.

Iverson was charged with four felonies—two counts of criminal trespass and one each of conspiracy and violating the Uniform Firearms Act—and ten misdemeanors. From a legal standpoint, there was unanimity from former prosecutors and defenders alike: there was no case here. Even former Philadelphia district attorney F. Emmitt Fitzpatrick was quoted in the *New York Times* as saying that "An arrest should never have been made."

Both Ira Berkow and William Rhoden of the *New York Times* weighed in; both mentioned Iverson's "record" and cited the bowling-alley-brawl conviction—without mentioning that an appeals court had overturned it. In the *Chicago Sun-Times*, Rick Telander wrote, "[Iverson] never expresses remorse, or even regret, for the things he does." In the *Philadelphia Daily News*, John Baer wrote that Iverson was "thug-prone," with "too much money, too much freedom, too much talent to hear the word 'no.' " Tom Knott in the *Washington Times*, before comparing Iverson to O. J. Simpson, wrote that, "America cannot say it was not warned if something truly bad ever happens to Iverson's naked wife . . ." The headline on the column by *Washington Post* media writer Howard Kurtz read FEW BOOS FOR GUN WAVING ATHLETE—despite the fact that not even Iverson's accuser claimed he waved a gun. Even Jay Leno got in on the act, unveiling the new Iverson signature shoe from Reebok. "It's called 'The Incarcerator,' " he cracked, pulling them from the box to show a chain link connecting one shoe to the other.

Iverson hired high-powered Philadelphia attorney Richard Sprague, a former prosecutor himself, to defend him. Sprague was out of the country, so the police allowed Iverson to turn himself in for arraignment upon his lawyer's return. In the meantime, they said, he wasn't under house arrest—but if he left his house, he'd be arrested. Iverson's critics howled about the special privileges being afforded him. Who else but a celebrity gets to make an appointment in advance to turn himself in? Actually, in Philadelphia, plenty of suspects. What was unusual here was the de facto house-arrest conditions.

So what did Iverson do? On the Saturday night before his Tuesday-morning arraignment, he threw an all-night party at the mansion while the gaping media looked on. "That's not guts," wrote Jim Spencer back home in the Newport News *Daily Press*. "It's not even arrogance. It is pure contempt—contempt for which Iverson will never be punished . . .

If the [rest] of us did what he does, we'd be behind bars or hanging on the street corner with no money and no prospects."

Just as passionate, on the other side, were Iverson's defenders. Reebok went far beyond the cautiously-supportive-PR-statement standard in such situations. "It is Allen's celebrity status, not the facts, that continues to fuel these proceedings," the company said in a statement. Interestingly, the *Wall Street Journal* reported anecdotal evidence indicating that Iverson's shoes sales were way up in the aftermath of his arrest. According to a Wells Fargo analyst, East Coast retailers had been "unable to keep the Iverson product in the stores."

Outside the Philadelphia Police Roundhouse, Iverson's arraignment was soundtracked by the cheering of fans, some of whom sold T-shirts proclaiming FREE IVERSON and THE ANSWER IS NOT GUILTY, just as had been done a decade earlier outside the courtroom in Virginia.

At one point, Ann came outside the mansion to confront the media horde. She counted five men standing around her with rings on their fingers and talked about how all couples have their ups and downs. "Do those ups and downs include throwing your wife out of the house naked?" asked one female TV reporter.

Ann let loose. "Get outta my face with that crazy stuff," she said while Aunt Jessie, next to her, shouted: "That's hearsay!"

"That's rumors," Ann continued. "Where you get that from? Did Tawanna tell you that? If you want to keep it real, keep it real with me, because I ain't frontin' no games."

Howard Stern had a lot of fun playing that audio clip over and over. But Ann had a point: Tawanna wasn't the complainant in this case. Plus, if the parade of lawyers-turned-pundits were right and the case against Allen was leading nowhere, and if the allegations—even if true—paled in comparison to a host of recent athlete transgressions, it begged the question: Why Iverson? Why this frenzy—again?

The way this country plays out its race traumas is—pardon the pun— very black-and-white. There is victim, and there is victimizer. Iverson's travails in the summer of 2002 were no exception.

Those reflexively denouncing him as a thug, just as those reflexively defending him as a victim of police harassment, might ostensibly have been talking about the case's evidence. But make no mistake: they were all trying to wrest control of what Allen Iverson symbolizes, what his story should *mean*. Many of us, whether we consciously realize it or not, similarly comprehend Iverson as symbol, which necessarily means we *invest* in him—either as a victim or as a victimizer. Those who demand the book be thrown at him today? Invested. Those who ten years ago beheld him as the catalyst for a "Rosa Parks" type movement? Invested.

It's not about the facts. In both the bowling-alley case and this most recent one, observers could sift through the testimony and appear impartial. And yet when people came down on one side or the other, they did so, almost to a person, along racial lines. Allen Iverson has now become a walking, breathing legacy born of the O.J. case; where you fall on Iverson depends on where you've invested yourself. (And in all likelihood, you invested yourself where you did long before Iverson came onto your radar.)

After all, it can't be about substance. Iverson's much-talked-about "record," his "rap sheet," consists of precisely one incident: the 1997 probation for having a legally registered gun under his seat. Those who refer to his litany of transgressions are inevitably including the overturned bowling-alley conviction, the missteps of his friends, and even his run-ins with Larry Brown.

So if it's not the substance, it's got to be the style. Sports' groundbreaking social characters, after all, always engender backlash: Jackie Robinson, Muhammad Ali, Joe Namath. Iverson burst onto the scene as the first athlete to wear cornrows, the first to so widely tattoo his body, the first to fire David Falk, the first to record gangsta rap, the first to cross over Michael Jordan and then say he didn't have to respect him. He instantly supplanted the likes of Mike Tyson as public enemy number one; to some, he represented the worst fears of white America, the latest and maybe best embodiment of what poet Amiri Baraka (then LeRoi Jones) wrote over thirty years ago of boxer Sonny Liston: "[Liston is] the big black Negro in every white man's hallway, waiting to do him in, deal him under for all the hurts white men, through their arbitrary order, have been able to inflict on the world."

For those who came down on his side, there was an appreciation for his ballsy nonconformity. But there are those, too, who reacted defensively when confronted by his unwillingness to sign on to the assimilation script. They are the ones who tend to see Iverson as a grenade with the pin pulled, as a kind of Tyson Redux.

But where Tyson is sideshow material (the cannibalistic threats, the *actual* cannibalism, the overall Poe-like derangement), Iverson is a threat. For Iverson succeeds. Born and raised in chaos, he thrives in it; depending on how you're invested, you can laud him for his survival skills and see him as a classic American figure, someone who succeeded not by overcoming the circumstances that spawned him—but *because* of them. He hasn't overcome the ghetto; he's taken it with him. Or you can see him as a walking refutation of all your own choices. Allen Iverson has never chosen safe or stable or comfortable.

Allen Iverson showed up for his July 29 preliminary hearing wearing a T-shirt, but not just any T-shirt. On the chest was Ra's picture, under the words CRU THIK SUPERSTAR.

In the six-hour hearing, Iverson's lawyer, Sprague, eviscerated the key witnesses against him. Hakim Carey, the upstairs neighbor, testified that when he saw that the man knocking on the door was Allen Iverson, he rushed to get paper and pen for an autograph. Iverson, Carey testified, demanded they get his "cocksucking wife" on the phone. Carey went on to say he didn't see Iverson with a gun and that Jones had urged him to go along with the story that Iverson had one.

Iverson's cousin Shaun testified that Iverson paid the rent on the apartment and had permission to come and go as he pleased. He also alleged that Jones had offered to drop everything for $100,000.

Jones was no match for Sprague, who quickly painted a portrait of Jones as a cocaine-snorting ex-con who couldn't even say where he'd gotten his cell phone from. It was a gift, Jones said, "from some guy Maurice." Sprague read aloud the numbers Jones had called in the ten hours before he dialed the police. The last of these was a twenty-one-minute call to a personal-injury lawyer that ended eighteen seconds before Jones called 911.

The judge had heard enough. He tossed the four felony charges and all but two misdemeanor counts for making terroristic threats. (The remaining misdemeanors were dropped in September.) "It sounded like you had a relative, looking for a relative, at the house of a relative. And you had the door opened by the guest of a guest," said Judge James DeLeon, a

Philadelphia Municipal Court judge, who determined there probably had never been a gun.

That didn't stop those who had already invested in Iverson's guilt from looking askance at the ruling. Eskin, for example, was unbowed. "He *had* a gun!" he shouted on the air, upbraiding the judge for admitting he was a fan of Iverson's and for showing deference to Sprague.

It's true that the judge may have been a bit cowed by Iverson's venerated counsel, but there was unanimity among legal observers when the ruling came down. "The case was dead on arrival," said Philadelphia lawyer George Bochetto, a former Republican candidate for mayor who secured the plum gig as ESPN's on-air legal analyst at the height of the Iverson story. "Before the first witness, the ability to prosecute that case was zero because of the nature and character of the witnesses, the star power of Iverson, and the complete absence of any victim or any harm."

To some, Iverson had evaded justice again. To others, he'd once again escaped the clutches of an unjust system.

The Sixers, who offered sound bites of support for Iverson through the ordeal, followed up the ruling by seeing to it that the headlines soon reverted back to matters of basketball. They let Matt Harpring go as a free agent to Utah and traded center Dikembe Mutombo to interdivision rival New Jersey for former Sixers center Todd MacCulloch (who suffered from chronic foot problems) and former Sixers draft pick Keith Van Horn. The remake raised all sorts of potential pitfalls: Could a front line of MacCulloch, Coleman, and Van Horn play anything but matador defense? Could Brown coach them if that were the case?

But lost in the summer talk of the Sixers' latest makeover, not to mention the fixation on Iverson's legal travails, was a simple fact that might have suggested positive developments for the player and his team: the Sixers consulted Iverson before trading Mutombo. Presumably, he'd signed off on the acquisition of Van Horn, someone with the potential, at least, to be the secondary scorer Iverson has always yearned for. Even if that turns out not to be the case, Iverson was afforded the respect of consultation. That, combined with the resentments of his summer experience, might be bad news for opposing teams in the NBA. If history repeats itself, on every drive to the basket, Iverson will not be seeing the faces of his defenders, but those of the cops, the prosecutors, and his poom-poom-pants-wearing accuser instead.

Just before the preliminary hearing, Iverson went ahead with his annual Summer Celebrity Classic. This time, the charity event took the form of an all-star softball game in Camden, New Jersey, just outside Philly. Before the game, Iverson showed up wearing a Phillies jersey, but not just any Phillies jersey: he was wearing Pete Rose's number fourteen.

Those around Iverson knew it was not coincidental. Iverson was always aware of the messages being sent by his style choices, by his game, by his tattoos. Together, they compose a plea to be taken at face value, to be taken as an athlete rather than as a symbol we manipulate in complicated ways, and for our own purposes. It's as though he has made himself a pictogram, and his tattoos, especially, speak for him.

On another level, while purporting to say, "This is who I am," the tattoos can also suggest a historical context. The branding of his black skin references a time when branding a black man's name onto his body *identified* him. Seen this way, Iverson's tattoos—and whole vibe—might just be a way to get in our face and say: "You don't know me. And you never will."

By the same token, when he didn't clean up for his mug shot, it was one part defiance, one part irony. "This is how you see me, this is what I'll give you," he seemed to be saying. Likewise, the choice of Rose's jersey resonated. Rose's style of play bore a striking resemblance to Iverson's. No one hustled more. Both men evinced a willingness, to put their bodies in harm's way on each and every play.

Rose's career ended in controversial disgrace, banned from baseball for allegedly betting on the game. He was also barred from the Hall of Fame despite the fact that his on-field exploits qualified him as a no-brainer inductee. Iverson believed wholeheartedly in merit; for him, there was a logical connection between him and someone who had been denied the accolades his heart and God-given talents had earned him.

Rose, who led the Phillies to the 1980 World Series championship, had always been a Philadelphia hero. In particular, he enjoyed a stellar relationship with the Philadelphia press, including a close friendship with, among others, Eskin. Could it be that, to Iverson, the media's embrace of Rose, compared with its hassling of him, had something to do with one of the few differences between the two icons—the color of their skin? Philadelphia, after all, has a history of being toughest on its black athletes, from Chamberlain to Dick Allen to Barkley to Randall Cunningham.

There Iverson sat in his Rose jersey, two hours before his charity game, signing posters of himself for a long line of kids from the Boys and Girls Club. They'd come up and shake his hand or shyly ask to hug him and he'd just as shyly oblige. Through it all, though, he was beaming and joking with his friends. This wasn't the Iverson who, when he grudgingly attended adult functions, would be bashfully distant. Instead, he was basking in the unconditional love of mostly disadvantaged black kids.

In line, however, was an adult black woman. When she got to him, she said, smiling, "Can I ask you a question?"

Iverson smiled. As he looked the woman up and down, though, the smile slowly dissipated. "You with the media?" he asked.

"Yes," she replied.

Iverson's shoulders slumped. Cru Thik instantly stepped in.

"No questions!"

"No media!"

"This is for the kids!"

After she was ushered off, it took Iverson a few moments to recover from the buzz-kill. Then he looked up and noticed, for the first time, that virtually all the kids were wearing white headbands that read RA.

"Where'd you get that?" an incredulous Iverson asked one tongue-tied eight-year-old.

"Th-th-they're giving 'em out," he said.

Iverson looked up to his left, where Gary Moore stood. "I had Reebok make some up," he said.

Iverson smiled and looked down the line, at a sea of kids showing love for him by honoring his man.

The locker room before the charity game had a party vibe. There was an elaborate buffet. There was Kevin Garnett chatting up Bow Wow—at fifteen, he no longer wanted to be called *Lil'* Bow Wow. There was Pat Croce, greeted earlier by Iverson with a hug and kiss on the neck, high-fiving Houston Rockets guard Steve Francis. Just outside the locker room, Aaron McKie was talking to the press about his teammate—who, owing to the legal case, would not be speaking publicly tonight.

"When we go to play road games, there are more of his jerseys in the stands than a lot of guys from the home team," McKie said. "His style of play, and him on and off the court—a lot of people would like to be like him, to be a free spirit, to live your life, to not think twice about what other people think of you."

Inside the locker room, the only person not seeming to partake of the party was Iverson himself. He stood in the corner, alone, hunched over a heaping bucket of chicken wings, gnawing away. "These are tough times, man," he said between bites. "Everybody's taking the chance to throw their darts at me."

He spoke softly, as though the weight of everything—the controversy, the allegations, the thirty-some-odd friends and family he supports—had sapped him. Royster, who had once marveled at how responsible Iverson was—who else takes it upon his shoulders to lift up so many people?— also saw the effects of the burdens Iverson bore. "He jokes around a lot, but the only time that man is happy is when he's on the basketball court or up in some pussy," the now former bodyguard had once observed.

I pointed out that so many people seem to be invested in a cut-and-dried view of him: victim or victimizer. "That's how it's always been," Iverson said. "I've always said, there are a million people who love Allen Iverson and a million people who hate Allen Iverson. It's just important for me to concentrate on the ones who love me."

But if you're neither sinner nor saint, is there a third option? "Man, I'm just a guy trying to do better, and sometimes I fuck up," he said. "But because of this talent, it's like I ain't allowed to."

"So who are you?" I asked.

Allen Iverson dropped a gnarled wing into the bucket before him. "Man, if someone's smart, they know," he said. "I'm that guy that you see out there."

Later, the crowd, some 4,500 strong, exploded when Iverson took the field. It was more than just applause; as he raced across the diamond to the dugout, the screaming and shouting bordered on hysteria, reminiscent of a time long ago when four other young pop-culture icons—John, Paul, George, and Ringo—raced across a stadium field. Call it Iverson-mania.

Then Iverson stood just behind the pitcher's mound and listened as, to the crowd's delight, speaker after speaker spoke of him in the most reverential way. Camden mayor Gwendolyn Faison handed him a key to the city and said, "We are not going to worry about all those people and what they say happened!"

After scoring 33 points to eliminate the Indiana Pacers in the 2001 play-offs, Iverson celebrates while holding three-year-old Deuce (Allen Jr.).

State Senator Anthony H. Williams whipped the crowd into a frenzy. "All you people who look at this young man because he wears his hair differently, wears his clothes differently—that does not mean he's a thug," he shouted. "Everybody has a crew. A CEO has his board of directors; that's his crew!"

"We cannot allow another young African-American millionaire to be taken down by a system that can't bear to see young African-American men who take care of their families," chimed in Philadelphia community activist Novella Williams.

Another speaker shared how Iverson had visited his leukemia-stricken nephew in the hospital. Shortly after the visit, the speaker solemnly intoned, the boy's cancer went into remission. The crowd roared; Iverson just looked down and shuffled his feet.

But then it was game time and Iverson seemed to respond to my earlier question—"Who are you?"—on the field. He was on third base, Bow Wow on second, when the batter cracked a shot in the right-center gap. Blaring over the PA system came Bow Wow's rendition of the Kurtis Blow classic "Basketball." Iverson took two steps toward home and stopped, struck by the music. And then he started grooving, moving his shoulders languidly, his feet approximating something close to a Michael Jackson moonwalk. Though Iverson never deigned to dance in the clubs, here he was, the center of attention, unable to resist. The crowd went nuts and Iverson seemed charged by the reaction, continuing the boogie.

After all the highfalutin accolades and shrill denunciations, there he was, finally. As had so often been the case, he was embattled, but intent on joyously expressing himself. He was dancing—the urge no doubt spurred by the same mysterious source as his drawing, rapping, and crossover—and the crowd rose up and joined in. Once again, all eyes were on him as he brought people to their feet.

Bow Wow approached and tried to run past him en route to scoring, but Iverson grabbed him and together they paused on their way home to bask in the music and the moment. It was as though Allen Iverson were saying, *Fuck all the talk. I am what I show myself to be.*